THE CINEMA OF THE SOVIET THAW

THE CINEMA OF THE SOVIET THAW

Space, Materiality, Movement

Lida Oukaderova

Indiana University Press

This book is a publication of

Indiana University Press
Office of Scholarly Publishing
Herman B Wells Library 350
1320 East 10th Street
Bloomington, Indiana 47405 USA

iupress.indiana.edu

© 2017 by Lida Oukaderova

All rights reserved

No part of this book may be reproduced or utilized in any form or by any means, electronic or mechanical, including photocopying and recording, or by any information storage and retrieval system, without permission in writing from the publisher. The Association of American University Presses' Resolution on Permissions constitutes the only exception to this prohibition.

♾ The paper used in this publication meets the minimum requirements of the American National Standard for Information Sciences—Permanence of Paper for Printed Library Materials, ANSI Z39.48-1992.

Manufactured in the United States of America

Cataloging information is available from the Library of Congress.

ISBN 978-0-253-02635-4 (cloth)
ISBN 978-0-253-02696-5 (paperback)
ISBN 978-0-253-02708-5 (ebook)

1 2 3 4 5 22 21 20 19 18 17

For Graham, Leo, and Sasha

CONTENTS

ix Acknowledgments

1 Introduction

25 1. The Persistence of Presence: Soviet Panoramic Cinema

49 2. Mimetic Passages: The Cinema of Mikhail Kalatozov and Sergei Urusevskii

86 3. The Architecture of Movement: Georgii Danelia's *I Walk the Streets of Moscow*

116 4. A Walk through the Ruins: Larisa Shepitko's *Wings*

150 5. The Obdurate Matter of Space: Kira Muratova's *Brief Encounters*

185 Conclusion: The Otherness of Space

193 Bibliography

205 Filmography

207 Index

ACKNOWLEDGMENTS

THE COMPLETION OF this book would not have been possible without the generous help of numerous institutions, colleagues, and friends.

I am grateful to the staffs of the Russian State Archive of Literature and Arts in Moscow and of the Russian State Documentary and Photo Archive in Krasnogorsk for their patient research assistance; to the Rice University Department of Art History and Dean of Humanities for their continued research support; to the Department of Romance, German, and Slavic Languages and Literatures at George Washington University, where this project was first conceived; and to John Steven Lasher of the Kinopanorama Widescreen Preservation Association for his kindness in sharing knowledge and materials.

Although work on this book began after I left the University of Texas at Austin, it has benefited greatly from conversations and friendships begun at UT. I am particularly thankful to Katherine Arens, Keith Livers, Joan Neuberger, and Janet Swaffar for their guiding support, and to Ben Chappell and Marike Janzen for their continued friendship. At GWU, Masha Belenky, Leah Chang, and Lynn Westwater were ideal colleagues and friends—conversations with all three were essential to the book's early development. At Rice, Linda Neagley and Diane Wolfthal provided consummate departmental leadership; Andrew Taylor was tireless in his image assistance; and Leo Costello, Luis Duno-Gottberg, Shirine Hamadeh, Gordon Hughes, Fabiola Lopez-Duran, and Kirsten Ostherr helped create an ideal professional and intellectual home. Last but not least, Michelle Piranio provided an astute eye and careful pen that were vital for the book's completion.

Sections of this book have been previously published or presented as lectures, which in all cases motivated the book's progress and improved its arguments. A version of chapter 3 was published in *Studies in Soviet and Russian Cinema* (vol. 4, no. 1, 2010) under the title "The Sense of Movement in Georgii Danelia's *Walking the Streets of Moscow*," and a section of chapter 2 appeared in *Film and History* (vol. 44, no. 2, 2014) under the title "*I Am Cuba* and the Space of Revolution"; I thank both journals for providing an initial public platform for the book's contents. Talks developed from the book's chapters were delivered at Rice University, George Washington University, University College London, the University of California–Irvine, and the annual conferences of the Society for Cinema and Media Studies and the American Comparative Literature Association. I am grateful to organizers and respondents at each of these venues, particularly to Julian Graffy and Philip Cavendish of the Russian Cinema Research Group at University College London, where my arguments were challenged and extended in unexpected and productive ways.

In addition to the colleagues already listed, numerous friends have assisted my work on this project through their knowledge, encouragement, and wit. In particular, I wish to thank Sarah Costello, Sandra Dorsthorst, Mary Giovagnoli, Frank Geurts, Yuri Goriukhin, Thekla Harre, Michael Kades, Jennie King, Aza Lukashionok, Vladimir Mironov, Svetlana Mironova, Carlos Pelayo Martinez Rivera, Tamara Rzaeva, Irina Teufel, Magda Walkiewicz, Maurice Wolfthal, and Eric Yvon; together, they have made me feel at home across continents. Family in both Russia and the United States also have helped sustain me during the book's development: In Russia, I thank Igor, Tatiana, and Maksim, and, above all, my mother, Ludmila, who has been unwavering in her patience and support, and my father, Vikentii, who is immensely missed. Shared celebrations with my Chicago family, Arlene Bader, Laura Bader, and Victor, Ben, and Lida Sturm, have made winters warmer across the years of the book's progress.

At the Indiana University Press, Janice Frisch has been a model editor and shepherd for this project. I am deeply indebted for her gracious guidance. Raina Polivka also is warmly thanked for her early support of the book, as are the press's anonymous readers; their careful reading and generous comments improved the manuscript considerably.

This book was written, finally, in the daily presence of—and out of deepest love for—Leo and Sasha, who have allowed me to perceive the world anew, and Graham, whose care and tenderness and ways of seeing are the book's foundation. It is dedicated to all three.

THE CINEMA OF THE SOVIET THAW

INTRODUCTION

IN MAY 1961 the Soviet film journal *Iskusstvo kino* (*The Art of Cinema*) published a short review of the just-released documentary *The City of Great Fate* (*Gorod bol'shoi sud'by*), directed by Il'ia Kopalin. The film—selected as an official Soviet entry for the shorts competition at the Cannes Film Festival taking place the very same month—is a visual lexicon of Moscow and joins numerous other Soviet productions of the 1960s that sought to define the image of the capital city within the more tolerant framework of post-Stalinist Soviet culture. The reviewer A. Zlobin unequivocally praised the film for its "interesting, original form" and for what he deemed to be its many inventive and investigative gestures.[1] He appreciated its focus on the boundless manifestations of urban movement, especially when contrasted with the static solidity of the city's buildings. He commended the film's presentation, through its study of Moscow's architectural and material surfaces, of the city's history as unfolding in space rather than time. And he admired the director's decision to develop his urban story through the visual buildup of its episodes, letting the images do the work most often left to voiceover narration in documentaries.

Zlobin's enthusiasm, however, began to falter as he moved into a discussion of the film's last section. Expecting to see a culmination of its episodic perceptions of the Soviet capital—a "philosophical generalization" of the diverse and disconnected routes of the film's previous parts—he found instead only random moments, isolated fragments, and cyclical repetitions: "a story about yet another house," an inquiry into yet another urban place.[2] The city's separate parts, the critic lamented, thus failed to cohere into a larger whole. Zlobin implied that Kopalin and his crew got so trapped in the abundance of Moscow's diversity, particularity, and materiality that they could find no clear path forward to a grand, narrative ending. As if unable to escape such an erratic multiplication of spaces, places, and people, the filmmakers, Zlobin claimed, abandoned the city altogether; instead, their film ends with shots of the moon.

Zlobin's points of critique, if somewhat exaggerated, are on the mark. The balancing act undertaken by *The City of Great Fate*—its desire to present the grand destiny of Moscow through attention to its divergent, frequently simple, everyday details—appears to have fallen asunder. The film loses its sense of a clear teleological progression as, despite all intentions, the city's spaces refuse to be organized into a narrative whole. One sequence stands out in this regard. It begins with a static image of a schematic map of Moscow (figure 0.1a), in the middle of which a large, irregular hole opens up; its contours coincide with Moscow's historical boundaries, and within them we see random moments from the city's past appear: a horse moving along, a streetcar passing through a city square, and the like (figure 0.1b). The cinematically recorded reality displayed within this singed gap, in its comparatively large scale and explicit depth, as well as fragmentary motion and transient specificity, overwhelms and sidelines the static and flat map, rendering it insignificant. It creates a desire to enter its space and to follow its streetcars and horses, rather than return to the simple lines of the mapped, general surface as a source for experience or knowledge.

Kopalin's sequence provides a relevant point of entry to the present book, for it concretizes, through the specifics of film's material form, the primacy of space and above all spatial experience to the cinematic production of the Soviet Thaw, the subject of the following pages. The Thaw period, known for its processes of political and cultural liberalization following Joseph Stalin's death in 1953, and evolving with particular force after Nikita Khrushchev's legendary 1956 speech denouncing his predecessor's crimes, witnessed a dramatic resurgence in cinematic production, the aesthetic and political principles of which departed significantly from the cinema of the Stalinist years. Although this departure can be traced along multiple paths—following different kinds of characters and conflicts, diverse settings and sensibilities—I argue that at its center were shifting relations to space, both filmic and social.[3] More specifically, the films of the Thaw period analyzed here were motivated by an urge to interrogate and reanimate spatial experience, and through this project to raise questions of ideology, social progress, and subjectivity that were particularly pressing for post-Stalinist Soviet culture.[4] As suggested by Kopalin's sequence, the cinema of the Thaw sought to unfold and *unmap* Soviet spatial realities rather than to forge their generalized understanding. This cinema, in other words, aimed to see beneath, and in pointed opposition to, the abstract representations of a paper map.

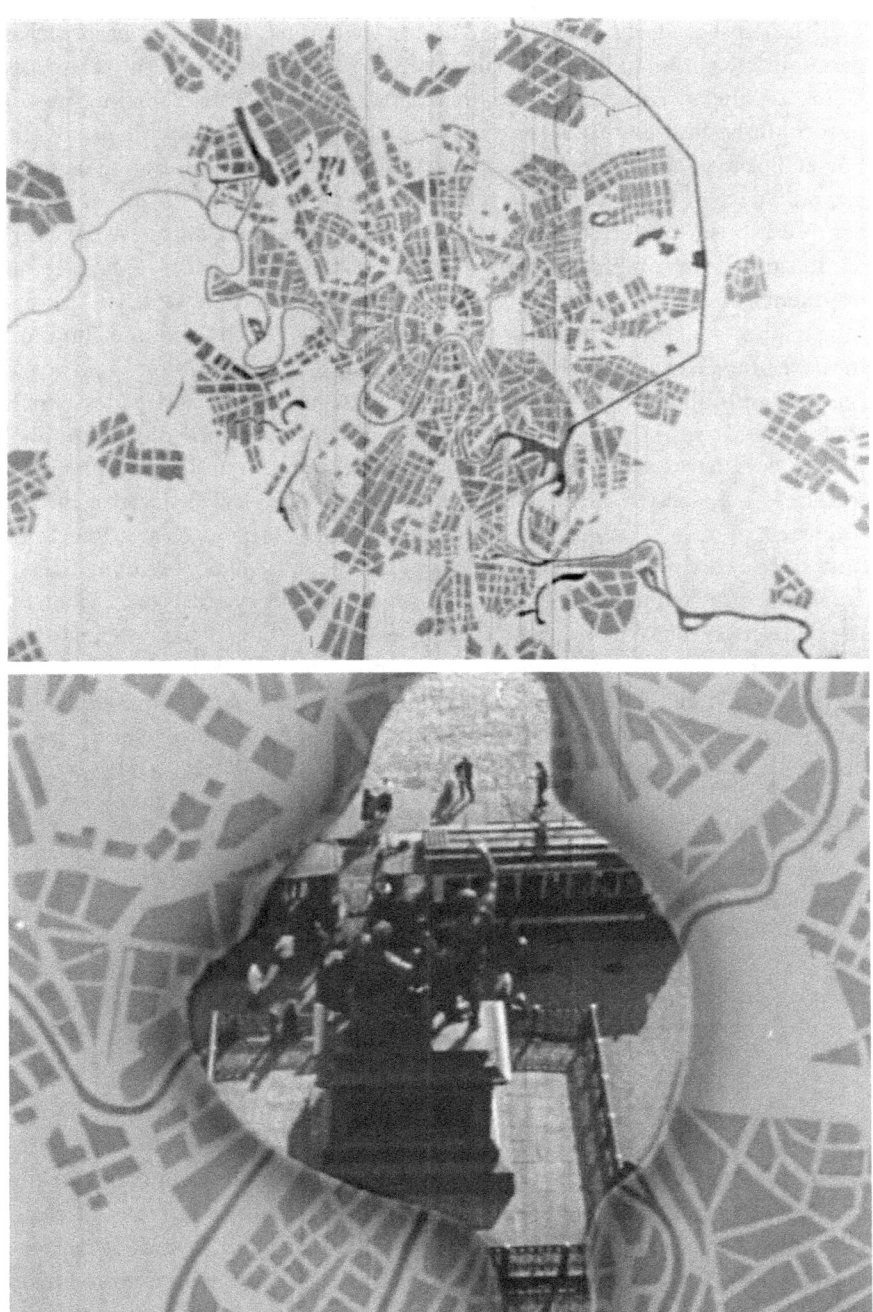

Fig. 0.1a–b Static map opening up to the motion and transience of film. From *The City of Great Fate*, 1961.

The present study opens with the Soviet Union's late-fifties embrace of panoramic cinema, followed by discussions of works by Mikhail Kalatozov, Georgii Danelia, Larisa Shepitko, and Kira Muratova—all crucial figures of post-Stalinist film culture, even if some had to wait until the collapse of the Soviet bloc to gain the national and international recognition they had long deserved. Space in these directors' works repeatedly poses formal and narrative complications: It exceeds the function of a setting; arrests narrative development; slows down time; acts as an embodied participant; persists in its material fragments; and actively attracts, confronts, and disorients viewers. The following chapters seek to unravel just why space assumes such form and function in these films. Answering this question, I propose, entails looking again at the political and cultural upheavals of the immediate post-Stalinist decades, which themselves were relentlessly preoccupied with the reorganization of public, private, and natural spaces. From shifts in architecture and urban planning to renewed pushes to conquer nature, from new practices of interior design to growing interest in urban walking, Soviet films of the 1950s and 1960s not only mirrored the broad spectrum of spatial phenomena occurring in Thaw-era Soviet culture but aimed in fact to prompt their reorganization. Driven by the conviction that true social transformation could take place only once the production and use of space had been critiqued and understood anew, the directors considered here sought to utilize film's specific spatial materials and technologies toward this end. The distinct spatiality of cinema, in short, was to be a primary engine for rethinking and reinventing social space itself.

The USSR in Construction

> Slender silhouettes of tower cranes became a characteristic detail of our Motherland's landscapes. A grand construction is unfolding everywhere: from the gloomy hills of the Kola Peninsula to the sunny shores of the Caucasus, from the foothills of the Carpathians to the Sea of Okhotsk. New centers of socialist industry are being created, along with new settlements: about 600 new cities have appeared on the Soviet Union's map in the last thirty-five years. Old cities too are experiencing an essential transformation, regaining their youth.
>
> —Andrei Ikonnikov and Georgii Stepanov, *The Aesthetics of the Socialist City*, 1963

When the Twenty-Second Congress of the Communist Party of the Soviet Union published its program outlining the impending developments of the country in 1961, it formulated them in a language that was direct and clear. Throughout the 1960s, the Soviet Union would focus on dramatically increasing economic production and improving standards of living in order to create "the material and technical basis for communism"; this would result, by the end of the 1970s, in a fully developed communist society with an abundance of material goods and a sweeping reassertion of communist relations and values.[5] Beaming with unbridled enthusiasm, the authors of the program described in detail the tasks of the party at hand. These included a renewed plan for the complete electrification of the country; great advancements in technology; an increase in the mechanization and efficiency of production; universal improvement of working conditions; the elimination of hard physical labor; the effective use of natural resources; and heavy investment in the development of the sciences and the education of the working classes. Achieved through the methodical planning and coordination of all branches of the Soviet economy, these developments would enable the USSR to become the world's leader in per capita production and simultaneously allow its citizens to enjoy a decrease in working hours, with plenty of time to engage in cultural, educational, and recreational activities.

The congress's call for widespread, grand construction—the planned comprehensive revival and reform of Soviet economic and cultural life—necessitated the development and reorganization of Soviet space on every conceivable scale. The projected image of this space was one of an integrated whole—a fresh, modern map of the Soviet Union envisioned as a dynamic totality and rooted in connectedness and economic interdependence among *all* its constituent parts, even its most negligible ones. The materialization of this image, which had already begun in the mid-1950s with Khrushchev's ascendance to power, was accompanied by detailed discussions in the professional and popular press of the expansive construction projects taking place throughout the country. These included the transformation of little-known and underdeveloped Soviet corners into vibrant industrial centers and new national spotlights; plans for improving the quantity and quality of transportation and communication systems; and the creation of a single water system and a unified power grid to transmit electricity throughout the entire county.[6] As part of these efforts, nature was to be increasingly exploited and natural processes, such as the course of rivers, altered with the goal of developing and integrating agricultural and economic production. If such calls for the country's spatial unity through industrial and agricultural development are reminiscent of the immediate postrevolutionary period, it is because the Thaw saw itself as directly continuing and expanding tasks outlined by Lenin. Lenin's famed phrase that "communism equals Soviet power plus the electrification of the entire country" was utilized by Khrushchev to motivate an intensive push for the development of the "electric" sides of things, since the political side—"Soviet power"—had long become a reality.[7]

The press was especially fervent in its discussions of changes in architecture and urban planning, including the massive construction of new neighborhoods throughout Soviet cities, as well as new directions in interior design that were meant to complement concomitant shifts in architecture toward rationality, simplicity, and efficiency (figure 0.2).[8] It is indeed in the realm of urban planning that the most substantial, or at least the most tangible, spatial reorganization of the Thaw era occurred, with new construction transforming the face of older Soviet cities and entirely shaping the appearance of new ones. Continuously growing urban populations, together with the perpetual housing shortage that had plagued Soviet city dwellers since the 1917 Revolution and particularly since World War II, required a fundamentally new approach to the organization of urban housing—not only a rapid increase in the number of available apartments but also a change in the quality and principles of their production. The shortage resulted in a turn toward the vast manufacture of new types of prefabricated, concrete-based buildings, the look of which veered completely away from the heavy, ornamental style favored during Stalin's regime. Nested together in open and free arrangements, these structures became the basis for new types of neighborhoods to which people moved en masse during the Thaw years. Although Khrushchev's aspiration to provide adequate housing for every Soviet citizen was never realized, his campaign toward this end brought significant results. If between 1946 and 1950 127.1 million square meters of housing had been erected, between 1956 and 1966 this number rose to 732.2 million, shifting the distribution of the population within urban centers and significantly improving living standards for tens of millions of Soviet people.[9] The majority of these constructions are still in place today, enduring as the most prominent legacy of the Thaw era, though no longer inspiring any of the enthusiasm with which they were initially met. Now deteriorated and infested, derided by many, and desired by very few, they persist as a sorry reminder of the unfulfilled hopes and failed policies of the period.

Khrushchev's projects in urban development serve as a relevant context for the present study not only because of the shifts they initiated in the physical appearances of Soviet cities, but also because of the discourse they generated on the theoretical, technical, and practical parameters of communist space and ways of living. In the best traditions of utopian imagining, the Soviet press frequently described the era's developing urban model as a perfect and beautiful organism: rational, human, ordered, and balanced (figure 0.3).[10] Materialized within the boundaries of an ensemble that integrated private apartments and a variety of public buildings, these developments were to alleviate all traditional problems and contradictions of city dwelling. Nature would play an integral part, with parks spread evenly throughout residential districts and easily accessible to the inhabitants. Private and family domains—and especially the lives of women—would be infinitely improved thanks to public services such

Fig. 0.2 Simplicity and functionality of Thaw-era interior design. From *Arkhitektura SSSR*, 10 (1962), 12.

as cafeterias, childcare, and cleaning facilities. Technology, from kitchen appliances to public transportation, would raise everyday efficiency, allowing more time for leisure and education, the resources for which also would be readily available. The development of environmentally responsible industrial processes would allow factories to be built in the vicinity of apartments, creating an organic synthesis of work and leisure sites and eliminating the time wasted on commuting.[11] Monumental artworks would complete and complement plain prefabricated façades, aiding in the aesthetic and ideological education of city dwellers.[12]

The new urban space then taking shape, in other words, would become the "material and technical basis" for communism (a phrase recited repeatedly in public discussions), preparing the ground for citizens' ethical and political enlightenment, economic well-being, and the ultimate assertion of a progressive consciousness. And though architects and historians at the time noted stylistic and technical similarities between Soviet housing projects and contemporaneous urban developments in Western Europe and the United States,

Fig. 0.3 Architectural model of a neighborhood development. Apartment buildings are integrated into a green landscape incorporating two children's boarding schools, a convalescent home, a park, a community and commercial center, a summer theater, a botanical garden, a stadium, and a fruit garden. From *Arkhitektura SSSR 6* (1961), 38.

they emphasized the *wholeness* of the planned Soviet approach, the harmony it would create among the individual, the social, and the space of the city. As historian Mark B. Smith has described such thinking, "the housing program was made self-consciously, explicitly, and even aggressively ideological. Its goal was no longer simply to benefit as many people as possible but to transform their consciousness in the context of proto-communism."[13] The discussions of the coming utopia, furthermore, were grounded in very present realities, with new construction sites sprouting up all over, instilling Soviet idealism and ideology with a sense of urgency and immanence. New socialist space was on the rise.

Transitional Motion

Writing on the spatial imagination of Soviet cinema and culture from the 1917 Revolution to Stalin's consolidation of power in the late 1930s, film historian Emma Widdis has argued that in these early years the project of creating a Soviet nation was inextricably connected to the organization of a new, specifically *Soviet* kind of space. Discussing fictional and documentary films, theoretical essays, and architectural proposals along with economic programs and emerging political structures, Widdis contends that the country's relation to space developed in accordance with two competing principles. One was the pursuit of spatial conquest—the domination and control of nature and the environment, and the organization of this process through a centripetal hierarchy, the rhetoric of which permeated public discourse throughout Soviet history. The other principle was that of exploration, referring to a decentralized, nonhierarchical, and dynamic organization of socialist society in which the periphery is of no less significance than the center, physical movement through the country's spaces is a source of primary experience and knowledge, and *sensory* connection to the environment is "envisaged as one of mutual benefit."[14] By the end of the 1930s, Widdis argues, the former principle had become dominant; the imaginary map guiding the conception of space in the Soviet Union "pictured an immobile space, hierarchically organized around a dominant centre from which lines of influence extended radially, and the relationship between centre and periphery encoded relations of power."[15]

The comparatively liberal policies of Khrushchev's government animated once again the principle of exploration for Soviet spatial consciousness. Freedom of mobility was celebrated, new possibilities of internationalism were emerging, and relationships between center and periphery were reconfigured. Just a few examples give a sense of the country's shifting relations with space in these years. A central reform of the period, for instance, was directly connected to decentralization, transferring the management of economic production to regional councils (*sovnarkhozy*), and thus loosening the panopticonlike organization of the Stalinist USSR.[16] In addition, the rehabilitation under Khrushchev of previously deported ethnic groups as well as prisoners of the Gulag instigated substantial migration within the country, often from its peripheral to central areas, as returning exiles claimed their old places of residency and former inmates sought new ones.[17] Young people were mobilized to participate in industrial development, which was propagated as an adventure by the government, and this in turn led to a significant exodus eastward, to the country's outer edges.[18] Tourism flourished during these years as never before. As historian Anne E. Gorsuch has noted, "some of the travel of the Khrushchev era was international, some was domestic, and some was imaginary, . . . but much was driven by a new sense of expansion and exploration, of being able to examine new topics and new places."[19] And Soviet urbanites, especially in Moscow and Leningrad, were increasingly able to engage with contemporary foreign cultures through books, films, and national exhibitions, with Moscow's 1957 International Youth Festival becoming perhaps the pinnacle of the period's new internationalism. In preparation for the event, the Soviet press published a flood of information about the 131 participating countries, giving rise to a striking "expansion of the geographic imagination" of its readers.[20] Simultaneously with these developments, newly democratic and specifically filmic options for the mapping of Soviet space were emerging, as portable movie cameras gave Soviet travelers the means to transform their *own* spatial experiences and encounters into moving images, thus increasing and diversifying the archive of Soviet cinematic cartography.[21]

But it would be an exaggeration to suggest that exploration became the defining mode of relation between people and space during the Thaw, which, as a transitional period, was marked by contradictory impulses. Khrushchev's policies of spatial expansion, occupation, and conquest, as well as *im*mobilization, continued, driven by urgent political and economic demands. Needing to find new routes for economic revival, the government turned to the untouched lands of Siberia and Kazakhstan in order to energize agricultural production—a campaign that enthusiastically embraced the exploitation of natural resources and resulted, as historians agree, in "the plowing up and exhaustion of soils followed by rampant erosion," which had dire consequences for the region's environment.[22] Soviet tendencies to spatial conquest are even more prominent in the realm of politics. Fearing a loss of influence in the socialist Eastern bloc, for instance, Khrushchev sent Soviet troops to Hungary during the antigovernmental uprising of 1956, suppressing all public opposition and substantiating Soviet power on foreign lands. Confronted with the daily flight of people from East Berlin to the West, he successfully propagated the building of the Berlin Wall in 1961, which divided the city for the next twenty-eight years and cemented the ideological boundaries between East and West in the most literal manner possible. Indeed, it is especially in proximity to borders that Soviet anxieties about free mobility became most palpable. As political historian Robert A. Jones has written, metaphors of bodily boundaries and openings were prevalent in Soviet political discourse in the 1950s. The leadership in Moscow, Jones argues, was "acutely aware of the 'porosity' of intra-bloc state frontiers: the 'spillover' or 'contagion' effect had been a significant factor in the explosions of 1956," referring to the Hungary uprisings.[23] To protect the "body" of socialism, in other words, the government had to subjugate it to a particular fixed spatial configuration—to close up, in essence, all its pores and orifices.

Soviet attitudes toward space during the Khrushchev era replicate the primary problem of post-Stalinist politics: that the sincere desire for systematic reform was paired with a simultaneous realization that the system's basic structure had to be preserved. As historian Donald Filtzer has noted, "There was a permanent tension between the perception that change was desperately needed, and a fear that reforms could bring the entire system crashing down, together with Khrushchev and the rest of the elite."[24] The politics of movement mirrored this tension: Movement could be flexible and dynamic as long as it remained contained within the fixed structures of socialism. But can a transition be successful if the process of transiting is not renewed and reimagined? This question is central to the cinema of the Thaw, which examines and engenders different modalities of movement and insists that arriving at a better place is contingent on the art of transit itself.

Spatial exploration during the Thaw was not, and could not be, of the same nature as in the immediate postrevolutionary period. The "ungraspable lands" of the Soviet Union in the 1920s provided the mobile gaze and body with the raw material "from which a new world was to be constructed," in Widdis's words.[25] In the 1950s these ungraspable lands had in fact been long in the making, having become integral parts of a system whose dismantling could be taken only so far. The exploratory gaze that materialized in the films of the Thaw period operates *within* this system even as it searches for modes of mobility that would push—intuitively, not programmatically— beyond its boundaries, unfold its constructs, and in some cases provide access to a raw material from which new spaces and relations, as well as new transitions, could be imagined again. A central task of this book is to trace the development of these modes of mobility and to probe their social and aesthetic parameters as they unfolded within this culture and its cinema's exploratory gaze.

Embodied Mapping

Post-Stalinist spatial politics permeate Thaw-era cinema in manifold forms, above all in its representations and narratives of natural exploitation, urban transformation, and of travel and mobility of all kinds. The conquest of the Soviet Union's virgin lands finds a broad cinematic representation with films such as *The First Echelon* (*Pervyi eshelon*, directed by Mikhail Kalatozov, 1955), *Ivan Brovkin in the Virgin Lands* (*Ivan Brovkin na tseline*, directed by Ivan Lukinskii, 1958), *Horizon* (*Gorizont*, directed by Iosif Kheifits, 1961), and *Alionka* (directed by Boris Barnet, 1961) depicting the first difficult years of agricultural developments in a warm and optimistic manner, and with a conventional resolution of conflicts structuring their narratives. More generally, movement toward, and between, the country's peripheral spaces becomes a common cinematic trope during these years. *Spring on Zarechnaia Street* (*Vesna na zarechnoi ulitse*, directed by Feliks Mironer and Marlen Khutsiev, 1956), for instance—one of the first widely popular and critically acclaimed Thaw-era dramas—depicts a young, educated woman from the city who relocates to a "remote village" (in the words of one character) and, after sundry trials and tribulations, joyfully accepts it as her home. Alternatively, the story of *Once Upon a Time There Lived an Old Man and an Old Woman* (*Zhili byli starik so starkhoi*, directed by Grigory Chukhrai, 1964) revolves around an old couple who move from their remote village in an indeterminate location to an even smaller settlement in the Arctic Circle, right at the feet of the unknown, unexplored, and uninhabited tundra. Filmed on location and with long stretches dominated by darkness and fields of snow, the film makes tangible the separation of this area from any Soviet center, which indeed never becomes relevant to any conflicts or affairs transpiring in the film. (It is also one of the few Soviet films of the period that directly, if only fleetingly, acknowledges the presence of labor camps in the Soviet north.)

Soviet worries about the porosity of state frontiers, furthermore, are directly explored in the melodramatic plot of *Over Tissa* (*Nad Tissoi*, directed by Dmitrii Vasieliev, 1958), in which an enemy border crosser infiltrates a local community and mendaciously wins the heart of a young woman—also the love object of a border patrol officer, who in the last moments uncovers the enemy's catastrophic plans. And the emergence of new cities and new architecture are repeatedly celebrated in Thaw-era films, including *The Girl without an Address* (*Devushka bez adresa*, directed by Eldar Riazanov, 1957), *Adult Children* (*Vzroslye deti*, directed by Villen Azarov, 1961), *Cheriomushki* (directed by Gerbert Rappoport, 1963), and *Two Sundays* (*Dva voskreseniia*, directed by Vladimir Shredel', 1963). *Adult Children* in particular warmly pokes fun at young, fashionable architects and their preoccupation with contemporary interior design. Cities, furthermore, are transformed in this period's films not only through new construction but also through celebratory events and everyday people. Thus in *A Sailor from "Comet"* (*Matros s "Komety,"* directed by Isidor Annenskii, 1958), the celebrations of Moscow's 1957 International Youth Festival bring crowds of thousands onto the capital's streets—a gigantic, insurmountable mass of all races and colors, complemented by seas of international flags obscuring the Stalinist façades from which they hang.

The popular 1960 Soviet–French production *Leon Garros Searches for His Friend* (*Leon Garros ishchet druga*, directed by Marcello Pagliero) encapsulates many such cinematic engagements with contemporary shifts in Soviet spatial organization and relations. Centering on a group of French journalists arriving in Moscow to report on Soviet culture and everyday life, the film takes us on an automobile tour throughout the USSR as the main protagonist, Leon Garros, decides to search the country for his old wartime friend Boris. By the end of the film, not only have we seen Moscow in transition—with new neighborhoods at its outskirts greeting the French journalists as they approach the city in the film's opening sequence—but we have witnessed the construction and development of the country's remote and ethnically diverse territories far beyond the Urals. The film's plot is driven by the glorification of mobility, as the task of finding Boris proves to be rather difficult: He has relocated several times, from one new industrial development to another. The travelers eventually catch up with him far in the east, in the recently developed city of Bratsk, where the wild and harsh environment of Siberia is shown to slowly yield to heroic Soviet efforts at industrial progress and human habitation. Boris has been participating in the construction of a hydroelectric power plant there, though he is about to move on yet again to another project.

In its eager celebration of post-Stalinist culture, *Leon Garros* strikes just the right balance between the new and the established. Presenting the Soviet population as relentlessly mobile, the film also shows it as inherently traceable, always having an identifiable place within the seemingly ungraspable Soviet expanse. Putting an emphasis on chance encounters on the road, the film makes them appear necessary to the overarching organization of socialist life. Suggesting that the country's previously centripetal organization has dissipated, with places like Bratsk assuming a central economic and cultural role, the journey of *Leon Garros* still begins and ends in Moscow, its spatial loop effectively subsuming peripheral events and experiences under the wing of the Soviet capital. Spatial exploration in the film is sublimated as spatial conquest; the two ways of relating to the environment are intertwined, especially as the travelers' journey culminates repeatedly in the awe-inspiring experience of Soviet industrial domination over nature. On the whole, *Leon Garros* celebrates new spatial relations—above all, the newly found freedom of mobility—but at the same time it structures them, rendering them an integral part of a balanced, and transparent, socialist life.

It is the disruption of such structured and stable spatiality that makes the films discussed in this book exceptional. Activating the same cultural tropes around which many Soviet productions of the period revolve—movement, urban construction, and natural conquest, among others—they nevertheless drift away from a "proper" Soviet reality, one that is whole, easily mapped, and transparent in form and meaning, even if also infinitely more dynamic and flexible than that of the Stalinist cultural imagination. These films fragment, obfuscate, and complicate that reality, while interrogating different modes by which spatial forms and meanings come to life. Examining how landscapes and cities, façades and interiors, can be approached, traversed, and known, as well as how movements and relations come to be mapped as part of a spatial whole, these films generate and put on display spatial experiences that resist assimilation into established narrative and ideological structures. They ask us to face, and to participate in, a different kind of Soviet cartography, one that undoes its own history of conquest, authority, and domination and explores instead the discursive and material practices through which space is produced and encountered. In such explorations, these films suggest, lies the potential for social transformation, the possibility of dismantling and reforming previously dominant organizing concepts of Soviet life—to rethink such overarching categorical pairs as time and history, revolution and subjectivity, and, perhaps most intricately, gender and politics.

Whereas the production of new Soviet spaces in films such as *Leon Garros* was held steadily in the hands of the state, the generative process shifted to individual subjects in the films under consideration here. More accurately, we see a shift to the agency of human—and increasingly porous—bodies, whose engagement with space is primary to individual subjects' goals and efforts. Moving through and contemplating space, these bodies privilege detail over the whole, material over conceptual, touch over sight, immersion over distinction, and fleeting moments of the here and now over teleological, linear time. It is in such moments of heightened encounter between self and space that the latter is revealed to be dynamic, unfinished, and open to the particularities of lived experience. And if such moments are only occasionally framed in explicitly political terms, they are nevertheless repeatedly impregnated with the possibility of social renewal: their constant reappearance in Soviet cinema during the decade-long period of the Thaw evinces a desire to create "something different"—to evoke the words of the philosopher Henri Lefebvre—from within the most structured and static of Soviet spaces.[26]

The Turn to Space

SOVIET CINEMA'S INTERROGATIONS of space in the immediate post-Stalinist years were born out of particular political and artistic circumstances. They are inseparable from the processes of ideological introspection that Soviet society underwent during the Thaw and from the history of spatial engagements specific to Soviet film from its inception. But these interrogations also parallel— indeed, expand and complicate—broader shifts that were taking place in theoretical debates during the early postwar period in Europe, and above all in France, where the understanding of spatial relations came increasingly to be seen as essential to social progress and revolutionary transformation. Such thinking was a two-way street: Lefebvre, a primary figure in these shifts, partially traced the evolution of his ideas to the main event that unleashed the Thaw—Khrushchev's 1956 speech denouncing Stalin at the Twentieth Party Congress. The speech, Lefebvre indicated, solidified his belief that the Communist Party—and with it, the basic tenets of orthodox Marxism—had lost its ability to instigate significant social change and that true "revolutionary movements [would move] outside the organized parties."[27] His examples of such 1950s movements are extremely diverse in both scale and kind, though all suggest new modes of spatial engagement: from Fidel Castro's guerrilla fighting in the mountains of Sierra Maestra, leading up to Cuba's 1959 revolution, to the psychogeographic urban drifting of the Situationist International, whose primary figure, Guy Debord, was a close associate of Lefebvre's between 1957 and 1962. For Lefebvre, the scattered nature of these movements, which, he noted, were "happening a little bit everywhere," was of particular conceptual interest. Castro and the situationists were not institutionally or otherwise connected, but both engaged space in spontaneous, diversely materialized ways. Lefebvre's subsequent studies of urban phenomena—of what people do in the city, how they use, organize, appropriate, and imagine the spaces in which they live—was driven by his belief that these micro-phenomena were themselves part of the broader, explicitly revolutionary movements.[28]

It is not surprising that the history of the Soviet Union repeatedly provided Lefebvre with material for discussing the failure of revolution. In his seminal 1974 book *The Production of Space*, he forthrightly grappled with the question of whether state socialism had been able to produce "a space of its own." He writes, "the question is not unimportant. A revolution that does not produce a new space has not realized its full potential; indeed it has failed in that it has not changed life itself, but has merely changed ideological superstructures, institutions or political apparatuses. A social transformation, to be truly revolutionary in character, must manifest a creative capacity in its effects on daily life, on language and on space."[29]

This passage captures the reasons for Lefebvre's disillusionment with developments in socialist Eastern Europe, and with Marxism as exemplified by Western communist parties. (He himself was expelled from the French Communist Party in 1958, and his justifications for having departed from orthodox Marxist thought, which he explored in detail in his 1959 book *The Sum and the Remainder*, were disdained and mocked by Soviet Marxists—his explanations denounced as an "ideological striptease."[30]) Lefebvre came to see the foundations of revolution not only in class struggle, or changes in economic relations and political structures, but in the phenomena of everyday life—"life itself"— within which space and spatial relations were of foremost significance. And though he recognized Soviet attempts to produce a revolutionary "space of its own" in the early experiments of the Soviet architectural avant-garde (with which he had become familiar primarily through the work of his collaborator, the Russian émigré Anatole Kopp), he saw the Soviet Union's subsequent history as antithetical to his theories on spatial and everyday practices.[31]

Lefebvre's critique might lead one to ask why the efforts at spatial reorientation that were central to the Soviet Thaw—especially the new models of city planning that constituted a significant turn in Soviet thinking about the production and use of socialist everyday environments—did not constitute a positive Soviet example. One can speculate from his writings how Lefebvre might respond to this question. Even if the new urban (and village) developments provided grounds for Soviet observers to see the emergence of a truly socialist space—fundamentally different from the excessive and economically impractical architectural methods of Stalinism and the utopian formalist experiments of the 1920s—these developments were still plagued by the same drive for functionalism and top-down overarching structure that sparked his critique of the state-sponsored massive urban creations sprouting up all over European cities in the postwar decades. In Lefebvre's thinking, the failure of these new projects lay in the structures' rigidity and inflexibility, and consequently their inability to entice a process of spatial appropriation, or dwelling and inhabitation. That process, for him, was one of the essential steps through which transformations of everyday life could be initiated: "For an individual, for a group, to inhabit is to appropriate something. Not in the sense of possessing it, but as making it an œuvre, making it one's own, marking it, modeling it, shaping it. . . . To inhabit is to appropriate space, in the midst of constraints, that is to say, to be in a conflict—often acute—between the constraining powers and the forces of appropriation."[32]

To my mind, Lefebvre's creative, indeed poetic, understanding of inhabitation as a process of shaping space and, most important, as a state of being in conflict captures something crucial about the dynamics of much Soviet Thaw–era film, which persistently puts into question the rhetoric of harmony, rationality, and progress that dominated contemporary discussions of Soviet urban planning, interior design, and even the conquest of nature. Though cinema in general was of no particular interest to Lefebvre, in the Soviet context it was nevertheless the arena where his idea of dwelling as conflict was most clearly manifested. It was precisely cinema that allowed the continuous negotiation between what space is made to be and what it *can* be—perhaps because the possibilities of a creative spatial production within actual Soviet environments remained severely limited. The films of Kalatozov, Danelia, Shepitko, and Muratova—as well as, inadvertently, the discourse on Soviet panoramic cinema—persistently make the necessity and value of such conflict visible and tangible. If Lefebvre saw alternative architectural forms as enabling a transformative habitation of private and public spaces, these filmmakers pursued a similar project through the basic material composition of moving images—the production, so to speak, of their own cinematic space.

The parallels between Lefebvre's spatial critique and Soviet cinema of the 1950s and 1960s should not be understood as a matter of direct influence or random confluence. Rather, as suggested earlier, these two cultural practices should be seen as part of the same paradigmatic shift in movements happening a little bit everywhere that began to consider space rather than time as a central category through which to explore social formations.³³ Political geographer Edward Soja, who has identified in Lefebvre's (as well as in Michel Foucault's) work the roots of a more recent spatial turn in social and humanistic studies, links this shift to an urgent need to reform Marxist thinking and to deprivilege time and history as the sole meaningful measures of evolutionary dynamics. Soja writes, "It was at this time [in the nineteenth century] that history and time began to be linked with process, progress, development, change.... Space, in contrast, came increasingly to be seen as something dead, fixed, nondialectical... always there, but never an active, social entity. Marx called space an unnecessary complication of his theory, and it was that indeed."³⁴

It makes sense that a challenge to Marxist preoccupations with time and history would rise in the country where the theory of dialectical and historical materialism was first put into practice and where an obsession with the teleological progression of time persisted in the most concrete, even violent, ways. Political philosopher Susan Buck-Morss has argued that the dimension of time dominated the political imaginary of the first socialist state from its beginnings, with class struggle driving the understanding of revolution in terms of a temporal advance. Furthermore, the idea of historical progress came to define the outcomes of conflicts, wars, and diverse cultural and political divisions throughout Soviet history.³⁵ The ideological difference between West and East, for instance, was understood in terms of historical rather than territorial separation—a difference, in Lenin's words, between "the old world of capitalism that is in a state of confusion... and the rising new world that is still very weak, but which will grow, for it is invincible."³⁶ Similarly, the so-called backward cultural traditions of diverse ethnic populations on the peripheries of the Soviet Union were seen as halting the progress of history.

It was especially during the period of rapid industrialization, beginning with the first Five-Year Plan in 1928 (the plan itself being a temporal construct that structured the development of Soviet society), that the Soviet rhetoric of time and progress intensified, implying a need for political control over the speed of time, and thus over history itself. For the historian Moshe Lewin "the sense of urgency in the whole upheaval is baffling. The pace imposed suggests a race against time, as if those responsible for the country's destinies felt they were running out of history."³⁷ Under these circumstances, the present moment, the immediate here and now, was to be constantly sacrificed, given up for the building of a better, communist future. In a different register but similar vein, Soviet linguist Roman Jakobson wrote the following in his 1930 poetic eulogy to Vladimir Maiakovskii: "We lived too much for the future, thought about it, believed in it; the news of the day—sufficient onto itself—no longer existed for us. We lost a sense of the present."³⁸ While the rhetoric of a straightforward march toward a communist future permeated Khrushchev's policies as well, Soviet cinema's profound turn to space during this period suggests a recognition, if only tangential, that the race against time had in fact been lost. Nothing is more consistent in the cinematic works discussed in the following chapters than their rejection of linear teleological time. Emptied of the potential for meaningful experience and critical knowledge, such time breaks apart and yields to spatially defined and ever-fleeting moments of the here and now, the significance of which rarely encompasses the dimensions of a bright future.

Materials of Cinema

The films discussed in this book were selected not only for their critical focus on Soviet spaces and spatiality, but also for their active engagement of cinema's own spatiality. They repeatedly foreground and utilize the architecture and materiality of moving images, seeking to generate perceptually challenging experiences for viewers. The most basic organizational elements of cinema, its own raw material—such as theatrical space and screen surface, camera motion and sound distribution—assume distinct prominence within these films, breaking apart the enclosed realistic unity of the representation on screen in favor of a spatially determined experience of the filmic event as a whole.

My concerns with space, materiality, and movement build upon recent directions in film scholarship that turn attention to the spatial foundations of cinematic practice. Numerous scholars have revived earlier modernist discourses that closely connected film to the histories of urbanism, architecture, and travel, all of which share modes of perception associated with the mobility and transience of modern life. Giuliana Bruno in particular has sought to create in her work a "new geography of modernity" by considering nineteenth-century spaces like trains, arcades, and exhibition pavilions as having "prepared the ground for the invention of the moving image" by essentially creating a protofilm spectator.[39] Stressing the affinity between filmic representation and the street—something explored initially by Walter Benjamin and Siegfried Kracauer—Bruno suggests that since the emergence of cinema, cultural images of cities have been governed by cinematic representations as much as by architecture, for they both participate in the building of city views.[40] Architectural historian Anthony Vidler, in turn, has reintroduced early discussions of cinema's production of space. He cites, for example, the journalist and art critic Herman G. Scheffauer, who described cinema's uncanny ability to create space that "has been smitten into life, into movement and conscious expression," extending the human *Raumgefühl*, or feeling for space.[41] As Vidler notes, referring to these forces at work in early cinema: "No longer an inert background, architecture now participated in the very emotions of film; the surroundings no longer surrounded but entered the experience as presence."[42]

As Soviet cinema in the Thaw era moved toward reinventing its role in society in the wake of Stalin's death, it did so, I propose, by reactivating the spatial roots of cinematic practice—by exploring and reshaping the spatial principles of filmic representation as a means of rethinking the organization of social space more broadly. Cinematic technology deserves special attention in this discussion, as it underwent substantial development during the midcentury decades, with new cameras, screen formats, and sound distribution systems driving formal experimentations and influencing the emergence of unprecedented cinematic environments. New technology expanded the possibilities of cinematic realism (particularly relevant in the Soviet context, given the culture's long-standing preoccupation with realist representation), which was put to work not only to increase the reality effect of what is shown on screen but to do so by specifically simulating the perceptual conditions of real life. The introduction of film panoramas in the second half of the 1950s was of particular significance. Their celebrated effect of presence—that is, their generation of the physiological sensation of actually participating in events on screen—mobilized audiences as active viewers and thus fostered new paradigms for thinking about cinematic perception and spatiality.

Arguably, much of this period's technical experimentation revolved around the ideal of viewer participation that was suggested by panoramic technology. The handheld, lightweight (five kilogram) "Konvas Automat" camera, for instance, produced in the Soviet Union from 1954 on, became one of the most popular pieces of equipment among Soviet cinematographers, especially those working in documentaries, because of its ability to transfer onto celluloid the active sense of the body in motion. Viewers' experience of this motion within a theater approached the physiological sensation of panoramic immersion, with Sergei Urusevskii (Kalatozov's collaborator) becoming one of the world's most celebrated practitioners of this filming style. The stereophonic sound system developed in conjunction with the widescreen format, furthermore, brought a number of related changes, including a better coordination of body and voice on screen and the distribution of microphones within the space of the audience, which resulted in its more complete integration into the spectacle on screen. All these developments sought to intensify viewers' physiological sensations and to frame their experience of film as one of integrated, immediate, tactile presence.

One of this book's repeated claims, however, is that the filmmakers studied here did not simply embrace such technologies' ability to represent and simulate reality; instead, they engaged this capacity dialectically, frequently negating the unified totality of realism promised by these new devices in order to activate the material seams, gaps, and frictions on which this totality was erected and which it was keen to suppress. It is precisely the realistic unity of space that repeatedly breaks down in these films, giving rise to a space that is not one with itself, that emphasizes its own social and material contradictions. As the following discussion outlines, it is through an active interrogation of the material conditions of filmic practice that Soviet ideology of space is dissected, accompanied by a reexamination and reimagining of the relations of space with the constructions of history, everyday life, and gender.

This interrogation begins in the discourse surrounding Soviet panoramic cinema at the end of the 1950s, examined in my opening chapter. Even as panoramic cinema sought to "erase" the presence of theatrical space as part of its experiential, participatory aesthetics, Soviet commentators were drawing attention to the fact that this space remained more present and tangible than ever before, through the activation of viewers' actual (not just imagined) mobility within the walls of the theater. This mobility, I propose, threatened to undermine the construction of a unified experience of Soviet time and history, precisely the goal of panoramic representation. Discussion of the present state of Moscow's Circular Panorama within the expansive Exhibition of Achievements of the People's Economy (VDNKh) opens and closes the chapter, contrasting the theater's original immersive intent with the fragmentary nature of its contemporary experience.

Building on this discussion of spectatorial immersion and fragmentation, the book's second chapter examines the participatory cinema of Mikhail Kalatozov and Sergei Urusevskii, especially their films *The Unsent Letter* (*Neotpravlennoe pis'mo*, 1959) and *I Am Cuba* (*Ia Kuba*, 1964). The physiologically immersive but simultaneously disorienting spatiality of both films, I argue, is rooted in an urge to create work in which space is perceived mimetically rather than topographically—that is, to abandon established Soviet divisions between people and their environment and to present human figures as indistinct from their surroundings. Particular attention is paid to Urusevskii's elaborate camera movement, which, while disrupting narrative coherence, seeks to embody the very process of spatial mimicry and, through this, to reformulate the guiding framework of progressive communist consciousness.

The notion of cinematic movement yields in the third chapter to an analysis of bodily movement in Georgii Danelia's 1964 film *I Walk the Streets of Moscow* (*Ia shagaiiu po Moskve*), made for the wide screen. Rather than utilizing this new screen format to generate a unified dramatic act, Danelia uses it to examine transient and scattered experiences in the Soviet capital. The chapter focuses in particular on the trope of purposeless walking and proposes that it functioned as a means for Danelia to imagine the regeneration of Soviet urban reality. In pursuing this analysis, I consider such diverse discursive threads as the embrace of transparent materials and pedestrian passages within post-Stalinist architecture, early 1960s Soviet film representations of children's mobile perception, and the Paris-based Situationist International's experimenting with the perception and use of urban space in the 1950s. Looking beyond abstract links between Western European practices and contemporary Soviet work, I explore concrete visual links between *I Walk the Streets of Moscow* and Jacques Tati's seminal 1967 film *Playtime* and propose that the two can be understood in direct correspondences to each other.

With a focus on Larisa Shepitko's 1966 film *Wings* (*Kryl'ia*), the fourth chapter examines the challenge posed by Shepitko's explicitly feminist project to Danelia's utopian vision of urban movement. Shepitko similarly concentrates on bodies and cities but turns her attention to who is doing the walking and why. Centering its discussion on Shepitko's figure of a middle-aged woman, burdened by history, who wanders the provincial city of Sevastopol, the chapter argues that *Wings* seeks to create, in dialogue with a host of filmic representations of walkers, a specifically *Soviet* female flaneur. Such a figure, I argue, was conceived by the director as a means of mobilizing female subjectivity in public places and, accordingly, to complicate the materialization of history and remembering in Soviet cities. Particular attention is paid to Shepitko's use of sound and voice in the film to elucidate the movement of women within urban and cinematic spaces—and in the process to question the foundational role of sexual difference for cinematic realism.

The final chapter continues the analysis of gender and space through a discussion of Kira Muratova's 1967 film *Brief Encounters* (*Korotkie vstrechi*), in which the filmmaker parses the relationship of women to space by exploring the materiality of film and of the film screen especially. My understanding of Muratova's unique spatial aesthetics unfolds through discussion of concomitant developments in Soviet interior design, consideration of the spatial rhetoric generated by the painterly genre of still life (which Muratova directly engages), and examination of feminist critiques of the production of space, especially in the work of Luce Irigaray. In a complete reversal of panoramic aesthetics, which sought to conceal the presence of the flat screen in order to achieve a seamless integration of audience and representational space, Muratova emphasizes the screen's material presence and flatness in order to illuminate the position of women within their everyday environments.

This book, it should be stressed, does not intend to cover every film in which changes in Soviet space of the Thaw period are depicted. Rather, it focuses on a few works that actively seek to produce—through the material conditions of cinematic presentation itself—new kinds of spaces, movements, and relations, and to position them as primary engines for social critique and transformation. This is also why, chronologically speaking, the films discussed here are weighted toward the later years of the Thaw—that is, from the mid-1960s on—including works produced after Khrushchev's removal from power. Soviet filmmakers, quite simply, needed time to process fully the complexity and potential repercussions of the spatial developments transpiring around them, including those taking place within cinema itself, before they could utilize them as a fount for new aesthetic possibilities. If the majority of films in the decade and a half after Stalin's death reflect diverse spatial shifts occurring in Soviet society during these years, it is toward the end of the period that filmmakers first take these shifts as a paramount—indeed, structuring—concern, transforming them into a basis for cinematic experimentation and social analysis.

As will become clear in the subsequent chapters, what began as an unintended evocation of the heterogeneity of cinematic space in debates about Soviet panoramic film turned into a consistent, increasingly precise and deliberate cinematic practice of dissecting the relationships between space, ideology, and subjectivity. The scope of this book culminates in 1967, one year before the Soviet military invasion of Prague—the event that marked the Thaw period's ultimate end. And yet the problems these films address persist to this very day, lending the works continued relevance. As contemporary Russia continues to redraw its map—literally and symbolically, ideologically and geopolitically—in a process of transition but without a clear destination, questions related to the production, use, and perception of space grow only deeper in their ethical and historical significance.

Notes

1. Zlobin, "Poiski, nakhodki, utraty," 106.
2. Ibid., 108.
3. For a detailed introduction to Thaw-era Soviet film, including the politics of film production, see Woll, *Real Images*. The development of Soviet film culture under Khrushchev, specifically through the import of Indian cinema, can be found in Rajagopalan's *Indian Films in Soviet Cinemas*.
4. Important precedents to this study are two scholarly articles that discuss the significance of space in the Thaw-era cinema. See Petrov, "The Freeze of Historicity in Thaw Cinema," and Izvilova, "Drugoe prostranstvo."
5. The program went on to confidently proclaim that "*a communist society will in the main be built in the USSR.*" Italics in the original. *Programme of the Communist Party of the Soviet Union*, 61, 62.
6. See, for instance, Neporozhnii, "Elektrifikatsiia i gradostroitelstvo."
7. Ibid., 3.
8. The discussions of architecture and urban planning took place primarily in two architecture journals published regularly during this period, *Sovetskaia arkhitektura* and *Arkhitektura SSSR*. Discussions of interior design appeared regularly in the journal *Dekorativnoe iskusstvo SSSR*.

9. Hanson, *The Rise and Fall of the Soviet Economy*, 64.
10. See, for instance, "Zabota o cheloveke—osnova sovetskogo gradostroitel'stva." The rhetoric of "organism" appears prominently in Tasalov, "Nekotorye problem razvitiia sovremennoi arkhitektury."
11. Aleksashina, "Promyshlennost' v gorode."
12. Lukin, "Nekotory voprosy sinteza monumental'nogo iskusstva i arkhitektury."
13. Smith, *Property of Communists*, 100.
14. Widdis, *Visions of a New Land*, 11.
15. Ibid., 8.
16. Detailed analysis of the reform can be found in Kibita, *Soviet Economic Management under Khrushchev*.
17. On the readjustment of Gulag prisoners to life outside the camp, see Cohen, *The Victims Return*.
18. McCauley, *Khrushchev and the Development of Soviet Agriculture*. On the disappointment many young people felt in the socialist adventure of the Virgin Land campaign and the ensuing protests, see Hornsby, *Protest, Reform, and Repression*.
19. Gorsuch, "Time Travelers," 205.
20. Gilburd, "The Revival of Soviet Internationalism," 380.
21. Thus *Iskusstvo kino* began a regular publication of a column for film lovers—that is, for people interested in making their own films. One example is an article about how to make a travel film by Shnaiderov, "O filmakh-puteshestviiakh."
22. Josephson et al., *An Environmental History of Russia*, 137.
23. Jones, *The Soviet Concept of "Limited Sovereignty" from Lenin to Gorbachev*, 143.
24. Filtzer, "From Mobilized to Free Labour," 154.
25. Widdis, *Visions of a New Land*, 10.
26. Lefebvre, *Key Writings*, 147.
27. Ross, "Lefebvre on the Situationists," 71.
28. Ibid.
29. Lefebvre, *The Production of Space*, 54.
30. Bykhovsky, "'Itog i ostatok' ili balans renegata," 122.
31. As Łukasz Stanek notes, Anatol Kopp's 1967 book *Town and Revolution* provided basic information about the Soviet postrevolutionary architectural avant-garde in France (Stanek, *Henri Lefebvre on Space*, 39).
32. Lefebvre, "L'urbanisme aujourd'hui," 222. Quoted in Stanek, *Henri Lefebvre on Space*, 87 (his translation).
33. Such parallels should be placed within the context of other broadly mirrored cultural developments in East and West, including shifting discourses about national pasts, legality, and human rights. See Kozlov and Gilburd, "The Thaw as an Event in Russian History."
34. Soja, "Vom 'Zeitgeist' zum 'Raumgeist,'" 245. Translation from German mine.
35. Buck-Morss, *Dreamworld and Catastrophe*, 35–39.
36. Lenin, "The Home and Foreign Policy of the Republic," 150.
37. Levin, "Society, State, and Ideology during the First Five-Year Plan," 59.
38. Jakobson, "On a Generation That Squandered Its Poets," 299.
39. Bruno, "Visual Studies: Four Takes on Spatial Turns," 23. For a broader and deeper history of the issues that Bruno addresses in this article, see also Bruno, *Atlas of Emotion*.
40. See, for instance, Kracauer, *Theory of Film*, and Walter Benjamin, "The Work of Art in the Age of Its Technological Reproducibility," *Selected Writings*, 4: 251–83.
41. Herman G. Scheffauer, "The Vivifying of Space," 77. Cited in Vidler, "The Explosion of Space," 47.
42. Vidler, "The Explosion of Space," 47.

1
THE PERSISTENCE OF PRESENCE: SOVIET PANORAMIC CINEMA

PERHAPS AS NO other place, first in the USSR and now Russia, Moscow's Exhibition of Achievements of the People's Economy, known widely as the VDNKh, has always operated as a sensitive seismograph of the country's ambitions and failures. An expansive complex to the north of Moscow's center, it has lived through several stages of construction throughout its history, each reflecting a particular moment in the developments of Soviet and post-Soviet economy, science, culture, and, most remarkably, ideology. The park opened in its initial form in 1939, with major additions during the first half of the 1950s.[1] In subsequent years the park's palatial pavilions, monuments, and fountains, generously spaced among carefully organized promenades, offered visitors an immersive environment in which to celebrate the USSR's power and accomplishments, its national unity, and its historical progress. While the concept of Soviet nationhood continued to be reworked and contested throughout the country's history, the VDNKh provided a space that transcended ethnic autonomies and divisions: the pavilions of Kazakhstan and Georgia, and so forth, showed how each constituent republic contributed, through its specific cultural and economic developments, to the creation of the Soviet whole, which was to be experienced as more than a sum of its parts. It became a space in which the Soviet community could be not only imagined, but momentarily lived.[2] As visitors strolled past Vera Mukhina's famous monument *Worker and Peasant Woman* (1937), were touched by the shiny drops of the Friendship of the Peoples Fountain, and contemplated the spectacular displays of immaculate collective farms and cosmic travels, they were meant to be overfilled with "energy," with a "physiological joy" of experiencing *here and now* the imminent, perfect Soviet future.[3]

As hopes for this radiant future officially shattered with the collapse of the Soviet Union in 1991, the park's architectural and symbolic unity began to break down as well, its carefully orchestrated manifestation of ideological enthusiasm becoming a pitiful collection of dilapidated and empty symbols. As the Friendship of the Peoples Fountain turned into an embodiment of failed Soviet ethnic policies, the previously splendid pavilions devoted to great national achievements transitioned into displays of disjointed stacks of imported commercial products, signifying the intensifying collapse of the post-Soviet economy. The park's groomed architectural ensemble became filled with temporary kiosks of all styles, shapes, and colors, selling mostly grilled meats, pilafs, and Coca-Cola.[4] A primary space of the Soviet utopian imagination fractured into pieces, its history and aspirations simply ignored or swallowed up by the emerging practices of nascent anything-goes capitalism.

In the last few years, however, calls to redevelop the exhibition complex have intensified. To prepare for the celebration of the park's seventy-fifth anniversary in August 2014, the Moscow government began a "global reconstruction . . . that already considerably transformed the appearance of the exhibition," restoring the pavilions, perfecting the promenades, and clearing the space of chaotic commercial traffic.[5] The park received back its original, and familiar to all, name of the VDNKh (after having been called All-Russia Exhibition Center for most of the post-Soviet period), and its territory was considerably expanded and enhanced with spectacular cultural and sports amenities. Commentators hailed this process as the center's chance for a "second youth," "the return to its roots," suggesting that it would very soon regain its past glory, become once more a place through which "paradise" could be imagined—now not only for the people of Russia, but, indeed, for the entire world.[6] The plans for what the VDNKh will offer in the future are still in development; the suggestions include making it a global exhibition center, or a modern entertainment park, or even a theme park dedicated to the USSR. Despite the disparity of the proposals, the common understanding is that the original architectural and landscape frameworks are to be preserved, with the most grandiose Soviet spatial rhetoric forming a basis for the park's operation within the culture of dynamic global capitalism. Soviet history will thus be neatly contained and yet functionally, and even glamorously, connected to the present, leaving behind the messiness in which it has been embedded, and lost, during the past two decades.

For our discussion here, one structure at the VDNKh is of a particular interest: the Circular Panorama, a movie theater of sorts featuring a circular eleven-panel screen, whose opening in summer 1959 coincided with the inauguration of the famous American National Exhibition a few miles away, at

Fig. 1.1 Moscow Circular Panorama. Photograph by the author, 2011.

Moscow's Sokolniki Park (figure 1.1).[7] Throughout the Soviet period, the Circular Panorama operated as a *mise en abîme* of the park's own aspirations, offering an extraordinary space for immersion into the happy Soviet life displayed on screen: the country's spectacular landscapes and urban promenades, the enthusiastic labor of factory workers, and the leisurely strolls of vacationers (figure 1.2). Today, the theater shows a modest repertoire of nine twenty-minute-long Soviet films made between 1967 and 1987, though their numbers are dwindling as film stock continues to deteriorate. As is the case of the exhibition center as a whole, the theater struggles to find its place in contemporary Russia, but the task here is particularly difficult. The Circular Panorama's cylindrical structure, designed for only one kind of moving image, which is no longer produced, cannot be easily adapted to other cinematic technologies.

To enter the space of the Circular Panorama today is like walking into an orchestrated historical installation: The entire structure and its function are arrested in time. Through its surround of images, the panorama transports visitors to a gauzy world of Soviet utopias, in which people and places of a bygone world appear in the present again. We are invited to take rides on the road, in the air, and on water; walk through well-known Moscow streets and through the centers of provincial towns on the Soviet periphery; visit the oldest architectural sites in Uzbekistan and stroll along the beaches of the Black Sea; and

Fig. 1.2 Strolling on a Soviet beach. From the Circular panorama film *Let's Go!* (*V dorogu, v dorogu!*), 1967.

simply encounter, "face to face," the people of the Soviet republics in the final two decades of the USSR's existence. These encounters, rides, and visits are effected through a nearly perpetual movement of the camera, meant to sweep spectators right into the center of brightly lit and joyful scenes.

In the 1950s, the Moscow panorama's primary draw was just this sense of spatial immersion: its elimination of the physical distance, and with it the ontological difference, between real and screen space. Today, the thrill appears to be gone, or at least substantially faded, comparing feebly with more recent cinematic technologies. Most often attended by no more than a dozen people, the worn-out and empty space of the theater is at the forefront of any spectator's gaze. But for these few visitors, the panorama's irresistible attraction lies in the material encounter it thus establishes with history itself: not just the images and sounds it presents, but also its own timeworn apparatus, space, and organization, not to mention its awkward place within the imminently expanding VDNKh. In contrast with the heavy-handed optimism and ostensibly timeless message of the original films, the theater imparts today a sense of impending disappearance. Rather than experiencing the intended physical sensation of being in another—invariably happy—place in which material present and utopian future are fused, contemporary panorama visitors are made acutely aware of the here and now of *this* place, of its uncomfortable position between an all-too-familiar (and un-utopian) past and an utterly unknown future.

Lacking financial and popular support, the theater has no clear path forward. At the same time, it displays a palpable unease with how it might relate to what came before. Its two small exhibition tables are covered with dusty

Soviet paraphernalia that appear random and lost, inviting neither nostalgia nor any particular historical interpretation. They are accompanied by amateurishly typed paper signs that read "We don't try to return to the past, we are just remembering it," as if apologizing for the theater's very existence.[8] There is no trace in this arbitrary presentation of the "marketing of memory"—what cultural critic Andreas Huyssen has discussed in relation to the global, often media-driven proliferation of memory narratives.[9] Rather, the display betrays a profound uncertainty about what should be remembered and how, if at all.

In its aching material obsolescence and problematic historical presentation, the Circular Panorama constitutes an exceptional display within the VDNKh. While the exhibition center seeks to move adamantly forward, the theater cannot leave behind its past. This past, however, unfolds as an experience of the present, effectively activating Soviet history and *placing* visitors within it. But in the process, the panorama also generates an awkward sense of distance, an awareness that we look at these moving images and inhabit the structure itself from a perspective that was hardly foreseen in their production. Experiencing the immersion, one cannot help feeling out of place within the panorama's represented world, because the future of these films' imagination stands at absolute odds with the future that has in fact arrived. Nowhere does this become more pronounced than in the rare moments when one of the filmed Soviet citizens gazes directly into the camera, looking trustfully at the viewer, initiating direct contact and encouraging a sense of seamless transition between the historical past and the viewing present. Whom are these people from the film looking at? Is it their own contemporaries, reincarnated in the bodies of today's spectators with help of the panorama's immersive forms? Or is it viewers from a post-Soviet future of whose existence they likely never imagined? Past, present, and future unfold here in multiple forms, layered one over another, impossible to separate. The result is a simultaneous production and disturbance of just the sort of historical contiguity the VDNKh as a whole seeks: both the seamless integration and the uneasy separation of past image and present circumstance.

The ambiguity and contradiction at the core of our present-day experience of the Circular Panorama invite us to look back at the early years of Soviet panoramic cinema—to reexamine its aspirations and assumed modes of operation in the 1950s and 1960s. As the panorama's immersive quality today suggests, and as many original critical discussions confirm, the spatial dynamics of panoramic films were well suited to the Soviet ideological landscape of the period. Projected within new, notably modern, theatrical spaces, of the kind that became popular all over the world at the time, these films seemed capable of advancing the aesthetic premise of socialist realism to a new level.[10] They not only depicted "reality in its revolutionary development" and displayed "revolutionary romanticism"—to quote from Andrei Zhdanov's original 1934 definition of socialist realism—but they also made visitors experience the "glimpse of tomorrow" as an immediate, enveloping, and physiologically sensed *present*, in which the tangible seamlessness of the grandiose Soviet space united the country into a great socialist nation.[11] But, as this chapter will further demonstrate, the same spatial organization of the theater that made this explicitly Soviet experience possible also appeared to work *against* its goal and logic. The rapidly multiplying critical voices of the time raised objections that the expansion of the screen and viewing space available to viewers would result in an increase of their real—not just imagined—mobility, thus allowing visitors to explore the theater itself as a contingently inhabited space. The outcome of such a mobile form of viewing would contradict what panoramas were meant to do: Rather than totalizing Soviet nationhood and subjectivity within the walls of the theater, it would fracture them and undermine the very idea of an integrated and perfectly unified consciousness of the country's history, time, and spaces.

Transcending the Attraction

When Moscow's Circular Panorama opened its doors in summer 1959, discussions and demonstrations of panoramic cinema in the USSR had already been around for a couple of years.[12] The first so-called kinopanorama film, *Wide Is My Country* (*Shiroka strana moia*, directed by Roman Karmen), had opened in winter 1958 utilizing technology developed at the Moscow Research Institute for Cinema and Photography (NIKFI) under the leadership of Evsei Goldovskii and closely resembling in its form US Cinerama, which had been developed in the United States by Fred Waller in 1952.[13] Although Goldovskii (who became one of the most vociferous advocates of panorama's use in the USSR) and others insisted on the superiority of the Soviet model, the difference between Cinerama and kinopanorama was negligible. The working parts of the two systems were largely interchangeable; the only notable difference between them was in their stereophonic sound systems, the Soviet version of which recorded and reproduced sound through nine channels, whereas the US version used seven. Otherwise, both used a three-panel, deeply curved screen with an aspect ratio of approximately 21.6 to 8.5, which extended the projected image far to the sides of the theatrical space, aiding in the creation of the panorama's celebrated effect of participatory presence.[14] Stereophonic technology, which distributed speakers throughout the space of the theater to create a more totalizing and organic correspondence between sound and image, substantially contributed to these effects.[15] And although Cinerama enjoyed great popular success at the Bangkok Constitution Fair in 1954, kinopanorama quickly caught up at the 1958 World's Fair in Brussels, with *Wide Is My Country* receiving the exhibition's grand prize. It was in Brussels, too, that the US Circarama, on which the construction of Moscow's Circular Panorama was based, made its international debut.

Kinopanorama's perceptual structure, widely hailed for creating the effect of presence, was scrutinized thoroughly in the Soviet press in the wake of the panoramic boom. Film critics suggested that it introduced an unprecedented viewing environment, one based on the elimination of the multiple boundaries that had traditionally structured filmic perception: between real life and the life depicted on screen, between spectatorial and represented space, between the physiology of perception inside and outside the theater. Rejecting these clear-cut distinctions, the new film form was considered a fundamental artistic breakthrough. As *Iskusstvo kino* critic Konstantin Dombrovskii wrote,

> From the times of Greek tragedy and the Roman circus, any spectacle—theater, film, or concert—was built around an opposition of the actor and the viewer. Actors' performances were bounded by the stage, proscenium, or the black frame of the screen. In the visual arts, . . . the essential compositional elements are the borders of the painterly surface. . . . Photography, painting, movie, or theater—for viewers it is a window into a world, a window behind which an action evolves that can be watched from the outside. . . .
>
> Panoramic film is grounded in a completely opposing principle. Here, the action takes place not behind the screen's frame, but immediately around the viewer—in front, behind, on the sides. Moviegoers, each separately and the whole mass that fills the theater, feel as if they participate in those events that unfold around them.[16]

Not only was the represented space freed from the separating and distancing constraints of the frame, but moviegoers' bodies, too, were unbounded from the visually conflicting conditions imposed by traditional viewing spaces. This was achieved above all through the activation of peripheral vision, which, as Dombrovskii and many others suggested, greatly added to the effect of presence. Whereas in traditional theatrical spaces the perimeter walls' persistent visual presence was at odds with that of the screen straight ahead, in panoramic cinema peripheral vision was harmonized and made contiguous with that of the screen. This peripheral vision, Dombrovskii suggested, operated more on the level of abstract sensation than on actual sight (we don't need to see exactly what is there, just sense that it *is* there), deepening—as in life—filmgoers' perception of the real, encompassing presence of the environment around them.[17]

Because the spatial structure of kinopanorama and the effect of presence that it produced were identical to US Cinerama, Soviet critics immediately sought to distinguish *Wide Is My Country* from previous productions in the United States. In the view of one such early reviewer,

> When the first Cinerama Theater opened on a noisy New York street, advertisement and newspaper reporters quickly spread the news throughout the world about the cinema's latest achievement, its "unheard-of effect": "without leaving the auditorium, you'll experience the beauty of flying." . . . The attraction, indeed, was potent. The film's authors didn't worry too much about the content. Success was in their hands: the illusion was so all-encompassing that viewers, taught by the bitter experience of their predecessors, hurried to stock up on lemons and mints before the show. A different method was chosen in the making of the first Soviet kinopanorama film. Soviet film workers didn't see it as their task to stun viewers with effective attractions and to cause dizziness.[18]

The experience of Cinerama, according to this description, was rooted in a series of fragmentary "attractions" that had little regard for film dramaturgy: sensational effects took the place of meaningful content. This terminology became a foundation for much subsequent criticism. Cinerama was described as an undeveloped formation whose practitioners remained unaware of its artistic potential, much as had been said of cinema itself in its earliest days, when excitement about the medium's technological newness temporarily arrested its artistic growth. Soviet kinopanorama, critics argued, was fundamentally different. Already in its debut feature, it emerged in a developed and mature form, immune to the "childhood illnesses" of its US cousin. The potent participatory moments in *Wide Is My Country*, rather than becoming ends in themselves and overwhelming the film's dramaturgical "texture," functioned hand in hand with this texture—evident above all, critics noted, in the film's masterly weaving of a poetic voiceover narration that effectively muted the essential fragmentariness, the spectacularized "attraction," of panoramic cinema.[19]

Roman Karmen, the film's director and one of the most established documentary filmmakers in the country at the time, echoed the terms of critics' subsequent praise in an interview given immediately before the film's release, stressing the significance of his film's content over the thrills of its participatory effects. *Wide Is My Country*, Karmen claimed, was to be a "tale about the Motherland" told through the dazzling representation of Soviet landscapes and cities and their industrial and cultural might (figure 1.3). The expanded material means of kinopanorama—above all, its enlarged screen—was especially productive in the pursuit of such patriotic aspirations: "Moscow highways and majestic panoramas of the city of Lenin; splendid Volga dams and sunny expanses of the Caucasus; spreads of yellow virgin fields and the industrial grandeur of Magnitogorsk. The measurements of the episodes narrating all of these could not better suit the specifics of kinopanorama, which allows

Fig. 1.3 Gliding through Moscow. From *Cinerama's Russian Adventure*, 1966 (the US-released Cinerama film, combining six Soviet Kinopanorama productions).

one to convey the magnificence and power, the ungraspable spaces, of the Soviet country."[20]

The discursive wrestling with US Cinerama that defined kinopanorama's emergence—rooted, again, in an awareness of the obvious similarities of form and intent that defined the two technologies—betrays the depth of issues at stake for Soviet representational practices at the time. Most important was the need to "translate" the spatial dynamics of Cinerama from one ideology to another, which meant essentially to appropriate and sublimate its original form into a higher Soviet order. If Cinerama *was* a cinema of attractions, organized around random (however programmed) moments of the corporeal experience of presence, kinopanorama sought to make this randomness necessary, to organize and imbed it within Soviet narratives and history. Physiological sensations—the aesthetic significance of which had repeatedly been debated within Soviet cultural discourse—supposedly assumed in kinopanorama a clear, progressive form.[21]

The repetitive, negative reference to the cinema of "attractions" within kinopanorama discussions begs for some explanation. The term, well known to film scholars today through the work of film historian Tom Gunning,[22] was indeed a primary concept for the Soviet avant-garde of the 1920s, formulated and exploited most thoroughly by Sergei Eisenstein, in direct connection to film's potential as a tool for progressive ideological development. Writing in 1923 about the organization of a theatrical play, Eisenstein defined attraction as "every aggressive moment in [theater], i.e. every element of it that brings to light in the spectator those senses or that psychology that influences his experience—every element that can be verified and mathematically calculated to produce certain emotional shocks in a proper order within the totality—the only means by which it is possible to make the final ideological conclusion perceptible."[23] An unambiguous and ideologically desirable meaning, Eisenstein thus made clear, could not evolve without viewers' sensory participation, without their experience of intense if fleeting "bursts of presence"; attraction was the means by which interaction with the story on screen was concentrated, and bodily and neurological reactions were channeled toward the calculated intellectual understanding of the matter at hand. Eisenstein's montage—and his "montage of attractions" especially—fell out of favor during the 1930s antiformalist campaign.[24] Yet we can see that he sought a similar sublimation of the physiological experiences of film spectatorship as that espoused by the proponents of Soviet kinopanorama several decades later, despite their continuously negative take on the notion of "attraction." For both, the startling, unexpected, and highly subjective experience of a moment was to be transformed into a sense that one was actively making and taking part in the objective development of history itself.

Viewing as Production

Kinopanorama was easily put to work to further socialist-realist traditions of advocating and celebrating the superiority of Soviet life, and, indeed, it substantially extended the very scope of socialist-realist aesthetics through its experiential effects. In the late 1950s, it appeared headed toward widespread critical and popular success. Kinopanorama offered something that previous films could not come close to matching: Not only was it better at conveying the USSR's distant, expansive, and "ungraspable" spaces, but it simultaneously brought these spaces close to the viewer and made them seem literally within one's grasp. As one Soviet viewer observed, "Already in my early years, I dreamt of traveling through the Soviet Union. And now, having visited the panoramic theater and watched the film *Wide Is My Country*, I think that my wish has almost been fulfilled."[25]

Although the desire to map the vast lands of the USSR on screen as a unified, representable whole had been present throughout Soviet film practice for decades, kinopanorama fundamentally shifted the terms of such aspirations, moving beyond the symbolic representation of such unity to pursue its *instantiation* as an embodied, haptic experience. Grigorii Alexandrov's seminal 1936 film *Circus* offers a particularly significant precedent in this regard (it also prominently features the popular "Song of the Motherland," the first words of which, "wide is my country," provided the title for Karmen's production some twenty years later). The enclosed circular arena of the circus at the end of Alexandrov's film, filled with a boisterous and explicitly ethnically diverse crowd, becomes a centripetal space that compacts, and absorbs, the entirety of the Soviet nation. It turns into an imaginary map of the country and its aspirational unity that viewers could easily read and recognize as such. Kinopanorama would later pursue this same project precisely by forgoing, and indeed actively countering, such symbolic or structural enclosures altogether. Viewers of *Wide Is My Country* were meant not only to recognize the Soviet map, but also to traverse it "from one end . . . to the other" in order to *live* its expansiveness firsthand.[26] Moscow's Circular Panorama epitomized this even more: The actual enclosed circular space of its theater would burst open onto the expansive territories of the nation.

In this process, the viewer's physiological experience of cinema took on a fundamental new importance. Indeed, it was the embodied viewers themselves—in lieu of a conventional protagonist, mostly absent in panoramic films—who became the central player, the literal focal point, of panoramic travel as realized in kinopanorama productions, with the camera operating as a virtual double for the spectator.[27] The possibility of such seamless placement of the viewer *within* represented space excited contemporary critics as opening up new possibilities for a specifically Soviet aesthetic experience. As Viktor Gorokhov noted in one of the first discussions of *Wide Is My Country* in the pages of *Iskusstvo kino*, "You could not tear your gaze away from the grandiose landscape of the new Moscow, opening from Lenin Hills. Before and behind you, the Peterhof fountains pleasantly gurgle. And travel through the country that has been transformed by the Revolution—beginning with Smolny, the Revolutionary headquarters—becomes your travel."[28] What Gorokhov suggests here is a complete entwinement of Soviet space, history, and subjecthood within the confines of the kinopanorama theater—a dynamic complementing and completion of these three over the course of viewing Karmen's film. Within this process, Soviet history is materialized as the force that has facilitated the homogeneity of the country's space, smoothly assimilating pre-Revolutionary areas, such as the groomed tsarist gardens of Peterhof, into its newly formed Soviet totality. Furthermore, individual and collective viewers are situated not only as subjects of but as active participants in this formation, marching "together" with Red Army soldiers toward Lenin in one of the film's sequences. And Soviet space—landscapes, factories, and construction sites of all kinds—is revealed as a medium, surrounding viewers from all sides and enabling them to *sense*, to physically feel and experience, the fact of their belonging to this nation and its endeavors.

As Gorokhov noted in his analysis, "It is a great joy to feel yourself, even if only for a moment, surrounded by coal miners who just finished their work, or among the workers of the virgin lands, or among the builders of the new apartment building.... You yourself, within the spaces of kinopanorama, can experience the intoxication of labor."[29] Kinopanorama thus seemed to perfect the very thing that places such as the VDNKh had originally sought to fashion: It generated, more directly and with greater orchestration, precisely the physiological joy that visitors to the exhibition were meant to feel—intoxicating them with pleasures of labor, infusing their bodies with enthusiasm for a communist construction. (The massive scale on which this process would transpire should not be overlooked. The Mir cinema in Moscow, built in 1957 as the first theater to project kinopanorama films in Russia, housed 1,226 seats, thus intensifying the collectivity of this experience and creating a festive mood in visitors from the moment they entered the theater. The Circular Panorama, designed for two hundred people, often packed up to five hundred, and by some accounts even one thousand, visitors.) And because *Wide Is My Country* was released soon after the celebrations of the fortieth anniversary of the October Revolution, its ostensible effects were to be even more powerful. The date was celebrated as both a process and a finishing line, with audiences initiating ideological transformation from within the space of the film and subsequently celebrating their successes as outside spectators of their own achievements. Viewers, then, were able to delight in productive participation, one that bore historic socialist results, instead of submitting themselves to the empty and meaningless pleasures of US Cinerama and its amusement park–like attractions.

The Reality of Mobility

But the unanimous praise for the "artistic breakthrough" of kinopanorama did not last long. As critics and technologists continued to scrutinize its space in order to perfect it, they brought attention to viewers' possible modes of behavior within the theater, some of which contradicted the very intention of panoramic aesthetics. It was Evsei Goldovskii, the credited inventor of kinopanorama and one of its strongest proponents, who introduced this fundamentally new angle into the discussions of panorama's spectatorial space, and he initially considered it to be the medium's greatest asset. The physiological activation of viewers, he suggested, not only created a sense of real participation in the spectacle represented before them, but also altered their behavioral patterns inside movie theaters themselves. One of the major hindrances to perceiving film realistically, Goldovskii repeatedly argued, is the unnatural stillness of the viewer's body while watching traditional cinema, in which the entire screen is easily seen from one point of view and no bodily movement whatsoever is called for or even provoked. Such immobility inevitably lends a sense of "artificiality, conditionality, to the film"—which, according to Goldovskii, became particularly pronounced with the heightening of film's realistic effect through the development of sound and color.[30] Panoramic film, on the other hand, demanded viewers' physical movement (at the very least, a turn of the head) and thus returned people's natural mobility to the experience of film viewing. This "principle of mobility" was for Goldovskii nothing less than the essence of the new cinema, which allowed expanding—explicitly and dramatically—the restricted point of view of a traditional movie theater into a "viewing situation."[31]

Goldovskii's conceptualization of cinematic realism as a simulation of real-life conditions, which depended substantially on viewers' bodily behavior, had little to do with the more proper understanding of realism in Soviet cultural discourse, which relied heavily on the inherent presence of a defined idea in the work of art that would be communicable to perceivers. This proper understanding of realism came unwittingly under Goldovskii's criticism when he wrote that in traditional cinema a "film is presented to the viewer in a completed form, so that he can look at it only in ways imposed by the filmmakers."[32] In contrast, with the introduction of mobility into the theatrical space, the viewer becomes an active participant, choosing the parts that interest him most, perceiving the film "in his own way."[33]

Just how foreign such a notion of democratic and interactive viewing was to Soviet aesthetic criticism is readily apparent in the discussions of both panoramic films and broader visual studies. The critic O. Beskin, for instance, bluntly stated the problem when he suggested, in a discussion of painterly panoramas, that the *wholeness* of artistic meaning (the existence of which is, by definition, a defining property of real—which is to say, *realist*—art) can be perceived only in the presence of clear boundaries, and distance, between the spectator's space and that of the work of art. The artwork's main goal, for Beskin, was to convey the ideas of its maker—expressed in its qualities as a composition in which all elements function together to create a single, organic, inseparable whole. In order for the viewer to perceive this entirety, the work of art *must* be separated from the space of the viewer, "circumscribed" in its own space. "In panoramas, where the viewer is surrounded by the representation on all sides and liberally tears out any of its parts," the wholeness of the composition breaks down and the idea of the work itself is compromised, and indeed becomes impossible.[34]

The essence of such criticism is familiar to contemporary readers of the history of expanded cinema, regarding such developments, for instance, as the integration of moving images into art museums, where the visitors' steady motion through the exhibition space might be at odds with the attention and immersion (and physical immobility) demanded by cinema.[35] Within Soviet criticism, this issue emerged as a rather unexpected byproduct of the original intent of panoramas, opposing the principle and premises of socialist aesthetics. In a 1960 article on the technological future of cinematography, an analysis of the viewing conditions in the Circular Panorama took an especially sharp turn when the two critics, A. Veklenko and B. Belkin, suggested that viewers' "freedom" to choose what to look at during a screening destroyed any possibility for a meaningful experience of the wholeness of its films. Analogously with Beskin, they argued that the goal of a director is to bring audiences to view the world through his or her eyes—a goal that becomes impossible in panoramic cinema. If initial reviews of panoramic cinema, then, had understood its spatial parameters to deepen the means by which filmmakers could realize an aesthetic representation of Soviet totality, subsequent critics saw it as shattering just this possibility. The natural mobility of viewers' bodies—for Goldovskii, the very essence of the new cinema—was seen in this new context to be simply excessive:

> If the story [siuzhet] is structured in such a way that all viewers turn simultaneously to the right, and then to the left, then why do we need these kind of turns that everybody tries to escape in life? Simpler and more comfortable, and considerably more natural, is to show the significant narrative moments directly in front of the viewer.
>
> If the director repudiates the device of "attachment" of the viewer's gaze to a certain subject, then a situation of complete freedom emerges, with some of the viewers looking left, others looking right, and some looking to the back. But this chaos leads only to the fact that after watching the film, viewers are not even capable of discussing it together, for it is as if they saw different things. Obviously, in such conditions, no director could create a whole [tselnyi] artistic work.[36]

These critics' discontent implied a conflict between the panorama's architectural and cinematic spaces. Constructed to operate in tandem, with the architectural space in effect dissolving into the represented space as part of the theater's immersive aesthetic program, they appear to have shifted their roles, with the architectural form taking prevalence over the cinematic representation. The totality of the latter was fragmented through the spectators' "architectural" viewing of the film —one in which they looked to the sides and freely moved around, as one would when observing an architectural site. Even kinopanorama's inventor, Goldovskii, could take this contradiction—and his "principle of mobility" of which it was a direct manifestation—only so far. For rather than embracing the unprecedented mobility of the viewer afforded by the Circular Panorama, he cautioned against the diffusion, or distraction, of vision it thus produced. "The viewer cannot see all screens at once," he wrote. "He is forced to turn his eyes, head, and body to observe these screens, losing the ability to look at the shots shown on other screens."[37] Like other critics, Goldovskii saw the space of the Circular Panorama as a threat to the coherence and contiguity of narration and suggested that its all-surrounding screens generate an event devoid of any meaning. The space, he argued, was limited to the status of "cinematic attraction." This term, initially reserved for US Cinerama, thus took an oblique turn in Soviet criticism: It fell to kinopanorama's very inventor to define the motivating principle of the Circular Panorama, right at the heart of Moscow's VDNKh.[38]

This "new" understanding of attraction departed significantly from the term's original meaning in the discussions of panoramas—that is, as a critique of the fleeting, physiological sensations of immersion that were not integrated into a purposeful narrative. Now it referred to the bodily distraction *from* the immersion, and to the architecture that facilitated this process. Perceiving "on the move," an individual viewer still engaged in a process of production, but of a very different kind than what Gorokhov had imagined—a production not of the Soviet history and nation, but of the viewer's own cinematic event, which he or she constituted out of the surrounding fragmentary possibilities. These could encompass a variety of things: an immersion, still, into the representation on screen; an absorption into the mechanics of this immersion; a reflection on how the perception of the spectacle might change with shifts in a bodily position; and, of course, the bodily movement itself. If there was any narrative arc—any dramaturgical "texture"—to connect all these, it was completely in the hands of the viewer. In such conditions, the wholeness of the cinematic experience, its collective nature, could *not* be more than a sum of its innumerable, unaccountable, and uncontrollable parts—always contingent on each individual visitor's state of physical and mental being.

What became an "attraction" then is the actual present, the physical reality, the contingency of which could not be integrated into the film and was, in fact, highlighted through the very structures that sought to defeat it. The extent of such a reality problem within Soviet aesthetic discourse is perhaps more apparent in the history of Soviet photography, in which the medium's "indexicality"—its actual material connection to what it represents—proved to be both a draw and a disturbance for Soviet representational practices. As art historian Leah Dickerman has argued, photographic images provided a critical material basis for documenting and "proving" emergent Soviet historical narratives, helpful especially in that they could be massively reproduced and circulated widely for public consumption. But as truthful and authentic representations of historical events, as a "permanent impress of a past moment in time," they also became potentially dangerous. The indexical and automatic nature of photography placed it beyond its makers' absolute authorial control, leading to images in which accidental details or unwanted figures contradicted officially established historical narratives.[39] To fix this, photographic images were manipulated or transformed into heavily edited painted versions. Politically dubious figures were thus simply airbrushed out or removed from scenes, allowing the official line to remain pure and straightforward for present and future generations.[40]

This simultaneous reliance on photography's truth value and anxiety about its "potentially ambivalent or mutable meanings" led to the particularly Soviet form of the "falsified document"—paintings and sculptures that formally resembled and thus epistemologically borrowed from well-known originals, but which mutated the originals' actual content to meet specific ideological needs. This process of translation from one medium to another included not only a modification of content but also a realignment of space—the creation of "proper" axes by which works were to be seen. Dickerman describes, for instance, the relationship between a 1927 sculpture of Lenin by the artist Ivan Shadr and an earlier photograph by K. A. Kuznetsov on which the monument was based:

> Lenin's sculptural elevation not only replaces the contingent and mobile vehicle [on which he stands in the photograph] with a fixed and permanent pedestal, but also lifts him out of the confused hierarchy of the photograph with its multiple points of interest. (For some members of the crowd, the truck seems far more interesting than Lenin.) ... The shift in scale re-monumentalizes the photo-figure, reversing the camera's operations of miniaturization, while its elevation onto a high pedestal creates a zone of isolated visibility within urban public space: both keep the spectator at a distance, establishing a barrier to approach.[41]

What is significant for our discussion is the resonance of terms between Dickerman's analysis and the negative criticism of panoramic cinema: focus on the lack of a clear hierarchy between what is important and what is not; concern with multiple points of view and the setting free or reigning in of viewers' mobile bodies; and attention to issues of proximity and the "equation" of scale between viewers and representation. Even more significant, conflicts over how to understand the space of panoramic cinema and the processes of perception it enacted were rooted in precisely the same concern with the reality effect that, as Dickerman argues, haunted Soviet engagements with photography.[42] In the case of panoramas, however, the conflict concerned not images but spectatorial space itself, raising questions about the extent to which viewers' *real* experiences of the here and now could be seamlessly integrated into the meanings generated on screen. It was this actual material space, populated with real, embodied viewers, that had the potential to become an integral part of—or alternately a threat to—Soviet ideology. The spatial experience instantiated by kinopanorama could create an effect of truth through the very corporeal participation of its own viewers, grounded in an active physical presence that, indeed, went beyond the mere indexical record. And yet this very same spatial experience escaped orchestrated control, threatening to take on meaning in and of itself as an independent, fluctuating form—"ambivalent and mutable" in significance, dependent on multiple variables in the here and now that could put into question the entire process of historical mythmaking, as set apart on isolated screens.[43]

One particular sequence in Karmen's *Wide Is My Country* suggests the extent to which Soviet panoramic cinema was interested in buttressing the indexicality of a documentary recording while at the same time further overcoming its contingency. It is a sequence that displays a sculpture of Lenin, followed by a "living shot" of the leader. (The descriptions of this sequence leave unclear whether it is a photograph or a documentary chronicle.) Gorokhov, in his *Iskusstvo kino* review, singles out this sequence as worthy of special praise, for here Karmen uses the screen as a triptych rather than as a contiguous surface, as in most panoramic films: "On the central segment of the spherical screen, a Lenin monument is succeeded by a shot that imprinted a living Lenin on a tribune. From the left side of the screen, the Red Army soldiers move toward the right side. Thanks to kinopanorama, the viewer feels that he, too, is in the thick of the people, marching together."[44] Karmen chose to represent the history of the origins of Soviet state through a formalized succession of distinct visual media, descending, so to speak, from the higher symbolic value of a sculpture, to the documentary realism of the photograph/chronicle, to, ultimately, the actual "mobile" bodies of the soldiers and the viewers, who would imbue the representation of Soviet history with truth-value through the panorama's participatory aesthetics. That is, the "documentary" quality of their physiological sensations of participation in the march toward Lenin, and socialism, would be uncontestable, defeating any contingency in the chronicle that might stand in the way of the intended meaning. But the almost immediate discontent of the panorama's critics with the perceptual heterogeneity it engendered demonstrated that it could in fact operate precisely in reverse: to intensify instead photography's uncontrollability, and thus to complicate film's ability to tell the proper story of the revolution.

The Multiplicity of Time

By opening up a road to conflicted perceptions, panoramas seemed to be capable of disordering not only the narrative of Soviet history and nation, but also time itself, in terms of both its use and its perception. If, on the one hand, viewers' time was seen as being spent productively, structured around a well-organized participatory tour through Soviet spaces and history, on the other hand, it was thought to be wasted, spent in a random, inefficient, and above all meaningless event with no overarching goal in sight. If the first version, furthermore, saturated the fleeting *sensations* of presence with a teleological progress that encompassed the past, present, and future, then the second version reinstated the *actual* present as a coincidental condition with no predetermined trajectory, no sense of integration into the broader order of Soviet time, and no consensus on how this present is lived by each individual in the theater. In this way, time became unstructured, contingent, and subjectively experienced—and as such, contradictory to the Soviet ideology of a homogeneous, measurable, and teleological time that had developed since the Revolution.

Such a rationalized and standardized temporal notion had been central to Soviet political discourse for decades, for only it could provide the organizing basis for the underlying narrative of spatial expansion and historical progress at the root of this discourse. These efforts began immediately after the Revolution in a diversity of practices—from Soviet obsessions with Taylorism, derived from the late-nineteenth-century system of scientific management advocated by the US engineer Frederick W. Taylor, to the more radical work of the well-known Bolshevik Platon Kerzhentsev and his "Time League," a short-lived but massive organization founded in 1923 whose goal was to establish "the correct and efficient use of time in all walks of social and private life."[45] Preoccupied with efficiency, members of Kerzhentsev's league thoroughly documented time use by measuring "every minute of their daily routine" in an attempt to completely eliminate temporal waste.[46] Less extreme practices of time rationalization continued to emerge in later periods, including, for instance, the establishment of Five-Year Plans for the country's development and the proliferation of statistical analyses on how Soviet citizens spent their working and resting hours. The Thaw period witnessed a greater interest in the structuring of time. Attempts were made to revive the methods of scientific management in industry and elaborate studies measuring time use were published, focusing in particular on leisure activities of young people in the hopes of eliminating "excesses of 'idle time' or 'inactivity' which breed various forms of anti-social behavior."[47] Filmgoing was viewed favorably in these studies, seen as serving the goal of structured relaxation and education and promoting healthy socialization. What is striking is that the whole origination of panoramic cinema was consistently described in terms of time efficiency—from the speed with which the technology was developed, to the theaters built, to the films produced—generating a sense that this efficiency, too, would be transferred into the viewing experience. The focus on a *productive* experience of panoramic viewing as just discussed also suggests a rational and calculated use of time within the new theaters.

But to what degree could cinema, in general, facilitate such efforts? Film scholar Mary Ann Doane has argued that early cinematic practices are inextricably connected to the project of rationalizing time within industrial modernity. Referring to such diverse developments as the expansion of railroad and communication systems, the distribution of pocket watches, and, once again Taylorism, Doane discusses this period as dominated by the tendency to transform time "into the discrete, the measurable, the locus of value" (not different, in essence, from the concerted efforts of those concerned with time organization in the Soviet Union)—a tendency that gradually replaced a more natural relationship with time associated with agrarian societies, in which the seasons and other biological and natural rhythms, including those of people's bodies, determined how time was experienced.[48] But it was also during this period, Doane argues, that a very different notion of time gained cultural significance. It was time as ephemeral moment, characterized by contingency and chance and escaping rationalization, "beyond or resistant to meaning."[49] It was especially in the discourse over photography that such notions of time took hold, because of the medium's indexicality, its "thisness," its ability to grasp the fleeting moment and yield it to representation. The emergence of cinema fell into the footsteps of photography, opening up even deeper possibilities of capturing such fleeting experience: "the technological assurance of indexicality is the guarantee of a privileged relation to chance and the contingent, whose lure would be the escape from the grasp of rationalization and its system."[50] Time, as a moment and duration, could regain its material form and become perceivable and accessible to experience while remaining still outside the abstract structures of rationalization. As Doane suggests, the impulse to document and archive time is particularly evident before the emergence of classical narrative film, in the turn-of-the-century actualities of the Lumière brothers, for instance, as they "appeared to capture a moment, to register and repeat 'that which happens,'" becoming a proof that any random, meaningless event could be filmable, its time thus archived and later reproduced.[51]

Doane's analysis resonates strikingly with an essay by Andrei Tarkovskii, "Imprinted Time," published at the end of the Thaw period, in 1967, in which he implicitly sets cinema's ability to record pure time against the project of time rationalization. He develops here a notion of the use and experience of time, specifically in cinema, that is contrary to nearly all Soviet discourse on the topic, arguing that the essence of film is to make time tangible "in its real and inseparable connection with the material actuality that surrounds us every day and hour."[52] It is only with the invention of cinema that people gained access to the "real matrix of time," which now could be stored, archived, repeatedly reproduced, and newly conceived and understood. Tarkovskii writes, "Why do people go to the movies? What leads them to the dark room where they sit for an hour and a half, observing the play of shadows on the screen? . . . I think that the typical aspiration of a person going to cinema is to find time—a lost time or the time that he could not yet have acquired."[53] In contrast to his many Soviet contemporaries, the filmmaker laments the tendency to structure films through literary and theatrical principles, and to focus on narrative and teleological progression, squandering thus the cinematic potential to imprint "the reality of time," which was present, he also suggests, in the Lumières' cinema but had mostly vanished since then. The documentary chronicle, for Tarkovskii, remains a particularly ideal cinematic form because it not only can record life but "reconstruct, resurrect it" through its unique relation with time.[54]

Both Tarkovskii and, more explicitly, Doane discuss the essential shift in the experience of time that film provided in its emergence, while also addressing a particular temporality that transpires during the process of film viewing. Life can be resurrected, according to Tarkovskii, or appear in all its multiplicity, according to Doane, only by means of cinematic technology. Otherwise, life itself is not reachable in the actual lived present; it passes before it becomes meaningful, or, in Tarkovskii's words, its time is "lost," or could not be "acquired." But in the darkness of the movie theater, this past, lived time returns as an *experience* of presence. In Doane's view, "Once the present as contingency has been seized and stored, it ineluctably becomes the past. Yet this archival artifact becomes strangely immaterial; existing nowhere but in its screening for a spectator in the present, it becomes the experience of presence. . . . What is archived, then, would be the experience of presence. But it is the disjunctiveness of the presence relived, of a presence haunted by historicity."[55] Cinema's rematerialization of the real flow of time, its return from the abstract and calculable into the domain of the tangible and even the embodied, does not enable viewers to be *in* the actual presence of what they see, but rather to have an *experience* of it, that is, an encounter still bracketed, not one with itself, not fully of an "actually lived" nature. What makes it different from the actual lived present, according to Doane, is the sense of disjunctiveness brought about by the persistence of the past within moving images, by the way spectators know and feel that what is shown on screen has already passed and no longer is.

This brings us back to panoramic cinema. For although neither Doane nor Tarkovskii discusses it in their writings (Doane focuses on the history of early cinema, and Tarkovskii explicitly states his lack of interest in experimental cinematic technologies), panoramic cinema was rooted, ultimately, in the very idea of experiencing presence that both the critic and the filmmaker take as their analytical focus. This experience of presence, one must acknowledge, was of a nature different from what Doane addresses, perhaps even of an opposing kind. Panoramic cinema, after all, was interested less in reconstructing "that which happened" and more in simulating presence as a *total*, unambiguous present, without the disjunctiveness or haunt of historicity central to her analysis. This could be achieved only through the perceived erasure of ontological boundaries between the actual and screened present and through the full integration of these into each other. The sensory, bodily reactions of the moment and the external rhythm of cinema were to finally find a unity, with physiological participation rematerializing the "strange immateriality" of moving images.

But, as I have suggested, the project appeared to fail precisely at the point where it needed to succeed. The specific architectural form of panoramic cinema—and especially of the circular panorama—invited viewers to initiate their own time within its walls, therefore placing the true contingency of the moment at the forefront of their perception. The result of doing so would not be the celebrated effect of presence within the moving images so much as an experience of experiencing that presence, so to speak. That is, it would be a process by which the audience would be integrated into the reality of the screen while simultaneously sensing this moment from a position external to it, highly aware of its actual present conditions, and of the entire apparatus generating the spectacle. If it is not an exact recovery of the lost time as Tarkovskii understood it, since time is not inscribed here and cannot be archived and repeated, it nevertheless *is* an encounter with time as a present moment— the *feel* of its presence, a sensation of "fully inhabiting it," precisely because of the distinct disassociation of one temporality from the other, and the mutual effect of them on each other.[56]

There are no explicit contemporary accounts of this divided and self-contradictory viewing experience, and so it remains a speculative possibility, emerging obliquely from critical discussions of the time. In the present, however, such a conflicted viewing is definitive for any visitor to the Moscow Circular Panorama. As suggested at the outset of this chapter, what structures our experience as much as, if not more than, the films themselves is the panorama's space in its current condition. For contemporary viewers, standing enclosed by the sunny faces and picturesque locales, our attention is necessarily drawn to the structure's own unforgiving presence: to the vertical gaps that separate its connected screens; to the projectors' lights visible throughout the space; and—perhaps most staggering—to the once-packed central floor that now stands nearly empty. It is this space once again that distracts visitors today from immersing themselves in the experience of these films as a total present.

Yet it is, nevertheless, the same space—*together* with the moving images that line its walls—that functions today as an astonishing archive of time, inching toward just the kind of cinematic inscription and preservation of time that Tarkovskii and Doane describe. Moving through the very same structure that viewers of the Soviet period encountered, "acting" within the spectacle of *their* panoramic films, stepping into *their* means of architectural distraction and cinematic immersion, contemporary visitors recover the time that has been lost, "capture its moment," and "repeat what happened." As we move through the theater's space today, we activate the time both of and within these images, carrying its ghostly passage into the present—a present thus haunted by historicity. Totalized Soviet time itself unfolds here as a fleeting and ephemeral experience—a series of moments, of fragments, the meaning of which escapes rationalization and easy assimilation into the ongoing flow of history.

Notes

1. For a detailed description of the appearance of the Exhibition in 1959, see Novakovskii, *Vystavka Dostizhenii Narodnogo Khoziastva SSSR*.

2. On the questions of nation and nationality in the USSR, see Martin, *The Affirmative Action Empire*. Martin finishes the book with the discussion of Stalin's doctrine of The Friendship of the Peoples as "the officially sanctioned metaphor of an imagined multinational community" (432). This concept was symbolically immortalized in the VDNKh's Friendship of the Peoples Fountain, one of the most prominent sculptural pieces of the exhibition.

3. Vladimir Paperny, *Architecture in the Age of Stalin*, 167. In a similar vein, Russian philosopher Mikhail Ryklin has described his personal childhood experience of visiting the exhibition in the 1950s as such: "I left the territory fully enchanted. If, I thought then, in this place, among all the palaces, sculptures, and fountains, wonder became true, then it cannot be different that this wonder repeats also in many other places." Ryklin, *Räume des Jubels*, 137 (my translation from German).

4. As one Moscow administrator described this chaotic commercial activity, "currently, [the center] has transformed in an indeterminate place, with indeterminate establishments on its periphery." Mikhalev, "Proekt rekonstruktsii VVTs priobriol konkretnye kontury."

5. Vladimirova, "Park kultury, otdykha i sporta."

6. Fedorova, "Vtoraia molodost' VDNKh," and Ishchenko, "Konchai bazar."

7. On Moscow's 1959 American Exhibition and the Soviet campaign to counter its attractions, see Hixson, *Parting the Curtain*, esp. chapters 6 and 7.

8. This description of Circular Panorama's interior refers to my visit there in December 2010. It has been renovated since then and might not have the same objects and signs as before.

9. Huyssen, *Present Pasts*, 21.

10. On the 1950s and early 1960s discussion of how to modernize representational realism, primarily in painting, see Reid, "Modernizing Socialist Realism." One part of these discussions focused specifically on new modes of viewers' engagement, since canonized models of realism, "far

from thrusting the viewer into the momentum of contemporary life and mobilizing him/her into action, abstracted her/him from life and induced passivity," 223.

11. Andrei Zhdanov's speech to the First All-Union Congress of Soviet Writers, reprinted in Bowlt, *Russian Art of the Avant-Garde*, 293.

12. According to the Soviet press, the development of panoramic technologies began in the USSR in 1956. "Sovetskoe panoramnoe kino," 92.

13. On the history of widescreen cinematic technologies, including Cinerama, see Belton, *Widescreen Cinema*. The history of reception—both the US reception of kinopanorama productions and Soviet discussions of Cinerama—is discussed thoroughly in Krukones, "Peacefully Coexisting on a Wide Screen."

14. The size of the screen and the aspect ratio varied from theater to theater. The largest panoramic screen at the time was installed in Moscow's Mir movie theater, where *Wide Is My Country* made its national debut. A pride of Soviet design, the theater's spaces were described in detail by Kotov, "Panoramnyi Teatr 'Mir.'" The theater, as part of a new series of experimental public constructions, is discussed in Ikonnikov and Stepanov, *Estetika sotsialisticheskogo goroda*, 225.

15. For a thorough contemporaneous discussion of Soviet stereophonic sound in panoramic film, see Vysotskii, *Shirokoekrannoe stereofonicheskoe kino*. The issue of sound and space will be discussed briefly in the second chapter, and more extensively in the fourth chapter of the present book.

16. Dombrovskii, "Novye khudozhestvennye sredstva," 36.

17. Ibid.

18. See "Fond Romana Karmena," 29. (The archival page contains an original newspaper article, without title or date, by N. Kolesnikova.)

19. Gorokhov, "Zritel vkhodit v ekran," 32.

20. "Fond Romana Karmena," 29.

21. See, for instance, Efimova, "To Touch on the Raw." As she argues on the subject of socialist realist painting, "More than any other art practice in the history of modernism, it was a theoretically and ideologically elaborated system with an intentional aspiration to affect the viewer on a sensory level" (80). What was new with panorama is the degree to which this affect could be imparted.

22. Gunning, "The Cinema of Attractions."

23. Eisenstein, "Montage of Attractions," 230–31.

24. See Goodwin, *Eisenstein, Cinema, and History*, 146–47.

25. "Pervye panoramnye kinoteatry," 16.

26. Liaskalo, "Ischerpany li vozmozhnosti kinopanoramy?" 153. The quote is from a letter by one of the journal's reader, who reviews two subsequent kinopanorama productions in a rather negative light, suggesting that they had lost the dynamism of *Wide Is My Country* and with it the connection to the audience.

27. This also marks a fundamental shift between the Stalinist cinema and the cinema of the Thaw. If in the 1930s, as Emma Widdis has argued, "the aerial perspective was granted primarily to the extraordinary individual"; panoramic cinema sought actively to return this gaze to any ordinary citizen—anybody who would bother to walk into a panoramic theater (Widdis, *Visions of a New Land*, 135).

28. Gorokhov, "Zritel vkhodit v ekran," 31.

29. Ibid.

30. Goldovskii, *Problemy panoramnogo*, 8, 9.

31. Vivian Sobchak, in her critique of theories of spectators, notes, "I don't have a point of view, I have a situation" (Sobchak, *The Address of the Eye*, 179).

32. Goldovskii, *Problemy panoramnogo*, 8.

33. Ibid., 9.

34. Beskin, "Iskusstvo dioramy," 13.

35. See, for instance, Balsom, "Screening Rooms," and Pantenburg, "1970 and Beyond."
36. Veklenko and Belkin, "K voprosu o sistemakh kinematografa budushchego," 23.
37. Goldovskii, "O sistemakh kinematografa budushchego," 17. Here, Goldovsky begins to sound much more reserved with regard to his earlier ideas on the freedom of perception. He in fact directly contradicts his earlier statements when writing that the only systems of cinematography that have the right to exist are those that "provide the conditions of perception in which the viewers see exactly the same representation and hear the same sound reproduction," 16.
38. It should be noted that despite the negative criticism of panoramic cinema, there were no suggestions to eliminate it. The concern was rather whether these films could develop into a true art form or would remain merely a popular entertainment. In the discussions on the future of cinematic technology, proposals were circulating about how to improve the imperfections of current panoramic cinema to enable its further ascendance toward true socialist art. See Goldovskii, "O sistemakh kinematografa budushchego." Goldovskii himself defended the right of "cinematic attractions" to exist, in contrast with "certain specialists" who think "cinematic attractions are not needed in our conditions," 17.
39. Dickerman, "Camera Obscura," 144.
40. The traces of such manipulation are thoroughly documented in King, *The Commissar Vanishes*.
41. Dickerman, "Camera Obscura," 152.
42. The relationship of photography to reality remained a convoluted problem within Soviet artistic discourse after Stalin's death. See Reid, "Photography in the Thaw."
43. The problem of the reality effect extended to the manipulation of documentary films as well, also during the Thaw period. See, for instance, a letter by a certain Savelii Khrabrovtskii to the Central Committee of the Communist Party, about the changes made to a documentary chronicle, eliminating undesirable figures—this time the general Zhukov and Stalin himself (Khrabrovtskii, "Letter to the Central Committee," 24–26).
44. Gorokhov, "Zritel vkhodit v ekran," 34.
45. Kerzhentsev, writing in *Pravda*, August 5, 1923, 3; quoted in Beissinger, *Scientific Management*, 54.
46. Beissinger, *Scientific Management*, 55.
47. Yanowitch, "Soviet Patterns of Time Use and Concepts of Leisure," 18. On Khrushchev's struggles with the revival of scientific management, see Beissinger, *Scientific Management*, 163–72. For an example of an exhaustive study on time management produced during the Thaw period, see Klimov, *Rabochii den' v obshchestve, stroiashchim communism*. Klimov defines "free time" in his study thus: "Free time—time for rest, time for mental, moral, and physical perfection, and political education. It includes time for study and growth of [professional] qualifications, sociopolitical activities, self-education, and time for child rearing, and entertainment" (141; my translation). As we see, there is not much space left in "free time" for a non-goal-oriented, idle rest. The author also stresses repeatedly that the amount of free time, with the advanced development of socialism and communism, will be considerably increased, thus allowing more time for the "development and perfection of men," 141.
48. Doane, *The Emergence of Cinematic Time*, 11.
49. Ibid., 10.
50. Ibid.
51. Ibid., 22.
52. Tarkovskii, "Zapechatlionnoe vremia," 70.
53. Ibid.
54. Ibid., 71.
55. Doane, *The Emergence of Cinematic Time*, 23.
56. Charney, "In a Moment," 279.

2
MIMETIC PASSAGES: THE CINEMA OF MIKHAIL KALATOZOV AND SERGEI URUSEVSKII

IN A 1962 roundtable discussion on the use of wide and panoramic screens in Soviet cinema conducted by *Iskusstvo kino*, the prominent Soviet director Mikhail Kalatozov advised against an overreliance on new film technologies but declared simultaneously his interest in "achieving the effect of widescreen cinema shooting with 16mm film."[1] Kalatozov's opinion carried significant weight. Since the mid-1950s, he had emerged as one of the most respected Soviet filmmakers, especially after his war melodrama *The Cranes Are Flying* (*Letiat zhuravli*, 1957) won the Palme d'Or at the 1958 Cannes Film Festival, an event that returned Soviet cinema to the attention of the international film community after years of virtual isolation. Furthermore, Kalatozov's collaborator Sergei Urusevskii, with whom he made three films, became one of the nation's most acclaimed, and obsessively emulated, cinematographers after the Cannes victory.[2] Urusevskii essentially performed with his camera the participatory effect that Kalatozov admired in widescreen formats. With the release of *The Cranes*, their films became synonymous with that effect, achieved through the combination of extremely long takes and subjective points of view, and especially by the handheld, mobile, and tremendously flexible camera, which allowed viewers to feel deeply immersed in the action on screen, to "stop being an external observer and become a participant in the events."[3]

On the heels of the Cannes victory, Kalatozov and Urusevskii's work was widely applauded for its virtuosity and formal intensity, which was thought to support the film's narrative trajectories, deepening viewers' understanding of the emotional and psychological world thus constructed.[4] But the matter became more complicated with the release of their two subsequent films, *The Unsent Letter* (1959) and *I Am Cuba* (1964). In reference to both, critics complained of a breakdown of Kalatozov and Urusevskii's representational practice, arguing that the dynamics of the camera had become wildly excessive, causing a disturbance in spatial perception and eclipsing the depth of emotional and dramatic developments.[5] *The Unsent Letter* was accused of blunt formalism, its spectacular shots seen as working against the logic and contiguity of meaning and ignoring the fate of the people and their relationships. In the words of one commentator, meaning in the film was abandoned in the service of abstraction, turning comprehensible images into a "suprematist amassing of some light and dark blotches."[6] With *I Am Cuba*—two years in the making and eagerly anticipated by Soviet and Cuban audiences—critical disappointment reached its peak.[7] Discussing the film's aesthetics in the pages of *Iskusstvo kino*, one critic stated that "behind the frenzied dynamics of the spatially free camera hides a temporal stasis. Everything is emotionally dragged out. The episode is clear, it seems the meaning is revealed—but no, one more run of the camera, one more panorama." Another critic added, "the camera spins around, rotates, oscillates—so the audience comes close to fainting."[8] Such utter condemnation effectively terminated the two filmmakers' cinematic partnership. Although Kalatozov did produce *Red Tent* in 1969, his collaboration with Urusevskii ended with *I Am Cuba*, and the film's international acclaim after its rediscovery in 1992 came after both filmmakers were already dead.[9]

Looking more closely at the immediate reception of *The Unsent Letter* and *I Am Cuba*, one is struck by two elements. First is the extent to which critics mapped the form-content opposition as one of space–time. Their complaint, in essence, was that space in both films defeated time: The latter drags on and is made seemingly endless by the "frenzied dynamics of the spatially free camera." The films' narrative failings, furthermore, were understood as a breakdown of temporal passage ("The emotional effect of the episode would have been stronger if it had a prehistory; if we knew what kind of people these are"; "Couldn't such masters adapt a gripping—yet clearly formed, perhaps a detective—plot?"), and their spatial elaborations were found to be distracting and destructive ("The camera dived under water. Then appeared again. Is it all? No, it dives down again"; "The architecture falls apart through the wide-angle lens [and] I no longer feel a meaningful wholeness of the camera movement").[10]

The second notable element is the recurrence of the same terms that had framed the discourse around panoramic cinema, especially references to a participatory mode of viewing, which Urusevskii's camera appeared to effect. The praise that the first kinopanorama film, *Wide Is My Country*, received, however—particularly for its success in integrating physiological effects of participation into the audience's experience of the film's temporal-narrative flow—was now gone. Instead, responses suggested an opposite view: that Kalatozov and Urusevskii had pivoted their films *around* such moments of "attraction" (although this term was not used directly), drawing them out, making them dominant in the perceptual experience of their films while simultaneously distancing viewers from the emotional depth of filmed events. Just as space took precedence over time, physiological experience came at the cost of psychological affect, and thus at the cost of meaning. The "effect of widescreen cinema," to follow up on Kalatozov's ambition, not only was achieved with a regular film format, but was also significantly magnified—so much so that the spatiality through which this effect unfolded absorbed each film's narrative logic and dominated its overall impression. As viewers were made to immerse themselves and participate—and even, it was claimed, to become faint—they remained at the same time emotionally uninvolved, distanced from the drama and its players.

For all its negative intent, the commentary of these critics points us directly to the aesthetic and political aspirations of *The Unsent Letter* and *I Am Cuba*. This chapter proposes that the formal operation of Urusevskii's camera, far from stagnating the films' narrative progressions, complicates them by making the very *process* of spatial perception and cognition primary to the experience of both films. The stories of *The Unsent Letter* and *I Am Cuba* are, after all, about space—about topography and mapping, locations and movement. Set and filmed in some of the most significant regions in Soviet and international political geography—depicting geological explorations in Siberia in *The Unsent Letter* and the revolutionary takeover of Cuba in the last years of the Batista regime in *I Am Cuba*—the films necessarily address the concurrent politics of spatial use and appropriation. But if the established political structures of the Soviet Union conceptualized and organized space through centripetal frameworks and an omnipotent gaze, with each territory having a stable place on a map that could be controlled from, and be subjected to, a distant center, *The Unsent Letter* and *I Am Cuba* persistently dispose of these aspects. The spaces that these films create frequently appear disorienting, defying the control and mastery of a centralized locus of power. Both films, I will argue, seek to grasp space through mimetic means, abandoning traditional subject–object distinctions and attempting to render people and their environment as mutually permeable on a sensory, physiological level—a process that is both depicted in the images on screen and experienced by viewers somatically through their perceptual encounter with Urusevskii's dynamic camera work. If the mimetic approach to space manifests itself in *The Unsent Letter* in intricate camera explorations that have no direct political implications, in *I Am Cuba* mimesis takes an explicitly political form: camera movement itself comes to embody a spatial awareness that, the film suggests, is potentially generative for progressive political consciousness.

Toward Indistinction

The Unsent Letter, which chronicles the events of a geological expedition to Siberia to find diamonds, is punctuated by images of heroic struggle against nature, of explorers conquering the wild, uninhabited "virgin" East. It begins with a group of four geologists arriving in Siberia to look for diamond deposits with the guidance of a map marking their hypothetical location. After a long, exhaustive, and seemingly hopeless search that takes up about half the film, the geologists find the stones, create a precise map of their location, and prepare to return to Moscow. During the night before their departure, extensive forest fires break out, severing their radio connection with Moscow and shattering the arranged plans for the group's return. What follows is an excruciatingly long walk to a major river during which all but one of the geologists die. Rescue airplanes twice fly right over the group but fail to locate them. After his three colleagues perish, the expedition's director, Konstantin, arrives at the river, builds a makeshift raft, and, barely alive, sets off aimlessly until an airplane spots him. Though his fate remains unclear, a medium close-up shot of his slightly moving eyes at the film's end suggests that he will in fact be saved—and, furthermore, that the diamond map also will be delivered to Moscow.[11]

The mapping of unknown territories at the center of *The Unsent Letter* and the struggle against nature that ensues place the film firmly within the politics of spatial conquest in the immediate post-Stalinist period. Its story emerges out of the context of the economic expansion, deemed necessary for the nation's development after World War II, within which Khrushchev's policies for the agricultural development of untouched terrains in Kazakhstan and Siberia became a primary example of economic exploitation of nature and the environment.[12] More specifically, *The Unsent Letter* reflects on the actual history of Soviet geologists who first discovered diamond deposits in Soviet territories in 1955, after eight years of repeated expeditions and grim failures.[13] With its representation of a personally fatal but politically victorious journey, *The Unsent Letter* initiates a dialogue within the relatively homogeneous Soviet discourse on the conquest of nature, just as it disturbs broader Soviet conceptualizations of nature as wild and untapped, needing to be explored, mapped, and developed in order to yield any political or economic significance.[14] Even the most distant and peripheral of the undeveloped territories had to be integrated into the national space—made visible and controllable from within the centripetal structures of the nation, with Moscow as the omnipotent eye.

The need for such a centripetal spatial organization of Soviet territories—not different in essence from the period of high Stalinism—manifested itself in diverse forms and was especially evident within the popular discourse of geographical explorations, as, for instance, in the travelogue *My Russia*, written by the prominent Soviet geographer Nikolai Mikhailov in 1966, on the occasion of the fiftieth anniversary of the 1917 Revolution. A tremendously popular author of numerous works on Soviet geography from the 1930s on and a recipient of the Stalin Prize for his 1947 book *Map of the Motherland*, Mikhailov, over the span of three decades, repeatedly presented Soviet readers with a mirror of their national space, registering its thriving development over the course of Soviet history.[15] He begins *My Russia* by musing on the best way to communicate his experience of traversing the vast territories of the USSR, ultimately settling on an approach that uses a set of coordinates to document objectively and scientifically his movement from the Soviet peripheries toward Moscow. Thus, at the beginning of each chapter we see pictures of two clocks and a map that together show the time and location of Moscow respective to the particular region through which Mikhailov was about to cross, thus insisting on the dependent relationship of the latter to the former. The book's section titles produce a map of trajectories that all radiate toward the political and geographical center of the Soviet Union (of which Mikhailov becomes a representative eye): "To Moscow, from the North," "To Moscow, from the West," and so forth. Combining chronological and geographical coordinates, Mikhailov creates a consistent, cogent, and, in his view, objective structure through which to convey and analyze national space.[16]

In its scope and expansiveness, Mikhailov's travelogue is best compared with representations of the nation that Soviet panoramic cinema sought to achieve, though it lacks the latter's experiential quality. Just as in panoramic films, Mikhailov creates an impressive and cohesive body of the nation in his writing, in which history, space, and people's individual and collective contributions work together to generate one unquestionable totality, and in which nature and civilization work together to the benefit of each. Filling his descriptions with exceptional details of breathtaking landscapes and the natural resources they offer, of specific industrial and urban developments, and of the progressive history of large and small settlements that emerged out of nothing, Mikhailov never loses the overall temporal trajectory of his narration, presenting the country "walking toward communism." The inexhaustible litany of facts he offers—"the logic of numbers"—becomes the most authentic expression of his personal patriotism, pride, and admiration.[17] And thus the reader takes part in a journey in which a "symphonic" world of diverse encounters and experiences is organically and totally subordinated to the Soviet structure of time and space, with Moscow as its constant, immutable center.[18]

The Unsent Letter likewise frames its territorial explorations through a centripetal approach to the organization of space. The film opens with aerial shots from an airplane arriving in Siberia from Moscow, and it ends with the presumed return of Konstantin, the group's lone survivor, to the capital city after he is spotted and picked up by another airplane. Throughout the film, the geologists, for as long as the radio functions, remain in contact with Moscow, listening to the directions from what they call "the center" and effectively operating as its extension. Both formally and narratively, the film is preoccupied from the very start with the process of mapping, with creating an intelligible and distinctive space that can be read and understood—an operation foregrounded especially in the geologists' need to uncover what is underground, below the level of normal visibility.

Much of the film is devoted to just this—making the uniform soil of the landscape open to readability. We constantly see the geologists examining the ground, breaking apart the surface and scrutinizing the minuscule particles of the grand Siberian space with microscopes, magnifying glasses, or the naked eye. Their bodies, in turn, are carefully delineated against the immediate environment. The sequence when one of the protagonists, Tania, finds the diamonds, for instance, is marked by a precise figuration of the geologists' bodies within a dug-out rectangle. Although they are below ground level, they remain perfectly visible and distinct from it (figure 2.1). In such axes of vision and perception (above or under the surface, aerial or ground view), the camera seeks an image of a unified and visibly ordered space, which is achieved through the privileged position of the omnipotent camera.[19]

But if *The Unsent Letter* initially suggests a cinematic version of Mikhailov's popular geography—channeling minute, detailed fragments and experiences within the Siberian landscape into the nation's centripetal forces and making the bodies operate as congruent agents of that force—this suggestion is forcefully challenged in the film's second half, in which stretches of blurred, swampy landscape begin to dominate, slipping away from the contained structures and defined trajectories of the centripetal order. Any potential unity of space is shattered after the forest fires break out, making the geologists invisible to the rescue airplanes that fly right over them and turning the landscape into an increasingly undifferentiated, repetitive, and at times flat and abstract surface that fails to offer viewers (or the protagonists) any sense of direction or orientation.[20] If previously the geologists seemed to *remake* the landscape as they moved through it—leaving with their work explicit marks behind them—in the film's second half they become incapable of

Fig. 2.1. Precise figuration of geologists' bodies within the landscape. From *The Unsent Letter*, 1959.

producing durable, distinct traces. Their footprints rapidly disappear in the swampy ground or are covered by snow; and the explicit silhouettes of figures against the landscape that dominated the film's first half, bestowing a sense of clear delineation between the figures and their surroundings, begin to lose their prominence, to the extent that the protagonists' bodies start to mimic the natural forms of the landscape through which they move, thus negating their distinct identities (figure 2.2).

One of the most striking sequences in this regard displays the final two protagonists, Konstantin and Tania, settling down for the night on a hill, soon after a second airplane has passed over without seeing them. The sequence begins with Konstantin and Tania lying together and conversing before falling asleep. This initial nighttime passage, shot in a series of close-ups and from a variety of low angles, alternates between the two protagonists' heads and faces, emphasizing their volumetric forms against the backdrop of the sky. Although the figures are clearly shot to stand out from the flattened, static sky behind them, they simultaneously merge with and in fact take the place of the landscape in which they lie. A slight pine tree blowing above the head of Tania at

Fig. 2.2 Mimicking natural surroundings. From *The Unsent Letter*, 1959.

the sequence's opening, for instance, soon disappears to be replaced by each figure's breezy wisps of hair. Their faces, seen in close-up, are relieflike, characterized by exaggerated volume and extreme physical expansiveness; viewed at a variety of angles that exclude all surrounding landscape, their profiles appear to be the land itself, a series of craggy cliffs.[21] It is as if they become the very terrain they are trying to traverse (figure 2.3).

The images that compose this sequence are strange. Although they display an exceptional attention to form and composition, they also seem to decompose from within, as any sense of clear spatial organization breaks down. Not only does the single marking tree at the outset vanish from view (compare figure 2.3a and figure 2.3d), but the two figures' placement in relation to each other defies any common sense of logically construed space. When Konstantin's face is shown in the lower triangle of the screen space (figure 2.3c), Tania's head, which is located right next to his and should still be visible, vanishes from view. The lack of a perspectival spatial organization culminates in the morning sequence to follow, which opens with an image of the first snow that fell during the night (figure 2.4a). The scene is completely devoid of cues to

Fig. 2.3a–d Geologists' bodies assuming form of the landscape. From *The Unsent Letter*, 1959.

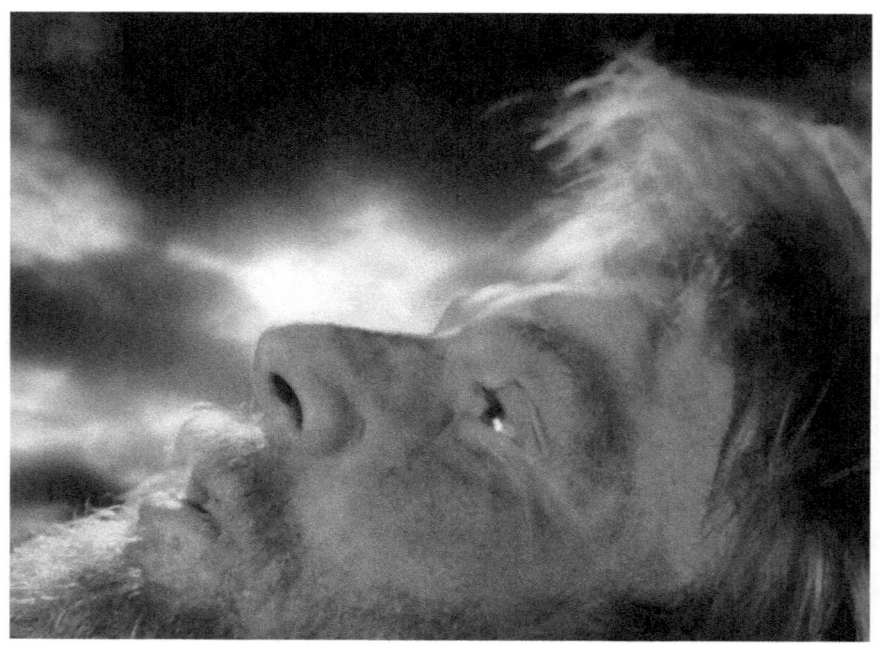

Fig. 2.3a–d (*Continued*)

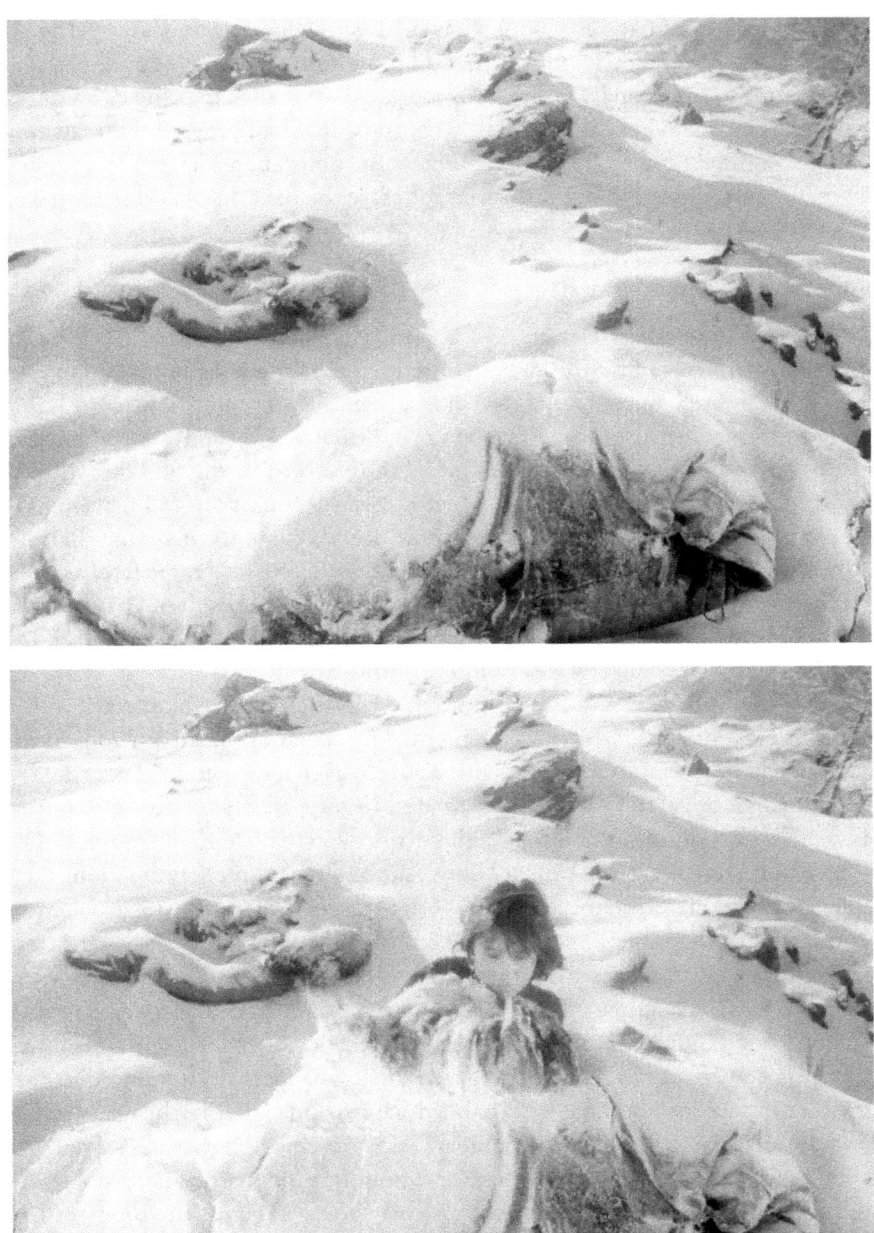

Fig. 2.4a–b Landscape devoid of cues of location or scale, bodies emerging to reveal them. From *The Unsent Letter*, 1959.

indicate location or scale, leaving viewers unsure whether they are seeing an empty snow-covered field or even distant mountain terrain. Not until the surface begins to break apart in the foreground do we realize that the two figures are emerging from beneath the blanket of snow that had covered them up during the night (figure 2.4b). At this moment, a comprehensible, readable space is again reestablished—but only briefly, before the next disorienting cycle begins.

From Pantheism to Mimesis

In one of the harshest critiques of Urusevskii's camerawork in *The Unsent Letter*, a certain Natalia Kokoreva contended that the issue in question was not his camera's formal excesses but rather the inappropriate worldview they expressed, which she described as "pantheistic."[22] "Pantheism," she explained, "inexorably considers people as if dissolved in the world . . . fused with nature. . . . This causes a coldness toward man, inattention to his inner nature." Kokoreva stated her core objection repeatedly, insisting that the film's apparent emotional indifference to its protagonists' tragic fate, as they are being "devoured" by the spaces of the taiga, was the result of Urusevskii's consideration of humanity as "nothing—that is, as equal with nature itself."[23] For Kokoreva, such a view was inherently anti-Soviet.

Referring to Urusevskii's coldness and indifference, Kokoreva implied that his camera work, which was renowned for its emotion-driven communication, had been emptied of its affective power, even if its technical vocabulary remained identical to that of the celebrated *Cranes Are Flying*. This evaluation is worth considering, for Urusevskii's work does develop substantially between *The Cranes* and *The Unsent Letter*. Although his camera is dynamic, flexible, and subjectively experienced in both films, in *The Cranes* it is frequently connected to the inner experiences of a protagonist, which Urusevskii externalizes through his camera motions. The subjective behavior of his camera in *The Unsent Letter*, by contrast, is not always connected to a specific figure. Instead, such moments make tangible the presence of space itself—as something that in effect has a body and gaze of its own, apart from human beings, rather than as simply their externalized expression.[24] Being thus subjective and objective, particular and general at the same time, the spatial body of *The Unsent Letter* lacks a psychological or emotional (or historical or political) motivation for its movements. As such, this "body" looks at the protagonists themselves as physical matter, as surface rather than depth, thereby excluding their interiority—and inviting, as a result, a pantheistic reading of the film's visual operation. What we observe here is not so much an anthropomorphism of space but rather a spatialization of human figures.

One of the most formally elaborate moments of this process takes place in the sequence of Tania's death, just a few moments after the shots of the first snowfall just discussed. The two protagonists are now walking through fields, with Tania becoming increasingly weak, until, as Konstantin suddenly realizes, she is no longer walking behind him. In a series of movements that, again, substantially confuse our spatial orientation, he searches for her and ultimately finds her collapsed on the ground. As Konstantin carries her retrieved body, it remains unclear whether Tania is still alive. That she has died is ultimately suggested through a medium close-up of her static, lifeless face (figure 2.5a), followed by a gradual fade that at first blends her visage with the surrounding branches (figure 2.5b), which then culminates in a blurred still shot of the frozen surroundings that appears to be a point-of-view shot, a kind of view from the dead (figure 2.5c). This sequence transitions from her face *as* the environment to her gaze looking out at it, producing an odd inside-out relation. She is the space, and at the same time she is gazing at it. Although she is dead within the film's narrative logic, she remains "alive" on a formal level, as a "space" still possessing an ability to look, through the suggestion of Urusevskii's camera work.

Although it is possible to understand the second half of *The Unsent Letter* as a reversal of fortunes—from man consuming nature to nature consuming

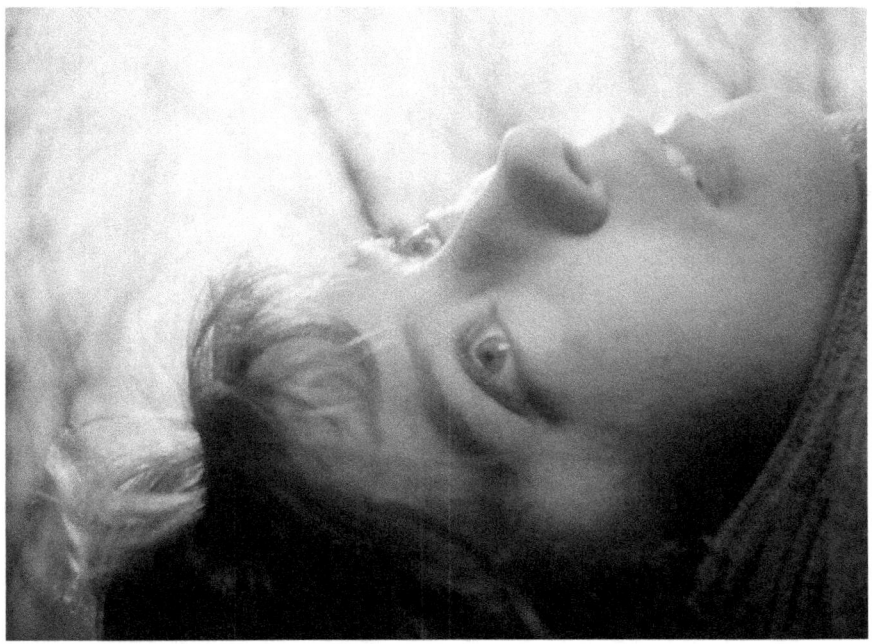

Fig. 2.5a–c Tania's death as dissolution into the environment. From *The Unsent Letter*, 1959.

Mimetic Passages

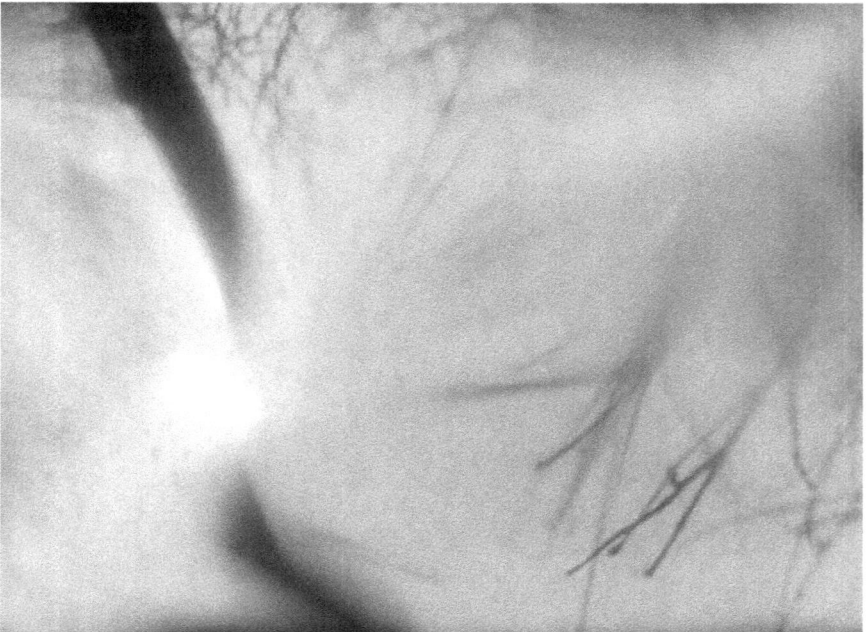

Fig. 2.5a–c (*Continued*)

man—there is more at stake in its images of bodily assimilation into the environment, as Kokoreva intuitively recognized in her critique. In its repeated displays of blended surfaces, the film searches for possible forms of spatial knowledge different from that of cartography. Corporeal integration with and unmediated proximity to the landscape, which Kalatozov and Urusevskii persistently give image to, turn into a new epistemological principle, one that seeks to perceive the environment through a mimetic approximation of it: to gain access to space by being *like* it on the most direct level, speaking visually and physiologically. It is striking, after all, that all three deaths in the film are presented as acts of spatial integration (though not all are as elaborate as Tania's), but not one actual dead body is shown explicitly on screen, perhaps suggesting that the geologists remain somehow alive within the texture of the space that has swallowed them. And although the filmmakers' insistence on seeing and producing formal similarities where there should be none (in accordance with the socialist division between nature and humankind) can be seen as entropic, the aesthetic overdetermination of these processes—their prolonged and poetic exposition—asks for a deeper understanding.

Writing in the 1920s and 1930s, Walter Benjamin discussed mimesis as a prevalent mode of being in primitive and prehistoric societies, referring to the realms of the sacred and the occult, the mythical and the astrological—noting that "the gift we possess for seeing similarity is nothing but a feeble vestige of the formerly powerful compulsion to be similar and to behave mimetically."[25] Although this compulsion has largely withered in modern bourgeois societies, Benjamin repeatedly insisted that it remains central to how children engage with their surroundings. By becoming similar, in play, not only to people and their actions but to any object around them—"not only a shopkeeper or a teacher, but also a windmill and a train"—children gain access to these objects preconceptually, through corporeal play, and in the process eradicate the difference between self and other.[26] While the urge to imitate disappears in the process of growing up, it never completely dies, continuing to be present for Benjamin, for instance, in childhood memories; nevertheless, it lacks a proper, acknowledged place within the modern world.

A more radical, and specifically spatial, discussion of mimetic capacities is elaborated in Roger Caillois's 1935 text "Mimicry and Legendary Psychasthenia," in which the French sociologist addresses the ability of insects to assimilate their external appearance to their environment such that they become completely indistinguishable from it. If this visual camouflaging had previously been understood as a kind of defense mechanism, Caillois argues for a strikingly different interpretation. He defines the process as one of "temptation by space," describing insects' visual assimilation as a desire to dissolve into—indeed, to become—space.²⁷ This desire is by no means limited to the world of insects. Caillois speaks of human "psychological potentialities" that lead to similar experiences of dissolution into the environment that encompass a wide range of practices in art, religions such as pantheism, and the psychic condition of "legendary psychasthenia," in which affected individuals feel as if they are literally eaten up by space.²⁸ As Caillois writes, "to these dispossessed souls, space seems to be a devouring force. Space pursues them, encircles them, digests them in a gigantic phagocytosis. It ends by replacing them. Then the body separates itself from thought, the individual breaks the boundary of his skin and occupies the other side of his senses."²⁹

What emerges in Benjamin's and Caillois's texts is a conceptualization of human subjectivity uncontained within the boundaries of the body, in which consciousness and sensation spill out into the world of other people, objects, and spaces and establish inseparable connections and contiguities. As Caillois describes this, "things that have once been in contact remain united."³⁰ These texts excavate mimetic practices from forgotten—or overcome—stages of human development, as something that can exist only on the margins of modern societies, and attempt to situate them as primary tools for the critical analysis of modernity. In comparing Benjamin's thinking to Jean Piaget's parallel analysis of children's cognitive development, philosopher Susan Buck-Morss notices that "Benjamin's own interest was not in the sequential development of stages of abstract, formal reason, but in what was lost along the way."³¹ The cultivation of the mimetic faculty, Buck-Morss further argues, was for Benjamin a matter of political significance, a potential source for rebuilding modern man's broken relationship with the world. It is interesting that, in describing his trip to Moscow in 1927, Benjamin fleetingly remarked, "the instant you arrive, the childhood stage begins. On the thick sheet ice of the streets, walking has to be relearned."³² His first moments of encounter with a revolutionary society, in other words, were experienced as a return to childhood—a renewed physical and bodily relationship with the surrounding world.

Soviet behavioral scientists, however, being *specifically interested* in the development of formal reason, and understanding children's maturation as a process of ascendance from the lower physiological to the higher cognitive functions, did not share Benjamin's enthusiasm. They conceptualized the mimetic urge as a faculty that does not disappear but rather gets absorbed into higher intellectual capabilities, where it remains in need of constant cultivation—but of a different kind than Benjamin had imagined. In one particular discussion of children's mimetic behavior, a certain psychologist and art critic named Mark Markov argued that the innate mimetic compulsion continues to operate primarily in the realm of art perception—indeed, as its basis—and evolved from the purely physiological need to master the environment to the psychological and conceptual capacity for artistic transference and identification. But in contrast to Benjamin's embrace of mimesis as a profound challenge to the abstract, conceptual forms of reasoning and knowledge, Markov found it useful only insofar as it could be exploited for these very things—and for their manifestations in Soviet ideology. He argued that the ultimate goal of artistic perception is "the alteration of consciousness, and, as a result, of the behavior of the perceiver."[33] If the mimetic compulsion never fully vanishes, it has to be cultivated in reverse, channeled into proper compliance with ideological form through limited, and meticulously shaped, imitative offerings. Writing this, remarkably, in the pages of *Iskusstvo kino* and thus for an audience interested in cinema, Markov suggested that film provided the most comprehensive form for just such a channeling—precisely because it created a place where physiological immersion could operate together with psychological transference, thus enticing viewers' mimetic capacities on a sensual level, but then immediately exerting an effect on a conceptual and ideological level.

I am expanding here on the discursive history of mimesis because *The Unsent Letter* engages its terms in direct and multiple ways. The film repeatedly shows images of visual contiguity and merger of bodies and space; it focuses on physical, corporeal contact between them, and on the apparent visual bleeding of one into the other; it keeps us close to the ground, in proximity to the surface of nature; it presents human figures looking at space from the perspective of space itself, as if "occupying the other side of their senses"; and it allows the conceptual organization of space—a recognizably mapped space—to disintegrate, yielding instead to the images of "dark and light blotches." But what is even more significant is that these mimetic processes carry ambiguous political implications. What occurs with the breakout of the forest fire midway through the film is a process of a complete, absolute separation of the protagonists from political and ideological institutions, as well as from the structures of vision, perception, and spatial organization they generate. It appears that Kalatozov and Urusevskii's own "temptation by space," to borrow Caillois's expression, could be staged only in the absence of such a political center, its elimination helping to liberate the mimetic potential of their cinematic language. Their extended representation of Siberian spaces through unmappable and sometimes nearly empty shots (empty of action, of narrative impulse, of any orienting clues to grasp) can be seen as a desire to understand how space could be—and could be perceived—outside any ideological permutations. Indeed, Markov's reasoning on the function of mimesis is nowhere to be found in this film. The physiological sensations of being in a space—of being space—are left unchanneled, for both the protagonists and the viewers.

But this is not to suggest that Kalatozov and Urusevskii's spatial mimicry is apolitical in nature. During one of the most prominent mimetic sequences discussed earlier—the conversation of Tania and Konstantin on the hill—the basic tenets of the communist imagination come into narrative focus, albeit ambiguously and even conflictingly. As the two protagonists lie on the hill before falling asleep, they begin to reminisce about their childhoods, specifically about entering the Young Pioneer organization (an obligatory step for all Soviet children) and reciting the oath that accompanied the ritual. The memory of their transformation from being simply children to becoming political, communist subjects could not sound more dejected here, as that experience seems so obsolete in the face of the unbounded, surrounding space that has all but consumed them. And yet this very same sequence underscores precisely the mimetic basis for *both* these experiences, as it is rooted in the subject's sublimation into the external environment, be this the "we" of communism or the surrounding landscape.[34] This is played up even more toward the end of the sequence, when the geologists' nostalgic recollection of becoming Young Pioneers takes a concrete spatial shape. Finishing the oath, Tania and Konstantin reaffirm their belief with a loud and repeated "yes," to which the landscape responds with an echoing confirmation. The voice of the Communist Party is articulated here through space, dispersing throughout the entirety of the visible terrain and enveloping the protagonists' emaciated and helpless bodies as they finally fall asleep with some sense of peace.

This superimposition of the political over spatial immersion remains direct only in this one sequence, which is left without any clear conclusions. What remains undoubtedly significant, however, is that both forms of mimetic behavior are staged here through each other. Communism is brought into focus less as a specific ideology and more as an idealized childhood experience, which, as Benjamin (and also Markov) reminds us, centers much more on mimetic interactions with the environment; furthermore, the direction of Markov's channeling here is reversed: Communist "behavior" is not just channeled but scattered into the unbounded nature, with no map to outline its routes and passages. If *The Unsent Letter* suggests the intersecting energies between communist and spatial mimesis, but leaves the issue on the whole latent, *I Am Cuba* returns to precisely this problem, with a renewed force and intensified formal language, to position spatial mimicry as the very basis of revolutionary consciousness.

Cuba's Space and Spatiality

One of the culminating sequences of *I Am Cuba* details the death of Enrique, a student revolutionary who has just initiated an open protest against the repressive police forces on the steps of Havana's university, in front of a prominently displayed *Alma Mater* sculpture. As Enrique leads the crowds to the bottom of the monumental stairs—with the sequence directly echoing the "Odessa Steps" massacre in Sergei Eisenstein's 1925 *Battleship Potemkin*—the water hoses of the police begin to break the protesters apart, spawning utter chaos, in which Enrique is ultimately shot.[35] We see an extended presentation of his death through a series of shots that closely replicate Tania's death in *The Unsent Letter*. As Enrique begins to lose consciousness, the contours of his body and especially of his face start to fade into the clouds of smoke. The camera shifts seamlessly then from this objective point of view to Enrique's perspective, looking at the surroundings, which become increasingly blurred, freezing ultimately in an abstract, undifferentiated pattern, followed by darkness. Just as with Tania's death in the previous film, we are presented here with an inside-out inversion of body and space, as the image of Enrique's fading into his surroundings is integrated with his view of the same space, now even more obscure and indefinite. But whereas such visual disintegration of bodily boundaries into the surrounding space was shown in *The Unsent Letter* as a poetic and devastating but largely meaningless death, in *I Am Cuba*, it coincides with a moment of willful political confrontation. For in direct contrast to the former film, *I Am Cuba* plunges its viewers into the thick of politics—the last years of Fulgencio Batista's regime and the revolutionary movement that defeated it.

The film as a whole consists of four separate stories that move through distinct Cuban locales. The first takes place in Havana and features a Cuban woman named Betty who is forced to work as a prostitute to comically lecherous US capitalists. The second transpires in the countryside and presents the sugarcane farmer Pedro, who, after years of hard labor, decides to burn the fields he works because their local owner has sold them to a US multinational. The third story moves back to Havana and portrays the actions of left-wing students and their confrontations with reactionary police forces. The final story takes place again outside the city, this time in the mountains, where a peasant, whose idyllic family life is shattered by an air raid, joins Fidel Castro's rebel forces to avenge his son's needless death, emerging in the last moments of the film as a convinced and committed revolutionary. These four stories are connected only by a shared female voice-over that intones "I am Cuba" throughout, which are the film's very first words as well.

As has been noted, one of the main shifts from *The Cranes Are Flying* to *The Unsent Letter* can be traced in the work of the camera—in a more distinct separation of its views from those of the protagonists, but its simultaneous ability to retain a behavior that is experienced as subjective by film viewers, thus effectively giving a body and gaze to space itself. *I Am Cuba* takes this development further, deepening the corporeal and subjective presence of the environment in which the film's events transpire. This occurs through the camera's intricate, mobile, and free plasticity, which appears to know no frames or boundaries; its sumptuous long takes that penetrate deeply into the filmed space; its ability to impart within one shot the views of film protagonists while at the same time presenting its own experiences of their environment; its handheld materiality, which persistently indicates the presence of a never-delineated body; and its repeated identification with the "I" and the voice of Cuba itself, leaving no doubt that it is Cuba's body that the camera's gaze and motions frequently present. If in *The Unsent Letter* Kalatozov and Urusevskii's interest in spatial mimesis was most evident in the film's images of bodily merger with the environment, in *I Am Cuba* it is conveyed through the camera's operation itself, above all in the way it situates Cuba simultaneously as a subject that looks and traverses and as an object being observed and traversed. And it is indeed the camera's movement—the apparatus itself being the most consistent and acting presence within the film—that is elevated to a material and intellectual principle in the film, one through which the revolutionary engagement of the country's inhabitants is mapped and revolution itself is enacted and experienced. *I Am Cuba* imagines progress toward revolution as an evolution of spatial relations, culminating in a balance between the spatiality created by the camera and that performed by the people. Although numerous sequences in the film demonstrate this point, four episodes in particular stand out: the hotel rooftop pageant at the film's beginning; Enrique's aborted assassination of a policeman; Enrique's funeral; and the short sequence showing guerrilla fighting in the mountains of Sierra Maestra.

The hotel rooftop scene at the opening of the first narrative act—justly heralded by many recent critics for its formal intensity—consists of a single extraordinary long take at a Havana hotel, elegantly moving from jumping musicians to prancing beauty-pageant contestants, then snaking down the hotel's side to a lower-level terrace and ending, dramatically, in the depths of the building's pool.[36] Gliding smoothly through the spaces of the rooftop, the camera assimilates in its views and motions both the immediate environment of the hotel and the distant space of the city, and although its trajectory is guided by the structure of the building and the behavior of the hotel's patrons, it also explicitly integrates the surrounding urban panorama, producing one contiguous space (figure 2.6a and figure 2.6b).[37] This contiguity, however, contrasts starkly with the way the hotel guests experience their environment. Although the sequence takes place above the rooftops of Havana—in a location designed specifically for surveying the city's broader space—it is only the camera that seems to notice the wider city at all. The figures on screen, understood

Fig. 2.6a–b On a Havana hotel rooftop. From *I Am Cuba*, 1964.

to be politically ignorant capitalists, are focused instead on the regimented spectacle of the hotel beauty pageant or on their own tan lines, busy lounging in plastic armchairs and ordering drinks. Their lack of interest in relating to the space outside is not merely suggested but explicit: One bikini-clad blonde, for instance, is shown wandering away from the building's edge as her cocktail arrives, while beauty-pageant cameramen turn their backs rigidly to the city below as they obsessively record the narcissistic spectacle playing out on the rooftop. As the camera finishes this sequence in the visual and auditory chaos of the hotel pool, it manages to accentuate both the unity of Havana's geography and the fractures of its geopolitical and social fabric, in which the indifferent culture of capitalism is equated with the spatial ignorance of the hotel guests.[38]

The spatial terms of this opening scene are most immediately taken up and elaborated in the film's third narrative act, which focuses on Havana's budding student revolutionaries. Enrique has decided to assassinate single-handedly the city's chief of police, against the wishes of his compatriots, who are planning a collective uprising. To do so, he ascends another urban rooftop, retrieves a concealed rifle, and stares down through the rifle scope at the chief and his family enjoying breakfast in their domestic garden. Sweating, tense, increasingly on the verge of fainting, Enrique is unable to shoot. Confronted with the unexpected presence of the chief's family and the sudden prospect of actually taking another person's life, he throws the rifle aside and frantically descends to the street below. Enrique's determined, if ultimately aborted, assassination attempt can be understood as a point-by-point reversal of the opening hotel sequence. The camera follows a specific figure rather than being divorced from any identifiable narrative agent; the scene moves up rather than down; and it culminates in a moment of resolutely focused critical consciousness—embodied on screen in a point-of-view shot through Enrique's rifle scope—that stands in pointed contrast to the chaotic flux of the underwater descent closing the earlier sequence. The movement of the hotel guests is random, unmotivated, and set against an open sky; Enrique's rooftop actions are specific and directed, and set within a structuring grid of buttresses that largely define the trajectories of his motions (figure 2.7a).[39]

Yet despite the correction that this sequence provides to the spatial inertia of the Havana hotel guests, Enrique's political act takes place in a strongly felt spatial isolation, emphasized by his extreme elevation from the seemingly lifeless and motionless city below (figure 2.7b). Its larger span remains similarly distant here, as Enrique trains his eyes primarily on the policeman's patio. And, as in the earlier sequence, the camera moves with fundamental autonomy from the protagonist, seeing what he does not see, behaving in ways that he

Fig. 2.7a–b Enrique's attempted assassination on a Havana rooftop. From *I Am Cuba*, 1964.

cannot. From the beginning of the sequence, it separates itself from Enrique in a graceful motion to take a different path toward the base of the building, enveloping the structure in its own passage—for no other reason, it seems, than to convey its own sense of the place. And as the episode progresses, the camera continues to float around Enrique, studying the areas through which he passes as if to create a morphology of space as it exists with and without his body. What we notice most obviously through this study is that although Enrique masterfully uses the space to act out his assassination attempt, the surrounding environment as such remains separate from him, outside his direct sensations and attention.

This distinction between how the actions and the setting are experienced by Enrique and the camera is intensified through the complex integration of sound into the sequence. A blind musician's song, encountered by Enrique on the street right before his ascent, remains present throughout the sequence, acting as a near double for the camera as it similarly moves freely and without limitations through the space. Even as the man's melancholy song emanates from a specific location below, it fluidly permeates the entirety of the surroundings, reaching all the way to the rooftop. Defying all boundaries and floating in every direction, the song infuses each visible point with its own vibrating, material presence. And it envelops Enrique inside and out, as we hear the song alternatively as an objective presence in space *and* as its distorted, subjective version, processed through the student's crumbling psyche. With movements that are inherently unmappable (it is, simply, everywhere), the sound begins to function as if it were the matter of space itself, subjecting Enrique to its constant presence, rendering his entire body permeable to its surroundings (as opposed to just his isolated and static vision, which otherwise had dominated the sequence) and forcing him ultimately to return to ground.

It is in the sequence of Enrique's funeral, shortly after this aborted assassination scene and immediately after that of his death, that the camera's spatial consciousness, as it were, becomes congruent with that of the Cuban people. As a spontaneous crowd forms to carry Enrique's body through Havana, we see him disappear from view, replaced by thousands of solemn mourners. Moving steadily through the city, the vast crowd maps itself so entirely onto its streets as to become their mobile fabric (figure 2.8a and figure 2.8b). The surrounding architecture begins to look pliant, as if absorbing and mimicking in reverse the pervasive energy of the marchers. And as the camera rises at the beginning of the sequence from a point-of-view shot identical to that of a lone mourner to a long aerial view of the procession as a whole, its trajectory positions these viewpoints as indivisible from each other, unifying the experience

Fig. 2.8a–b Enrique's funeral. From *I Am Cuba*, 1964.

of protesters on the ground and the mobile gaze from on high as equally belonging to Cuba itself.

This aerial view is notably different from the centripetal, and clearly mapped, organization of space discussed earlier. What we perceive here is a camera floating at the top of three-story buildings, not so very high; it is tightly embraced on all sides by the city and its inhabitants, who keep joining the procession from behind the building façades and above the ground. As part of its long take, for instance, the camera sweeps into the window of a cigar factory and follows the workers there as they drape a Cuban flag on their balcony, before continuing out to follow the marchers from above. The gaze looking at Enrique's funeral procession, furthermore, offers something other than the straightforward perspective one might expect from an aerial shot. It shows the streets as somewhat warped and distorted, formed and incomplete at the same time, and ultimately embodied, sensuous, and in motion. Political consciousness, made present in the scene through the calm order of the procession and the collectivity of action, is not only joined but also counterbalanced by the mimetic interaction of all the participants (individuals, crowd, camera, façades)—the physicality, plasticity, and *dis*order of which ("the architecture falls apart," to repeat the earlier mentioned criticism) cannot be contained by centripetal hierarchies of vision and spatial organization. To return to Markov's discussion of mimesis once more, although the physiological sensation of being one with space is presented here as a form of political channeling, it also exceeds such channeling, and in doing so actively disturbs the sequence's conceptual clarity.

Movement as Perpetual Displacement

As the funeral sequence makes particularly evident, *I Am Cuba* imagines spatial mimesis as rooted in near perpetual movement—a shift from *The Unsent Letter*, in which the most striking mimetic passages culminated in a series of nearly static images. Here, movement is present incessantly, and on diverse registers: the movement of the crowd, which Urusevskii films and viewers observe; the camera movement, through which he films and viewers experience the sequence; and the movement of the built environment—the seeming pliability of architectural surfaces—which Urusevskii generates through the specificity of his camera lens and viewers perceive as grounded in the filmic reality. Movement drives *I Am Cuba*'s aesthetics and the participatory mode that it enacts, fostering an immediacy of perception and producing an experience of space as fluctuating, living, and physical, as if accessible to touch.

Urusevskii advances with his practice the proposition put forward by film theorist Christian Metz that "in the cinema the impression of reality is also the reality of the impression, the real presence of motion."[40] Metz argues that cinematic movement transcends the usual logic of representation and notes that "the strict distinction between object and copy... dissolves on the threshold of motion. Because movement is never material but is *always* visual, to reproduce its appearance is to duplicate its reality. In truth, one cannot even 'reproduce' a movement; one can only re-produce it in a second production belonging to the same order of reality, for the spectator, as the first."[41] The perception of movement in a representation, Metz thus implies, is in essence no different from its perception in real life, involving the same sensory activation in the perceiver; as a primary perception rather than a representation, it deepens the effect of immediacy of the filmed space and of viewers' participation in it, blurring the ontological boundaries between representation and reality.

Urusevskii's own remarks on his working methods suggest that he conceived of cinematic movement along the same lines as Metz does, putting all resources into creating the kind of mobility that would substantially increase "the reality of the impression." In a 1966 meeting with Moscow cinematographers—during which he offered the most arduous defense of his "formalism"—he stressed just this point while describing his complete dependency on the handheld camera and noting that he could not make his cinematic image "breathe" as if alive using a traditional stationary device.[42] Indeed, his employment of the lightweight handheld camera increased from film to film, culminating in *I Am Cuba*, for which it was used exclusively. What Urusevskii liked most about it was its sensitivity to the hand that holds it, its ability to register the slightest motion of the body in a state of "excitement" and to translate this excitement into moving images. As he reported, "if this excitement emerges, if there is a unity [of the cameraman] with the actor's excitement, then the camera itself strives intuitively to move or freezes, approaches the actor or shifts away, and thus exactly and emotionally expresses the meaning of the scene."[43] On occasion, Urusevskii made his actors themselves hold the camera, so they could "film themselves" on the move, with the lens adapting to their bodies and thus imaging directly—not through any symbolization—what they ostensibly sensed and felt.

Urusevskii's goal, it appears, was to subordinate the recording device to the physicality of the entire body ("hand camera" in Russian—*ruchnaia kamera*—can, coincidentally, be understood as "tamed camera"). This subordination enables the machine to be enclosed within a bodily circuit, to become integral part of the body's sensory and nervous system, or even turn into its third hand, for Urusevskii placed so much emphasis on holding rather than looking. Otherwise, how else would the camera itself move intuitively?

The result was not to be the camera's perfection of human vision, its liberation *from* "human immobility," as Dziga Vertov would have it, but rather its liberation *of* human mobility in the process of mimicking it—and of presenting it as dynamic space itself.[44] Under such conditions, the movement of the camera would impart more than a "reality of the impression." It would generate a sensory contiguity between the (filming) body and space—a mimetic synchrony by which bodily sensations and affects are located immediately within the screened space, and in which film viewers would participate through "the real presence of motion."

Benjamin, writing at the height of industrial modernity and in the wake of World War I, saw cinema as possessing the capacity to counter the disastrous, numbing effects of technology on the human sensorium by restoring the lost mimetic bond between man and the world in all its immediate, tactile, and heretofore unexperienced proximity.[45] Urusevskii's work suggests a similar investment in the power of cinema, namely, its potential to oppose the dominant spatial politics of his time. The fact that Kalatozov's film crew arrived in Cuba shortly after the Cuban Missile Crisis of October 1962, in which the deployment of nuclear weapons became a real possibility, makes this opposition all the more powerful—and the director himself declared the film to be "his answer" to the crisis.[46] *I Am Cuba*'s long, embodied camera expositions and the film's extended, sensuous space itself negate the disembodied practices of military surveillance that came to the fore during the crisis, above all, the ability to control, map, and use a territory from afar. Indeed, this Cold War military exercise distilled on a global level the kind of spatial relations that *The Unsent Letter* sought to suspend aesthetically.[47] Rather than creating a map of the island from without, through a distant and disconnected gaze, *I Am Cuba* seeks to produce the nation's spatial wholeness from within, through a gliding plasticity of the body presented as a changing, and always in motion, space.

Urusevskii's belief in the aesthetic and political potential of cinematic movement is inscribed directly into *I Am Cuba*'s narrative: the film introduces its student revolutionaries at the beginning of the third episode in an act of an explicit *cinematic* revolt, set, above all places, in a drive-in cinema. As the uninterested audience members sit isolated in their cars during a propaganda film triumphing the achievements of the dictator Batista, we see Enrique and his fellow students sneaking toward the screen, hurling Molotov cocktails to disrupt the film and then gliding away in their open convertibles as the drive-in descends into chaos (figure 2.9a and figure 2.9b). The spatially static and compartmentalized experience of film viewing at the drive-in could not be farther away from the destabilizing, panoramic dynamics of *I Am Cuba* itself,

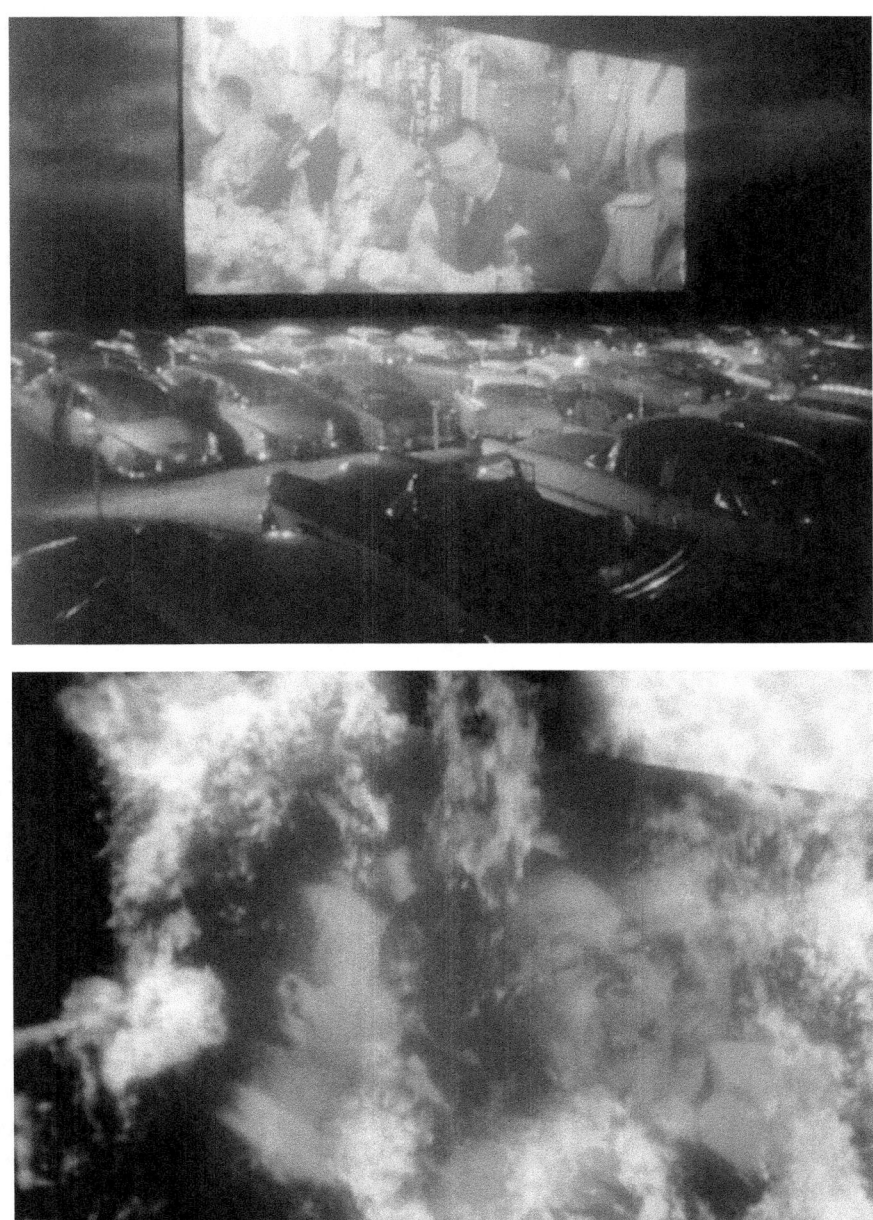

Fig. 2.9a–b Student revolt at a drive-in cinema. From *I Am Cuba*, 1964.

Fig. 2.10 Cinerama theater façade in *I Am Cuba*, 1964.

which seeks to integrate viewers into its actions, as if to physically mobilize them. Only a few sequences later, at the very closure of the sequence featuring Enrique's assassination attempt, a panoramic theater itself appears on screen. As the student descends to the street in a daze and is nearly run over by a car, a Cinerama theater is visible prominently in the background—representing a self-reflexive directorial gesture, I think, as well as an embrace of dynamic, full-body experiences of space as part of political struggle, at which Enrique, in fact, has just failed (figure 2.10).

But what is arguably *I Am Cuba*'s most significant cinematic reference is also its most oblique. After the triumphant procession of Enrique's funeral, the film cuts to a nearly black screen, across which a trail of armed figures wading through a swamp becomes just barely visible. After a few moments in which this band is followed in near-total darkness, a barrage of flashlight beams accompanied by gunfire suddenly halts and illuminates them (figure 2.11). As the projected light drags across their bodies, three guerrilla fighters—as we understand the figures to be—are asked, "Where is Fidel?" to which each laconically responds that he is the revolutionary leader: "*I* am Fidel." Arms around one another, the figures move defiantly forward, followed once again by the camera's

Fig. 2.11 Guerilla fighting in an indeterminate location. From *I Am Cuba*, 1964.

gaze. With its quiet dark space that is suddenly pierced by beams of projected light and a barrage of sound, this scene mimics almost precisely the material presentation of cinema itself. But the brief sequence is noteworthy not only for its suggestion of the abstract structure of cinema, but also for its materialization of the film's essential spatial logic. For in answering the question of "where is" with the statement of "I am," the three figures conflate *spatial* knowledge with *self*-knowledge and situate this conflation as the very substance of advanced political thought. The stakes of Kalatozov and Urusevskii's mimetic practice are articulated here most directly. As the figure of Fidel disperses onto the body of each guerrilla fighter—their individual declarations of "I" becoming one communal "we"—their collective bodies move indistinguishably in a field of almost complete darkness, and this unity constitutes the core tactic of their revolutionary struggle.

By locating the force of revolution—in a word, Fidel—as both everywhere (for thousands of other Fidels clearly stand in waiting, spread across the countryside) and nowhere (in the murky and dark nonspace of the unlocatable swamp), the guerrilla-capture scene resonates with the particular significance of Cuba for revolutionary thought within the broader rubric of the sixties as a cultural period. Situated within that context by the cultural critic Fredric Jameson, the Cuban experience was noteworthy for precisely the spatial upheaval its revolutionary process embodied:

> The strategy of the mobile guerrilla base ... is conceived as yet a third term, as something distinct from *either* the traditional model of class struggle (an essentially *urban* proletariat rising against a bourgeoisie or ruling class) *or* the Chinese experience of a mass peasant movement in the countryside.... The [Cuban] guerrilla operation ... is conceptualized as being neither "in" nor "of" either country or city ... but rather in that third or nonplace which is the wilderness of the Sierra Maestra ... a whole new element in which the guerrilla band moves in perpetual displacement.[48]

The uniqueness of the Cuban model, Jameson argues, is essentially spatial, rooted in a roaming and "perpetually displaced," revolutionary presence. Cuban revolutionary potentiality, he contends, resided somewhere *between* country and city, and advanced political thinking within the Cuban situation was above all a matter of reconceptualizing space—of being able to "out-map" the pro-Batista forces.

If an explicitly aesthetic, sensory connection to space is not part of Jameson's discussion, his description of revolutionary movement as a "perpetual displacement" in a "third or nonplace" evokes directly Kalatozov and Urusevskii's practice, in both *The Unsent Letter* and *I Am Cuba*. For already in the earlier film, the filmmakers defined the relationship between Soviet space and ideology as one of control, omnipotent gaze, and mapping while simultaneously creating conditions for space to escape from just these constraints. The swampy, murky, and unmappable territories of the taiga in *The Unsent Letter* visually and conceptually precede the guerrilla sequence in *I Am Cuba*, suggesting that the nearly mythical, mobile power of the Sierra Maestra fighters not only provided Kalatozov's team with new material but also extended and clarified the political and aesthetic vision already present in the earlier film.[49] In engaging space directly through their bodies and their mobility, and in making their environment an integral actor of political processes, the Cuban revolutionaries of the later film offer a conclusion to the unresolved relation between communism and space that was staged in *The Unsent Letter*'s conversation-on-the-hill sequence.

But the spatial experience of the Cuban fighters appeared to offer even more to Kalatozov and Urusevskii by solidifying their understanding of *cinema's* political significance. By equating the essential material presentation of film with the spatial program of the revolutionaries in the guerrilla sequence, the filmmakers invite us to think of cinema as itself a "third or nonspace," the experience of which is rooted in perpetual displacement. In their incessant urge to upset viewers' sense of physical equilibrium and stasis, to tear their gaze from the position of control, and to mobilize them into a dynamic, if also disorienting, experience of the environment constructed by the camera, they seek to render viewers' selves—individually and communally, as a collective, political body—aware of, and permeable to, their surroundings.[50] There could be no better place than the dark cinematic theater in which to explore space as a powerfully sensed reality, a presence from within which a political movement could be imagined, and mapped, anew. What such a reimagining entails is not articulated as an explicit program in either film; but in *I Am Cuba*, movement as spatial mimicry—and movement into spatial mimicry—rises to become an essential operation in the process of giving shape to a progressive, socialist reality.

Notes

1. "Kakoi ekran luchsche?" 92.
2. Markel', "Dolzhen li operator videt'?" Markel argues that while Urusevskii's camera work in *The Cranes Are Flying* and *The Unsent Letter* served as a catalyst for the development of new visual possibilities in film, it also became an empty model of imitation for many filmmakers, who used Urusevskii's style without any formal or dramaturgical motivation.
3. Dyko, "Tvorcheskiie poiski Sergeia Urusevskogo," 102. The cooperation between Kalatozov and Urusevskii should be understood as what Philip Cavendish, in reference to Soviet avant-garde film, has described as codirecting. Examining the efforts of Eduard Tisse, Anatolii Golovnia, and Danilo Demutskii—the cameramen for Eisenstein, Pudovkin, and Dovzhenko, respectively—Cavendish argues that they contributed equally, if not more, to the latter's work than the celebrated directors themselves (Cavendish, *The Men with the Movie Camera*).
4. On the reception and detailed analysis of *The Cranes Are Flying*, see Woll, *The Cranes Are Flying*.
5. Such negative reactions developed progressively; some of the first assessments of *The Unsent Letter* speak more favorably of the film, emphasizing the same terms of the participatory camera aesthetics as had dominated in the discussions of *Cranes*. See, for instance, a detailed description of Urusevskii's camera work in *The Unsent Letter* by Bogdanov, "Kamera v dvizhenii."
6. "Delo fil'ma 'Neotpravlennoe pis'mo'" [File on the film *The Unsent Letter*], 7. These pages are particularly aggressive toward *The Unsent Letter*, partially because they comprise the responses from party members (rather than film critics) who were interested more in the ideological correctness of the work than in its aesthetic experimentation. This archival file is especially rich with accusations of formalism; a typical comment: "many of the scenes became just a form, not filled with anything important" (4).
7. The film was not a success in either the USSR or Cuba upon its release. A frequently quoted Cuban review was indeed titled "No soy Cuba" (I am not Cuba) and described the script as a caricature. Another review noted, "The film has much of Urusevskii and Kalatozov, but little of Cuba." Quoted in Domínguez, "The Mammoth That Wouldn't Die," 111.
8. "Novye filmy: 'Ia Kuba,'" 28, 30.
9. *I Am Cuba* was taken out of circulation one week after its initial release and spent nearly thirty years on the shelves in Soviet archives. It was screened as part of a tribute to Kalatozov at the

1992 Telluride Film Festival, leading to an international rerelease with help of Martin Scorsese and Francis Ford Coppola. Although the film's didacticism was criticized by many, it also achieved great international acclaim, hailed, in one typical phrase, as "one of the most stylistically vigorous films of all times." See Guthman, "Soviet Bird's-Eye View of Cuba."

10. "Novye fil'my: Ia Kuba," Page numbers in order of quotes: 31, 26, 25, 25.

11. Alexander Prokhorov notes that the original ending was changed immediately before the film's release: in the initial version, all four of the protagonists die (Prokhorov, "The Unknown New Wave," 12).

12. See Taubman, *Khrushchev: The Man and His Era*, 262–63, 364–65, 606–9. Kalatozov had explored the conquest of virgin lands in an earlier work, his 1955 film *Pervyi eshelon* (*The First Echelon*). This is a much more traditional cinematic representation of the topic, organized around Soviet people's arrival in new territories, overcoming their difficulties there, and successfully cultivating new crops.

13. Epstein, *The Rise and Fall of Diamonds*, esp. chapter 17.

14. Having examined a thorough collection of newspaper articles from the era, Alla Bolotova argues that "between the 1920s and the 1960s, the hegemonic discourse on nature remained practically unchallenged.... The ideas of man's power over nature and the necessity of struggle with nature were implicit in the vast majority of articles, and newspapers routinely carried glowing descriptions of drastic alterations of the environment in correspondence with human needs" (Bolotova, "Colonization of Nature in the Soviet Union," 111–12). Official Soviet attitudes toward natural territories, Bolotova's article implies, did not change with Khrushchev's arrival; if anything, they intensified with a new push in agricultural and economic development.

15. See a detailed discussion of Mikhailov's work, especially his *Map of the Motherland*, in Dobrenko, "The Art of Social Navigation." Dobrenko discusses the centrality of the map within the operation of Soviet centripetal space, noting Khrushchev's remarks during the Twentieth Party Congress that Stalin rarely left Moscow during his rule: "The Kremlin hermit ruled the largest country in the world, transforming it exclusively on maps. The map was indeed the equivalent of power" (190).

16. Mikhailov, *Moia Rossiia*.

17. Ibid., 101.

18. Ibid., introduction, unpaginated.

19. It should be noted, however, that we are rarely free from slightly disorienting camera motions that somewhat disturb the stability of the ordered space, serving as a premonition of things to come.

20. Critics repeatedly noted the lack of narrative logic (or simple common sense) in the sequences of spatial disorientation. One commentator, for instance, complained, "Right next to them is a clean, comfortable spot—but no, they have to get into some bushes, to climb somewhere. These people simply got lost in a broad daylight. They walk, circle around, as if they were blind" ("*Delo fil'ma* 'Neotpravlennoe pis'mo,'" 23).

21. Sequences of this kind received particularly harsh treatment from Soviet critics. One, for instance, noted that the film is simply "anti-humanist," arguing that "we cannot do this, we cannot show our people like that; everything is done here for some aesthetic effect, for some sick beauty. And look, the man never stands as he is supposed to—vertically; no, everything always goes crooked, up, down" ("*Delo fil'ma* 'Neotpravlennoe pis'mo,'" 25).

22. Kokoreva makes an explicit point that it is Urusevskii, and not Kalatozov, who presents such a worldview, grounding her argument in the continuity of formal language between *The Unsent Letter* and *Forty First* (*Sorok Pervyi*), a film that Urusevskii made with the director Grigorii Chukhrai in 1956.

23. "*Delo fil'ma* 'Neotpravlennoe pis'mo,'" 30.

24. In an excellent discussion of *The Unsent Letter*, Evgenii Margolit makes a very similar observation about Urusevskii's camera, arguing that for the first time in Soviet cinema, nature acquired its own point of view. He notes, furthermore, that "what is cataclysmic from the point of view of a human is uneventful for nature and nothing disturbs its flow. That is, the epic of nature turns out to be the humans' drama—a drama precisely because nature simply does not notice them, because nature does not distinguish a human within a series of its other creation, and because nature is indifferent to human pain" (Margolit, "Landscape, with Hero," 39). Although our discussions of Urusevskii's constructions of nature's gaze are similar, our understandings of the film as a whole differ significantly. Whereas for Margolit this film is a manifestation of humankind's total separation from the natural world, for me it is a search for new routes of connection.
25. Benjamin, "The Lamp," 693.
26. Benjamin, "On the Mimetic Faculty," 722.
27. Caillois, "Mimicry and Legendary Psychasthenia," 28.
28. Ibid., 27.
29. Ibid., 30.
30. Ibid., 25.
31. Buck-Morss, *The Dialectics of Seeing*, 263.
32. Benjamin, "Moscow," 23.
33. Markov, "Nekotorye zakony vospriiatia iskusstva," 98.
34. Bertolt Brecht grasped such a process of sublimation in specifically mimetic terms. In his 1930 didactic play *The Decision*, he writes, "Who do you think is the Party? . . . We are it. You and I and them—all of us. Comrades, the clothes it's dressed in are your clothes, the head that it thinks with is yours" (Brecht, *Collected Plays*: 3: 82).
35. In both *I Am Cuba* and Eisenstein's 1925 *Battleship Potemkin*, a dramatic and violent clash between protesters and progovernment forces takes place on prominent steps and is framed by similarly looking sculptural figures. But in contrast to Eisenstein's sequence, which progresses through an elaborate montage that fragments and even distorts the spatial organization of the Odessa steps, the sequence in *I Am Cuba* puts emphasis on the formal unity of space, which is fragmented nevertheless by the violent acts of the police forces.
36. Roger Ebert described this shot, for instance, as "one of the most astonishing I have ever seen" (Ebert, "I Am Cuba"); Jonathan Rosenbaum, describing Urusevskii's work more generally, writes, "this is some of the most exhilarating camera movements and most luscious black-and-white cinematography you'll ever see" (Rosenbaum, "I Am Cuba"). The choice of site for this sequence could not have been more appropriate. It was filmed at Habana Libre—the tallest hotel in Latin America at the time of its 1958 construction—operated by Hilton before the revolution but turned into Fidel Castro's headquarters in the first months afterward.
37. These and a few other sequences in the film are shot with a 9.8 mm camera lens, which Urusevskii used enthusiastically because it provided a vision angle wider than that of a wide-screen format; this enabled him to condense the vast built environment of Havana into one shot, making it surround tightly, if distortedly, the rooftop area.
38. The hotel rooftop sequence is rich with cinematic references. One interesting aspect is the dialogue it generates with the opening of Orson Welles's *Touch of Evil* (1958).
39. Brazilian filmmaker Vicente Ferraz includes a discussion of this scene in his documentary *Soy Cuba, o mamute siberiano* (*I Am Cuba, A Siberian Mammoth*), exploring the making of Kalatozov's film.
40. Metz, "On the Impression of Reality in the Cinema," 9.
41. Ibid. Building on Metz's reflections, film historian Tom Gunning has suggested recently that movement be elevated to an "alternative theory of the realistic effect of the cinema," opposing it to the photographic indexicality that is often presented as an essential hallmark of film (Tom Gunning, "Moving Away from the Index," 56).

42. Urusevskii, "O forme," 31. Urusevskii's discussion directly addresses contemporary phenomenological studies on the tactility of film, such as Laura Marks, *The Skin of the Film*, and Jennifer Barker, *The Tactile Eye*.

43. Ibid.

44. In contrast to that of Vertov, Urusevskii's camera work could be likened to handwriting or painting, with the camera operating as a pencil that transmits the hand's touch, rather than a modern machine that records mechanically and at a distance. Urusevskii's conception indicates a desire to humanize the camera (rather than to mechanize the human), the roots of which lie perhaps in his original training as a painter at the end of the 1920s, with the painterly practice, as some critics have suggested, remaining at the core of his work as a cinematographer. See Kamenskii, "Khudozhnik Urusevskii," 90–93. Furthermore, Urusevskii's transference of nervous, sensory energy onto the camera itself can be linked to Walter Benjamin's concept of innervation, which itself is directly connected to mimesis, and, as Miriam Hansen has argued, "entails dynamics that move in opposite, yet complementary, directions: (1) a decentering and extension of the human sensorium beyond the limits of the individual body/subject into the world . . . ; and (2) an introjection, ingestion, or incorporation of the object or device, be it an external rhythm, a familiar madeleine, or an alien(ating) apparatus" (Hansen, "Benjamin and Cinema," 332).

45. In a much quoted passage, Benjamin writes, "Our bars and city streets, our offices and furnished rooms, our railroad stations and our factories seemed to close relentlessly around us. Then came film and exploded this prison-world with the dynamite of the split second, so that now we can set off calmly on journeys of adventure among its far-flung debris. With the close-up, space expands; with slow motion, movement is extended" (Benjamin, "The Work of Art," 265).

46. Kalatozov, in a Soviet radio broadcast, declared his film to be "my answer, and that of the whole Soviet people, against the naval blockade, this cruel aggression of American imperialism." For a discussion of the film within the context of the Cuban Missile Crisis, including a clip of this broadcast, watch *Soy Cuba, o mamute siberiano*.

47. *I Am Cuba*'s employment of cinematic technology can be understood as a response to the Cuban Missile Crisis more extensively. The Soviet general Ivan Zavialov discussed in 1965 how the emergence of nuclear weapons virtually eliminated distance between hostile territories, making them much more susceptible to sudden attacks and destruction. He essentially implied that in the context of contemporary warfare, global space became a network of disconnected points, in which in-between spaces lost all significance. They stopped operating as places of either defense or blockade, or even of passage from one place to another, since they could be traversed in a brief amount of time, completely devoid of bodily measures of distance, time, and movement. On the other hand, Zavialov also suggested that the actual field of military operations would grow exponentially in a nuclear war, because the sheer power of the new weapons requires expansive territories for destruction, eliminating the whole concept of a military front, in that nuclear weapons consume and destroy national spaces all at once. See Zavialov, *Skorost', vremia i prostranstvo v sovremennoi voine*, esp. 161–86. *I Am Cuba* operates in reverse: Its camera movement stresses the contiguity of space; it comprehends space explicitly through dimensions available to human body; it alternately slows down and increases the time of passage; and it communicates with space as if one step at a time, each moment of passage articulating a specificity of the relationship between the camera and its immediate environment.

48. Jameson, "Periodizing the '60s," 202.

49. Descriptions of the Sierra Maestra mountains, as a symbol of Cuba's revolutionary struggle, circulated widely in the Soviet press. Kalatozov's film, furthermore, had a predecessor, a documentary production called *Pylaiushchii Ostrov* [Flaming Island] that included Cuban documentary footage of the guerrilla fighting. Roman Karmen, the director of the film, described in great detail his experiences of working on the film in Cuba, including a month and a half he spent in the province

of Oriente, where the mountains are located. See Karmen, "S'emki na pylaiushchem ostrove." In turn, the "docu-fiction" sequences in Karmen's film showing Fidel Castro's troops moving through swamps look very similar to the swamp sequences of *The Unsent Letter*, suggesting a direct visual dialogue between these films.

50. In his analysis of mimicry, Caillois engages with the work of psychiatrist Eugène Minkowski and his discussion of darkness as conductive to mimetic experiences. Caillois's rhetoric can be applied to Kalatozov and Urusevskii's cinematic space as well: "While light space is eliminated by the materiality of objects, darkness is 'filled,' it touches the individual directly, envelops him, penetrates him, and even passes through him: hence 'the ego is *permeable* for darkness while it is not so for light'" (Caillois, "Mimicry and Legendary Psychasthenia," 30). Not only do film experiences take place in the dark space of the theater, but Kalatozov and Urusevskii intensify this darkness in some of the key sequences—such as the "I am Fidel" scene—that allow for hardly any light at all, even on screen.

3
THE ARCHITECTURE OF MOVEMENT: GEORGII DANELIA'S *I WALK THE STREETS OF MOSCOW*

THERE IS A surprising correspondence in the opening seconds of two very different films: Georgii Danelia's *I Walk the Streets of Moscow*, a Soviet production from 1964 that is relatively unknown to international audiences, and Jacques Tati's *Playtime*, a widely discussed French masterpiece from 1967. The Soviet film begins at a Moscow airport, with a young woman dancing and humming as she moves along a glass-curtain exterior wall (figure 3.1). The French film, set in Paris, begins with two nuns walking first on the outside of and then on the interior side of a glass terminal façade, eventually disappearing around a waiting-lounge corner (figure 3.2). The formal language, represented spaces, and sounds and movements of both sequences strangely mirror one another. Filmed from the same straight-on angle in long shot, the female figures in both films glide along almost identical glass façades of airport terminals. *Playtime*'s opening moments, however, appear not only to replicate, but also to comically reverse the earlier Soviet film. Whereas the young woman in Danelia's film moves in an unrestricted and dancelike fashion, Tati's nuns appear to march, their bodies pulled tightly together and seeming to advance along invisible straight lines. In contrast to the quiet humming of Danelia's figure, *Playtime* opens with only the cold sounds of the nuns' steps. And while Danelia focuses in his opening moments on a single figure but uses a complex series of reflections in the glass wall along which she moves to create doubling and difference, Tati presents two distinct figures whose faces, clothes, and motions, it is no exaggeration to say, make them indistinguishable from each other.

Fig. 3.1 Dancing along a modern façade. From *I Walk the Streets of Moscow*, 1964.

Fig. 3.2 Marching along a modern façade. From *Playtime*, 1967.

The visual and tropological parallels of these opening shots are so striking that one suspects Tati framed his opening sequence as a specific response to Danelia's film. Although, to my knowledge, no documentary evidence exists to confirm this supposition, circumstantial facts support it. *I Walk the Streets of Moscow* premiered internationally at the 1964 Cannes Film Festival, where it was nominated for the Palme d'Or along with such films as Glauber Rocha's *Black God, White Devil*, François Truffaut's *The Soft Skin*, and Jacques Demy's *The Umbrellas of Cherbourg*, to which it ultimately lost. Tati was just beginning work on *Playtime* that summer, assembling his so-called Tativille, the miniature city outside Paris that he described as "the real star of the film."[1]

Recent Soviet cinema, furthermore, must have been on Tati's mind, as his own *Mon Oncle* had lost out on the 1958 Palme d'Or, for which it had been favored, to Mikhail Kalatozov's *The Cranes Are Flying*.[2] Danelia's feature, furthermore, was purchased for distribution in France and reviewed in the French press, becoming, by some accounts, a popular film among audiences in that country.[3]

But even if Tati had no knowledge of *I Walk the Streets of Moscow*, that would make *Playtime's* intricate formal echoes of Danelia's opening sequence all the more compelling. Both directors, working at almost precisely the same moment, take urban space—and specifically, the body's movement through urban space—as their primary focus. And both begin their filmic examinations with similar shots in identical settings dominated by 1960s architecture, thus raising the question: What precisely were the cultural tendencies on both sides of the Iron Curtain that could have contributed to such an unthinkably direct mirroring?

Playtime is not the focus of this chapter, but its inversion of Danelia's opening—intentional or not—prompts a reexamination of *I Walk the Streets of Moscow*, particularly its place within a range of Soviet and European discourses on architecture, urban development, and the moving body. For if *Playtime* throughout its two-and-a-half-hour running time, presents a comic and dystopian tribute to the failures of contemporary urbanism—showing human bodies driven by, but fundamentally out of synchrony with, modern architecture and design—*I Walk the Streets of Moscow* offers precisely the opposite: a utopian portrait of the dialogical interaction between bodies and urban space. Driving this dialogue is movement itself. Emerging from and expanding upon a broad shift that appeared in Soviet culture in the years after Stalin's death, Danelia portrays the fundamentally sensory experience of space as both a primary goal of new architectural forms and an essential means to reimagine familiar structures and spaces anew. In doing so, he both responds to and revises earlier avant-garde precedents and, as *Playtime's* parallels with *I Walk the Streets of Moscow* suggest, develops powerful correspondences with contemporary European discussions of the political efficacy of walking and everyday urban experience.

Straight Lines and Curves

The narrative of *I Walk the Streets of Moscow* can be recounted only loosely, as it consists of a series of lighthearted, interrelated episodes taking place on a summer day in the Soviet capital. A young Siberian writer, Volodia, has arrived in the city for the day to see acquaintances and meet with a prominent writer. Volodia meets Kolia, a young worker who has just finished his night shift working on the construction of the Moscow metro. The two spend part of the day together, and Kolia introduces his new friend to Aliona, his "love," who sells records at GUM, the central shopping arcade next to Red Square. Volodia and Aliona become attracted to each other, and Volodia expresses the hope that she will perhaps join him at some point in Siberia. Meanwhile, Sasha, an old friend of Kolia's, is about to leave for his compulsory military service and is in a hurry to get married before his departure. Sasha's romantic relationship encounters a few obstacles, but the film ends with a reconciliation between him and his new wife, Sveta. The film regularly digresses from these main narrative threads, however, shifting its attention to other cursory plotlines: Sasha and Kolia, for instance, take a ride in a taxi to help a Japanese tourist find the Tretyakov Gallery; Kolia runs into a church to search for the owner of a lost dog; Kolia, Volodia, and Aliona chase a criminal in a park; and so forth. The camera frequently abandons these main protagonists, furthermore, simply to project diverse corners of the city within the film's widescreen format, or to glance upon nameless strangers having nothing to do with any narrative strand. The young woman who opens the film, for instance, is never seen after that initial sequence.

This loose narrative structure and lack of a central dramatic conflict disturbed Soviet critics, even as they praised the film for its fresh, enthusiastic, and untroubled representation of Soviet youth. Rostislav Yurenev, a prominent voice in Soviet film discussions at the time, wrote that "the protagonist's lack of precise, conscious aspiration to anything, his lack of conflict and difficulties that need to be overcome—that is, the lack of what in olden times was called a unified dramatic act—creates an impression of being lightweight, even thoughtless."[4] Mikhail Bleiman, a well-known scriptwriter, similarly questioned the seriousness of a film that had no clear dramatic progression: "I agree that this film consists of observations and genre scenes. And I don't debate the lawfulness of such art. But I need to clarify something else: what quality do these observations possess—are they superficial or deep?"[5] Although these critics understood that their desire for such coherent narrative development was somehow old-fashioned, they nevertheless insisted that the informal plot structure of *I Walk the Streets of Moscow* and its lack of obstacles for the characters to overcome prohibited it from becoming significant socialist art. In their view, the film could offer little more than a pleasant entertainment.

In focusing on character and plot development, these early critics paid only marginal attention to the film's concern with the spaces of contemporary Moscow. Bleiman, in his minimal remarks on the film's urban imagery, disparaged Vadim Yusov's camera work for being untruthful, for making Moscow appear static and devoid of new development—a particularly surprising argument, because so much of the camera's focus is on urban change and construction. In general, critics tended to divide the film into two facets: its spatial city aspect and its narrative or dramatic aspect, with the former serving as nothing but a charming backdrop for the latter. We can understand this opposition more essentially as one of spatial versus temporal unfolding, with space serving as a vessel within which time and its events transpire. That this opposition might be reversed—that the film's narrative strands might serve to provide a context in which to explore spatial dynamics, with the film's representation of urban space at the very core of its dramatic conflict—remained beyond these considerations.

It is just this aspect of Danelia's film that Tati's *Playtime* appears to engage, both in the opening sequence and throughout the entirety of the film. The French director described *Playtime's* story of a man's bumbling encounters within a homogenized urban landscape somewhere in Paris in terms of straight lines gradually becoming curves: "At the beginning, the people's movements always follow the architecture, they never make a curve, ... they go from one line to another. The more the picture continues, the more the people dance, and start to make curves, and turn around, and start to be absolutely round—because *we* have decided that we're still there."[6] For Tati, then, *Playtime's* primary story was about modalities of movement, the possibility of subjective curves—understood as a confirmation that ours are still there—in an environment composed almost entirely of straight lines. Just such an imbrication of traditional, straight plot and formal exploration is likewise suggested by the opening sequence of *I Walk the Streets of Moscow*.

Examining the sequence again more closely, we see that the space outside the airport terminal is shown twice: first through its reflection in the expansive glass wall of the terminal building and then, when the young woman turns after having stopped her quasi-dance, as an actual, inhabitable space under open sky. The difference between these two could not be more striking. In the reflection, the airy, spacious exterior, together with the woman's figure, becomes densely embedded into the fabric of the windows and the interior structure of the building. Her body, of which there is of course only one, is shown in duplicate and triplicate in this reflection while the multiple airplanes behind her are visible as only a single machine. Our perception of these contrasts unfolds as we follow the woman's moving body; indeed, it takes a moment even to recognize that she is actually dancing outside rather than inside the building, as she seems to glide effortlessly through, and behind, the glass wall.

This focus on space, the body, and the ambiguities of perception is further heightened by a short dialogue that touches upon both the thematics of movement and the most conventional narrative concerns of romantic relations and marriage. The conversation between the young woman and Volodia, who has just arrived from Siberia, proceeds as follows, with Volodia asking:

—Are you arriving or departing?

—I'm meeting somebody.

—Who?

—My husband....

—You are already married?

—Yes.

—And everything is well with you?

—Yes, it is.

—That can't be.

—Yes, it can!

This is a short and lively, but certainly strange, dialogue. Although the man wants to situate the woman within the most linear narrative framework of departure and arrival, she announces her presence along what we might describe as a perpendicular axis to this: she is *meeting* somebody—that is, neither arriving nor departing, but precisely staying put in this singular place. This process of meeting is presented to us in the film's opening moments as a kind of expulsion from time and absorption within space, an opposition that is stressed by the way the woman fully ignores a chime announcing the hour and focuses instead on her own quiet singing, which guides her movement. Danelia's decision, in the sequence as a whole, to set intricately articulated spatial experience against the most banal tropes of filmic narrative (arrival, departure, marriage) appears as a self-consciously declarative opening gambit: to present his film's central project as that of creating a narrative of space, of proposing space itself as narrative. Indeed, this opening corresponds almost perfectly with Tati's logic: the straight lines of departures and arrivals are opposed here to the curves of the young woman's dance along and seemingly through the glass-curtain façade. But if, for Tati, modern geometric glass structures obstructed such movements, for Danelia, they serve to facilitate them.

New Architecture, Expanded Screen

Contemporary critics, as already noted, essentially ignored this aspect of the film. It is striking that Yurenev did recognize the particular significance of movement and architecture for the film's opening scene but describes them incorrectly. Mentioning in passing the woman's dancelike motions, he suggests that she is moving *inside* the terminal building: "When, in the stream of the morning sun, a young woman moves, dancingly, *through the deserted hall* of the airport, you feel both joy and anxiety, as if at the door to the future. *Behind the wall*—the tarmac, boundless expanses of the country, vast and turbulent life."[7] With this mistake, Yurenev's observation could fit seamlessly with Tati's *Playtime* whose gags frequently revolve around the imperceptibility of glass walls in contemporary structures. Yurenev's comment, however, is indicative not so much of inattentive viewing as of inattentiveness to the particular nature of the new built environment emerging in the Soviet Union of the 1960s. Glass especially gained a new significance in Soviet architectural developments of the post-Stalinist period, primarily in public projects such as airports and leisure and cultural facilities. Its transparency was infused with aspirations to create new kinds of spaces—to organize the exterior and interior of buildings into a "unified architectural environment," generating an essential contrast to the heavy and separating stone façades that had dominated Soviet architecture since the 1930s.[8] In place of excessive decorations, heavy materials, and labyrinthine vertical structures, Soviet public architecture of the 1960s most often mobilized simple horizontal forms and transparent materials, clearly looking both to Soviet architectural experiments of the 1920s and to contemporaneous architectural modernism in the West.

The architectural choices of the film suggest that Danelia (a former architect) was obviously conversant with the contemporaneous discourse of urban planning. The new terminal at Moscow's Vnukovo Airport, where the film most likely opens, presents the very essence of new architectural developments with its extended horizontal form and glass façade—and was completed at the very same time as Danelia's film. Another modern structure that the director pointedly integrates into the film is a café right across from Kolia's apartment building: essentially a glass cube, the café not only operates as a nodal point of the street, facilitating people's circulation, but also provides a framework for vision, with the camera surveying the street from the interior and through its window reflections in one long circular take (figure 3.3a). As if enchanted by this small building, the camera keeps returning to it, examining it from different angles, inside and out, but always occupied with its glass walls, positioning them as central to the production of a unified architectural environment, in which the interior and exterior spaces fuse to generate new perceptual experiences. Danelia organizes the shots of Kolia's street, furthermore, as a spectrum of architectural possibilities. The café appears on one end of the street, in the screen's foreground, as a structure that explicitly mobilizes the senses (vision, sound, and bodily movement), and far on the other end a

Fig. 3.3a–b Glass café as a model for new perceptual experiences in the city. From *I Walk the Streets of Moscow*, 1964.

Stalinist skyscraper stands. Though in the same frame, and even framing the street, it remains nevertheless beyond the reach of direct bodily and sensory interactions, displayed more as a static image in the background than as a participating space (figure 3.3b).

An even more significant architectural composition that did not make it into the final version of the film, but was present in the director's initial plan, is the Palace of Young Pioneers, which, with its emphatic aspiration to move beyond Stalinist spatial conventions, became one of the most discussed architectural projects of the period.[9] The Palace of Young Pioneers—built in 1958–1962 on the Lenin Hills (now Sparrow Hills) in southwestern Moscow and in the general vicinity of the exceptional Stalinist skyscraper of Moscow State University—was, despite its name, quite unpalatial. Hardly visible from the street and not structured around a main entry or façade, it was embedded in its natural environment and extended horizontally as a network of several distinct buildings. Glass made up a significant part of its exterior walls, reinforcing an interaction between the building and its surroundings, blending interior and exterior spaces, and thus creating a new environment for Soviet children's leisure and education.[10] Although the palace was cut from the final version of the film, Danelia's original interest in it betrays once more his desire to present the Soviet capital through the framework of the most contemporary structures.

The director's preoccupation with new architecture extends, however, beyond the structures represented on screen to include the *form* of the screen itself. Released on a widescreen format with an aspect ratio of 2.35:1, *I Walk the Streets of Moscow* was certainly not the first Soviet production of its kind. The first such film, *Il'ia Muromets* (directed by Aleksandr Ptushko), appeared in 1956. Produced in color and featuring lavish landscapes, it was meant to be a true cinematic spectacle and was followed by a few dozen other films produced with the new technology. According to the cinematographer Leonid Kosmatov, who worked on the trilogy *A Long Ordeal* (*Khozhdeniie po mukam*; directed by Grigorii Roshal'), released in three parts on the wide screen between 1957 and 1959, the broader use of widescreen formats at the time "increased the significance of space surrounding the actor," urging filmmakers to rethink how to organize the events within this recently developed cinematic expanse.[11] On the whole, however, the 1950s widescreen films remained relatively static in their orchestrations of space. In *Il'ia Muromets* in particular, the surroundings have the appearance of a decorative setting, separated from the actors and not constituting a dynamic relation with what transpires within the film.[12]

Danelia, by contrast, integrates the exaggerated horizontality of the screen into the architectural ensemble of the film. His engagement with this horizontality is worth considering in light of Kosmatov's insightful discussion of the new aesthetic possibilities generated by the expanded screen. The camera operator urged his fellow filmmakers not to clutter the bigger frame with random details and advocated instead a careful, minimalist mise-en-scène, one that would help produce an active space, capable of emotionally influencing film viewers. He particularly praised the relation of bodily movement to the new screen, arguing that the latter liberated actors' mobility and thus allowed the activation of not only central but also peripheral spaces. At the same time though, Kosmatov addressed the difficulty of filming close-up (and even medium close-up) shots in the format, revealing that he had to "fight the superfluous fields that remained empty," which he filled, after all, with unnecessary details, despite his own warning to his colleagues.[13]

Danelia was not very concerned with close-ups (especially when filming outside), and his spatial organization on screen follows Kosmatov's suggested principles: He leaves only what is necessary within the frame, seeking to make the surrounding environment active. This process is most obvious precisely in the sequences showing newly built structures, whose horizontally extended façades work naturally in tandem with the shape of the screen. In the opening sequence in particular, we see the airport terminal stretch across the entirety of the screen, organizing our visual field and activating central *and* peripheral spaces—or rather equalizing their roles through the repetitive pattern of the façade's window frames and the liberated movement of the young woman who dances across the screen. Indeed, if her reflection in the image (figure 3.1) occupies the center of the camera frame, her actual figure moves to its left, and the configuration of the two shifts as the woman keeps dancing, stirring up the entire field of the screen. The architecture and the screen thus reinforce each other's significance—with both operating to shape and represent contemporary urban experience. Notably, Stalinist skyscrapers could fit into the wide screen only if shot from a distance, and thus separated from the immediacy of experience; conversely, if shown in proximity, they were then necessarily fragmented and thus deprived of their grandiose verticality. Danelia deemed the wide screen the most appropriate and logical window for looking at post-Stalinist Moscow, asserting a new principle of perceptual organization within the architecture of the movie theater that closely matched the goals of contemporary urban design.

The Sense of Movement

The goals, as well as the conceived effects, of the new constructions were manifold. They included, among others, the already mentioned creation of unified architectural environments, rooted in the dialogue between inside and out; the more human scale and inviting openness of new urban compositions; and the economic efficiency of building methods and materials. Most significant, they brought a renewed attention to the human body—in generating new spaces and vistas, it was necessary to engage the entire body, to make it move and thus feel and sense the environment in a fundamentally new way.[14] In discussing the initial Soviet reception of the Palace of the Young Pioneers, art historian Susan Reid points out the focus placed on bodily movement through the space, as opposed to static visual perception. She writes, "*Komsomolskaia Pravda* described the initial encounter with the complex in terms of the spatial experience of a young body *moving* through it, rather than of instantaneous *visual* comprehension. Coming into the new palace, even an adult became like an excited child: 'You, too, suddenly feel like a little boy and want to run around and see everything at once.'"[15]

The understanding of movement as essential to the perception and production of space was not a new development within Soviet architectural thought. In his influential 1996 study *Architecture in the Age of Stalin: Culture Two*, Vladimir Paperny argues that Soviet avant-garde culture of the 1920s (what he terms "culture one") can be differentiated from the subsequent totalitarian culture from the 1930s to 1950s ("culture two") through the categories of movement versus immobility. Soviet avant-garde projects of the 1920s, Paperny writes, are saturated with discourses of spatial transformation and instability; within their designs, as the critic Nikolai Punin wrote, you "should not stand or sit; you must be carried up and down mechanically, drawn against your own will."[16] Mobility was a driving force in the architecture of the time; houses—Paperny quotes here another cultural critic of the period, Konstantin Zelinsky—should "turn to the sun, be collapsible, combinable, and mobile."[17] The early Stalinist period of the 1930s, on the other hand, is defined by an increasing attempt to stabilize such fluidity in both architectural practice and society at large. To keep the population spatially fixed, Paperny argues, the government introduced measures of control, from an extensive surveillance apparatus to "work-books" that officially recorded an individual's places of employment. Architecture, too, compared to the plastic experiments of the 1920s, became formally rigid and explicitly grounded. Thus Moscow State University, built between 1949 and 1953, certainly does not suggest folding and unfolding at will.

But for all its interest in an expansion of what Paperny terms "culture one," Soviet culture in the wake of Stalin explores a very different notion of bodily movement than that of the earlier Soviet avant-garde. Post-Stalinist architectural discourse envisions the dynamism of urban space not as an imperative for movement so strong that it works against one's will, as Punin described, nor through the mobility of architectural forms themselves, as Zelinsky would have it, but through the natural movement of the individual body. This is readily apparent in discussions of urban development during the 1960s, which repeatedly emphasize the role of a walking figure in the unfolding of the built environment. Addressing the integration of green and built spaces in the city of the future, for instance, one architect specifically noted that it is the passage of pedestrians through the new, more open architectural compositions that generates a great multiplicity of vistas, while allowing a simultaneous "sensing of a structural unity of the entire complex, of its built and natural spaces."[18] Through the free movement of people, he implies, space becomes multiple and heterogeneous, just as its structural unity remains dynamic—understood as an individual, sensory experience of the passage. This conception is very different from that of architectural compositions of the past, he suggests, which were static and outside bodily experiences. They could be perceived only from an airplane, because green spaces were confined to enclosed courtyards and were therefore inaccessible to accidental pedestrian meanderings.

Andrei Ikonnikov, one of the leading Soviet architectural historians of the period, described in an even more explicit way the significance of the moving body in the newly emerging neighborhoods of Moscow, which consisted of open compositions: "The multiplicity of perspectives, and, most important, the opening and uninterrupted change of new spatial images (caused by the movement through the architectural complex) appear to unfold the composition in time, in the 'fourth dimension': from the static three-dimensional to the dynamic four-dimensional compositions that organically include movement."[19] Walking through the built environment, Ikonnikov proposes, creates an indispensable and structurally significant component—a fourth dimension that renders space alive and transforms the repetitive patterns of new housing blocks into an original composition, making it change continuously and spontaneously. Static structures become renewed with each human passage through them, their feel and appearance affected by pedestrians' routes, bodies, minds, and modes of mobility.

Ikonnikov's description is particularly remarkable in our context, if we consider its cinematic nature. Movement, multiplicity of perspectives, uninterrupted flow of images, unfolding in time: the architectural historian could be writing about the experiences of cinematic perception, if only we replace the actual physical movement through space with the imaginary one created by a camera's long take. This camera would itself be of a bodily kind, communicating spatial experiences as seen organically—that is, employing its mechanical capacities only to approximate the perceived capacities of a mobile human body. Thus, while Danelia integrates Moscow's new architecture as a model for the organization of new sensory experiences on a wide screen, Ikonnikov does the reverse: His conception of the spatial experience of the new constructions corresponds with the patterns of cinematic unfolding. What unites both is the embodied peripatetic vision (of the camera or the human being) that ultimately opens up and completes urban spaces.

The difference between organic and mechanical perception and dynamism of the city can be elaborated further by looking at Dziga Vertov's seminal 1928 film *Man with a Movie Camera* [*Chelovek s kinoapparatom*]—without any doubt, an emblematic work of "culture one." Like Danelia's film, it presents one day in the life of a city but, unlike Danelia's film, it is permeated by views of urban spaces that only the camera can afford. The city here is in a state of perpetual movement and transformation, driven by mechanics: of the camera, the automobile, the train—of modern technology in all its forms. These mechanics—and above all, that of the cinematic apparatus itself—are meant to compensate for the body's imperfections, particularly its kinetic and visual ones. For Vertov, the camera—the "kino-eye"—was inherently superior to human eye: "Now and forever, I [the kino-eye] free myself from human immobility, I am in constant motion, I draw near, then away from objects, I crawl under, I climb onto them. I move apace with the muzzle of a galloping horse, I plunge full speed into a crowd, I outstrip running soldiers, I fall on my back, I ascend with an airplane, I plunge and soar together with plunging and soaring bodies. Now I, a camera, fling myself along their resultant, maneuvering in the chaos of movement, recording movement, starting with movements composed of the most complex combinations."[20]

The movie camera's inexhaustible capacity for motion is far more dynamic than the innate mobility of the human body. Indeed, Vertov is interested in bodily motion insofar as it can approach—or be extended by—the perfection of the machine. Throughout *Man with a Movie Camera*, Vertov's camera-eye insists on improving and intensifying people's corporeal activities—at work, on the sports field, in leisure—through specific manipulations of cinematic technology.[21]

If we look now at Danelia's *I Walk the Streets of Moscow*—and specifically at a passage in which shots of participants arriving for Sasha and Sveta's wedding are followed by a sequence showing an anonymous young woman walking through the city's rainy streets—a strikingly different project is evident. At the beginning of the sequence, we see members of the wedding party arriving in the pouring rain; as they exit their cars and rush inside the state registry office, they protectively hunch their bodies against the downpour. We then see these same guests waiting impatiently behind the registry window for Sasha, to whom the camera cuts as he runs anxiously down a nearby street (figure 3.4a). Similarly bent in upon himself in a useless attempt to escape the sheets of rain, he bumps into fellow pedestrians, passes by others clustered under awnings, hurriedly buys a bouquet from a kiosk, and finally, completely drenched, enters the registry building.

At this point the camera shifts from the wedding party to focus on an anonymous female figure walking barefoot through (we assume) the same downpour. She moves slowly toward the camera, holding her shoes in her hands and taking obvious pleasure in this summer activity; indeed, her pleasure is so boundless that her walking soon turns into a loose and graceful dancing (figure 3.4b). A male bicyclist catches up with her, and, trying to hold his umbrella over her head, accompanies her through the street, at once complicating and embellishing her movement. As if studying their joined motion, the camera zooms in on the bicycle's wheel, which provides a perfect spinning frame for

Fig. 3.4a–c Modes of walking in the city. From *I Walk the Streets of Moscow*, 1964.

the woman's feet as they step forward harmoniously within it (figure 3.4c). The abundance of "empty" space surrounding the figures in these shots is never superfluous, but in a direct interaction with the bodies, activated by—and in turn, activating—their movements and senses. These two young people seem to merge completely with their environment, their faces almost indistinguishable in the showery atmosphere of the street, as if dissolving.

In contrast to Vertov's shots of urban movement—which invariably concentrate on trams, automobiles, carriages, and filmic manipulations—Danelia's walking-in-the-rain sequence emphasizes the natural experience of the body itself, a kind of organic will to move and sense. Feet are bare, expanses of skin are exposed, bodies are deluged by and seemingly merged with the pouring rain. The machine's mediating role is superfluous: the bicycle wheel through which we see the woman's feet complements and accentuates the body's movement rather than driving it. The figures' experience of urban space, furthermore, is primarily tactile rather than visual. The woman makes a precise gesture of closing her eyes as she turns to face the rain, and the metaphorical coupling of bodies in the formal merging of feet and bicycle wheel stresses the sensuality that pervades the entire scene. If the iconic figure of *Man with a Movie Camera* is the eye of the camera that Vertov's protagonist carries through the urban environment, in *I Walk the Streets of Moscow* it is skin itself.[22]

The cinematic language of Vertov's and Danelia's respective films provides a vivid manifestation of the differences in the dominant conceptions of movement in the 1920s and the 1960s. In contrast to the cuts, superimpositions, changes in film speed, and countless other cine-technological turns that drive Vertov's project, the camera work here is much more restricted, emphasizing longer takes and spatial continuity. *I Walk the Streets of Moscow* allows and encourages viewers to contemplate fluid patterns of movement within individual shots and to establish an identification with the natural mobility of the body rather than with the mechanical kinetics of the camera. This opposition is analogous to the contrast that film theorist André Bazin outlined between what he saw as the two primary modes of cinematic representation; one grounded in "the reality of dramatic space" and the other, encompassing montage and expressionism, in the manipulation of images. Danelia's cinematography is firmly in the former camp, aiming to be "evaluated not according to what it adds to reality but what it reveals of it."[23]

It is significant that the sensory commingling of bodies suggested in the walking-in-the-rain sequence comes immediately after the frenzied rush to Sasha and Sveta's wedding and that the ceremony's culmination is shown only briefly much later in the film. The anonymous merger of two figures moving through urban space as if in a dance, in other words, replaces the culturally sanctioned union of marriage. This narrative opposition of carefree happiness and rigid cultural practice is mapped as one of two distinct modalities of movement: the dispersed and sensorially charged passage of the two figures in the street is set against the self-enclosed, goal-oriented movement of the arriving wedding parties. Just as in the film's opening sequence, ideas of marriage and happiness are woven together here with the trope of bodily movement and the experience of space. And as I suggested is the case with that earlier passage, the opposition thus established can be understood as one of time versus space, of the temporal drive of traditional narrative against the essentially spatial focus of Danelia's film. For not only is marriage (particularly within tradition-bound Soviet culture) perhaps *the* central step in a person's life when viewed as a narrativized sequence of events, but, throughout the film, Sasha and Sveta's main concern is the endless planning of their seemingly never-to-arrive future. Sasha keeps changing the date of his departure for military service, and the two are constantly arranging their wedding through a series of telephone calls (they are in fact shown to physically share the same space only for a very brief moment near the film's close). Sasha and Sveta's future together appears as an ever elusive phantom, draining the immediate experience of the here and now. It is, of course, this experience that is realized by the anonymous couple walking, indeed dancing, in the rain.

City as Playground

The essential terms employed in the discussions of the developing architecture—that of sensory experience of movement within the newly emerging environments—find an important parallel in the 1960s Soviet films depicting children, though not always produced *for* children. Indeed, if a genealogy of curved lines were to be established within post-Stalinist Soviet cinema, it would be rooted in just these films, as nowhere else is the production of new city space associated so directly with bodily movement and perceptual spontaneity.[24] It is worth taking a short detour here to connect Danelia's spatial tropes to this period's cinematic preoccupation with the uninhibited perception of children—their ways of transforming urban appearances by rendering the city, its architecture and its spaces, their boundless playground. Alexander Mitta's *With No Fear and Reproach* (*Bez strakha i uprioka*, 1962), for instance, is a film that sets the perpetual roaming of children throughout Moscow against the backdrop of the city's overwhelming Stalinist buildings; the scale of those structures, looming large over the human figures below, is so at odds with the size of the children and their unstructured, close-to-the-ground mobility as to become completely irrelevant to their experiences of the city. Andrei Tarkovskii's short diploma work, *The Steamroller and the Violin* (*Katok i skripka*, 1960), filmed, as was *I Walk the Streets of Moscow*, by the camera operator Vadim Yusov (after Tarkovskii had failed to hire Sergei Urusevskii for the work), focuses on a boy's skewed and poetic perceptions of Moscow under construction as he strolls through the city, and on the seductive powers of urban surfaces—glass shop windows in particular—through which the child transforms his surroundings into playful and impermanent ornaments of lights, patterns, and colors.[25] Danelia himself, it should be noted, had turned to childhood in his previous film, *Seriozha* (1962), in which the world of adults and the spaces they inhabit are viewed from a child's perspective—although that film takes place in a village rather than a city.

One of the most compelling examples in this regard is Mikhail Kalik's *Man Follows the Sun* (*Chelovek idiot za solntsem*, 1961), the sole focus of which is a child's drifting through, and perception of, the city. Set in Kishinev, the Soviet capital of Moldova, the film follows a charming boy, about five or six years old, on his pursuit to "get" the sun, because, as another child tells him, "If you go straight, you will be able to get the sun, walk around the globe, and return to the place of your departure but from a different side." The protagonist's going straight, however, turns very quickly into a variety of curves, as he gets distracted by urban sights and sounds and is pulled into unexpected encounters and experiences—all the while compelled to circle around various gridded surfaces (figure 3.5a). In the process, the solid Stalinist architecture dominating the panoramas of major boulevards retreats into the background. The child opens up views of the city that are fluctuating, ephemeral, and of the moment. They also are constantly modified through the boy's encounter with random and found objects and surfaces: pink balloons and colored glass pieces, fences, fountains, and even a spinning lottery machine become his camera through which to generate new views, constantly changing the palette and texture of urban appearances. Kalik imagines children's playfulness, and the modes of mobility associated with it, as the very basis for his camera's perceptual principle. Estranging shots of the city (at times reminiscent of Alexander Rodchenko's constructivist photography), as well as a series of kaleidoscopic montages conveying the boy's dream at the end of the film, situate the camera's mechanical capacities not as superior to human vision, but rather as being rich and spontaneous, like the perception of a child (figure 3.5b). The boy's senses are what edit reality and generate a new one, with the camera operating as nothing more than a mediator of his sensory activities. Most important, this child, with his naturally uninhibited modes of perception and mobility, comes to naturalize Soviet ideology itself. The purity and transformational power of his sensory experiences are equated with ethical rightfulness, and are seen as inherently—and truthfully—socialist.[26]

Fig. 3.5a–b Child's uninhibited engagement with the urban environment. From *Man Follows the Sun*, 1961.

Even as Soviet cinema of the early 1960s invested repeatedly in the visual trope of a roaming child in order to give new shape to the depiction of Soviet cities, it demonstrated a profound uncertainty about how to validate this practice within the world of adults.[27] As criticisms of Danelia's film make clear, playful and aimless drifting through urban settings was not easily appropriated as an activity for grown-up city dwellers. Although a number of popular films seem to be drawn to just this practice, allowing adults to spill aimlessly into the street, they also seek immediately to contain them—to integrate them into familiar and purposeful structures of everyday living. Alexander Pashkov's comedy *Come Tomorrow* (*Prikhodite zavtra*, 1962), for instance, begins with disorienting perspectives of Moscow's cityscape seen from the point of view of a young woman who has just arrived from a remote Siberian village in order to study at Moscow's prestigious music academy. Before her classes begin, though, we see her walking streets with childish curiosity, enthralled by the urbanites and their spaces. But as soon as she is integrated into her proper work and study routine, the street as a space of exploration vanishes and begins to function primarily as a site of transition from one point to the next. Lev Kulidzhanov's *When the Trees Were Tall* (*Kogda derevia byli bolshimi*, 1961) depicts a grown man who has no work and spends his time bumbling down the sidewalks, creating a physical disturbance in the paths of other, busy pedestrians. He eventually relocates to a village, pretending to be the father of a young woman whose parents disappeared during the war, and, after trials and tribulations, gets integrated into a family and the village collective, leaving the capital's streets free of his annoying and purposeless presence. And in yet another production, Alexander Ptushko's *Fairy Tale about Lost Time* (*Skazka o poteriannom vremeni*, 1964), lazy and loafing children are magically turned into adults, only to become the focus of ridicule as they roam childishly through Moscow.[28]

One crucial exception to these films is Marlen Khutsiev's *I Am Twenty* (*Mne dvdtsat'*, 1961–64), an essential work of the Thaw period, known particularly for the scathing criticism it received from Nikita Khrushchev (and others commentators) and for the subsequent editing that went on for two years, after which the work was released in a truncated form. As film historian Oksana Bulgakova has suggested, the harsh disapproval of the film stemmed not from its thematic content—there is nothing particularly subversive about the actions or statement of the young men and women in this feature—but from the presence of "undisciplined bodies" throughout.[29] Khutsiev's protagonists gestured, talked, and walked in ways that did not conform with the familiar norms of public behavior—their relaxed and laid-back body language evoking depictions of troubled youth in contemporary Western cinema more than ordinary Soviet archetypes. Thus the sequence of a May Day parade, instead of showing the geometrically structured, uniform rows of marching people, presents an impressionistic, fragmented, and subjectively oriented passage through the streets, with the intimate attractions of individual figures taking precedence over the ideological inspirations of the collective that have generally dominated Soviet cinematic representations of this event.

If Khutsiev integrates long passages of uninhibited strolling to create a particular urban ambience, one that supports the film's loosely organized thematic concerns with history, ideology, and personal responsibility, Danelia takes such a movement one step further, raising it to a driving cultural venture in its own right and freeing it from any of the narrative, moral, or age constraints that qualified the films discussed in this chapter. Notably, Danelia described the walking-in-the-rain sequence as having provided the initial core of his film. The original screenplay, written by Gennadii Shpalikov (who also wrote the screenplay for *I Am Twenty*), apparently consisted of nothing more than a description of a young woman walking barefoot down rainy streets and a bicyclist's attempt to shelter her with an umbrella.[30] The rest of the film grew out of this most arbitrary and unmotivated situation.

Situations

> "The only progressive way out is to liberate the tendency toward play elsewhere, and on a larger scale."
> —Situationist International, "Preliminary Problems in Constructing Situations," 1958

If the films just discussed suggest that playful urban walking gained cultural significance in the wake of Stalin's death, no real theoretical discourse emerged around that fact. It is here again that Tati's parallels to Danelia's film are of particular interest, for France in the early postwar decades produced one of the twentieth century's most rigorous theoretical investigations into the nature and experience of space and the built environment, providing a broader context in which to explore Tati's work, and opening Danelia's film to a contemporaneous international discourse of which he most certainly had no knowledge. Beginning in the mid-1950s, the situationists, led by Guy Debord, placed an interrogation of the instrumentalization of urban space at the center of their radical critique of capitalist culture. "Capitalism," Debord wrote in *The Society of the Spectacle*, "true to its logical development toward absolute domination, can (and now must) refashion the totality of space into *its own peculiar décor*."[31] To revive space as something concrete, social, and lived—in place of such a capitalist décor—the group engaged in the production of "situations," which they also referred to as "play" or "games."[32] Debord defined them as "the concrete construction of momentary ambiences of life and their transformation into a superior passional quality."[33] Always transient and ephemeral, "without a future," the situations were meant to foster a dialogue between specific material environments and the participants' actions, with the aim of creating a potential foundation for transforming people's everyday lives, their behavior, and through this, ultimately, the spaces they traverse and inhabit. One of the fundamental practices of the situationists was that of the *dérive*, which Debord described thus: "in a *dérive* one or more persons during a certain period drop their relations, their work and leisure activities, and all their other usual motives for movement and action, and let themselves be drawn by the attractions of the terrain and the encounters they find there."[34] The ultimate goal of such wandering would be to perceive the space of the city in its specific materiality and sociability and to expose the contradictions that traditional, abstracted representations of urban spaces (such as typical maps) seek to conceal.[35]

If the situationists' critique of urban space and the everyday grew out of particular postwar capitalist conditions, it is worthwhile to explore their critical terms in the context of Soviet culture. Debord himself—like Henri Lefebvre, as discussed in the introduction—repeatedly drew comparisons between capitalist and socialist countries, arguing that the Soviet Union and other socialist states failed in their revolutions because they failed to transform the everyday, resorting to old, conservative superstructures similar to those that organized life in the West. In turn, the Soviet dogma of socialist realism served for Debord as an umbrella term to describe the conservative institutional organization of culture on both sides of the Iron Curtain, the aesthetics of which, he argued, expressed "the cultural degeneration of the workers movement but also of the conservative cultural position in the bourgeois world."[36] He continued,

> Revolution is not limited to determining the level of industrial production, or even to determining who is to be the master of such production. It must abolish not only the exploitation of humanity, but also the passions, compensations and habits which that exploitation has engendered. We have to define new desires in relation to present possibilities. In the thick of the battle between the present society and the forces that are going to destroy it, we have to find the first elements of a more advanced construction of the environment and new conditions of behavior—both as experiences in themselves and as material for propaganda.[37]

Danelia's walking-in-the-rain sequence is, certainly, far from a situationist action. Above all, the events captured in the film's passage are rather intuitive, not motivated by the kind of intellectual rigor that drove the situationists' artistic and theoretical pursuits. But the sequence speaks, in a particular Soviet register, to a similar set of concerns and desires that was emerging in the Soviet Union in the early 1960s. If the situationists' *dérive* was intended to fragment and destabilize from within capitalist spaces of control and domination, Danelia's film repeatedly isolates uninhibited movement through the city as a form of disruption of the stalled cultural and spatial practices of the Soviet Union, making such passages the potential building blocks of the "advanced construction of the environment and new conditions of behavior."

I Walk the Streets of Moscow, in a number of brief narrative sequences, develops contrasts between spontaneous, itinerant, and sensory experiences of space and the static rigidity of systems. In one such scene, Kolia—the film's central protagonist—enters a church to look for the owner of an abandoned dog. The sequence opens with a slow tilt from the church's upper corner to its floor, stressing the excessive verticality of its interior and the seeming black void of its upper reaches. Incongruous with this verticality are the human bodies that come into view as the camera tilts toward the ground, mostly old women who appear diminutive and fragile within the grand space of the church (figure 3.6a). Kolia acts here as a disruptive stranger. Upon entering the church, he greets the priest, disturbing the hierarchical organization of the service as his voice and figure level the dominating voice and figure of the priest; and then, after pausing briefly at a column, he moves back and forth among the women with his inquiries about the dog's owner. His movement is specifically *not* motivated by any particular logic, least of all that of the church interior, which appears to enthrall and immobilize the women. From the scene's opening, Kolia's resistance to the church's ordered space is framed as a kind of sensory appropriation of its interior. Before he starts moving around, we see him standing at a large column painted with icons, his hand touching it on one side (figure 3.6b). As he moves away, his shadow remains for a moment on the column, as if having incorporated itself into its pictorial program. In both its shadow and manner of movement, Kolia's body appears momentarily to inhabit the church interior rather than being overwhelmed and dominated by it—suggesting a kind of structural transformation in line with the new architecture of the time, toward imperatives of flexibility, mobility, and sensory directness. It also establishes, once again, an opposition between temporal and spatial experience: between the teleological narrative of the Orthodox Church—in which the here and now of human life exists primarily for the purpose of future salvation—and Kolia's essentially directionless back-and-forth drift in that very moment.

Kolia's church visit is ironically echoed in a later scene of a tourist group visiting Saint Basil's Cathedral on Red Square, in which the priest has been

Fig. 3.6a–b Kolia's disruptive entrance into the hierarchical organization of the church. From *I Walk the Streets of Moscow*, 1964.

replaced with a tour guide, and younger but similarly immobile visitors stand in for the earlier sequence's worshippers. The passage opens, just as in the earlier scene, with a slow pan from the top of Saint Basil's to the ground as the guide relates the history of the cathedral in a dreadfully monotone voice.[38] The tourists' eyes and heads move obediently—and seemingly mechanically—up and down to the guide's words, their bodies immobile as they survey the cathedral's exterior walls, echoing almost precisely the vertically oriented rapture of the earlier worshipping women. As the tourists continue to stare—with close-ups emphasizing their dull-looking faces—another group, consisting of Young Pioneers, cuts through them in a manner that recalls Tati's nuns, seemingly moving along invisible straight lines and with nothing impeding their precisely measured and directed motion.[39] And, once again, the tourists' spatial anesthesia is emphasized by their subordination to time—and specifically, to time as an instrument and symbol of political power. For as the hour is marked by the Kremlin chimes behind them—a sound recognized by any Soviet citizen as a symbol of the country's centralized base of power—Danelia again focuses on the tourists' faces looking upward, this time in orchestrated awe at the Kremlin's clock; only a child in a man's arms is looking somewhere else, off to the side. It is not insignificant that the group's mechanical and vertically oriented turn toward the clock stands in direct contrast to the woman dancing at the airport in the opening of Danelia's film, whose indifference to a similar hourly chime specifically defines her movement as physically and motivationally unhindered.

The Movements of Narrative

Soviet culture's simultaneous interest in and apprehension of free bodily movement are reflected directly in theoretical discussions on the nature of cinema transpiring during this period. The critic Efim Dobin, a frequent contributor to Soviet film debates of the 1960s, placed just such movement at the center of his contemplations on the era's cinematic tendency toward "dedramatization"—that is, the frequent disappearance of any clear narrative trajectory in films of the era. Dobin begins his discussion by quoting the words of the Italian scriptwriter Ennio de Concini, who directly addressed the relationship of movement to plot: "Today, cinematographers tend to guide their narration as freely as possible, destroying the structure that holds it together.... At the root of new cinematic works... are not iron constructions, not strict and inviolable architectural forms," but rather "intuitive movements forward, in the direction of transient experiences. Movement that is interrupted by silent pauses along with full repudiation of any effort to develop a plot and concrete content."[40] Although Dobin agrees that the adherence to iron constructions and strict architectural forms produces nothing but empty imitations, he spends the rest of his article arguing against de Concini's embrace of dedramatization, while admitting that some of the greatest masters of contemporary cinema, including Michelangelo Antonioni, build their entire aesthetics on just such a principle.

Although it is not clear exactly what kind of movement de Concini is referring to in this quoted excerpt—and how his discussion is related to bodily movement especially—Dobin's ensuing analysis easily conflates de Concini's conceptions of unstructured narrative with physical and material manifestations of motion. Building his discussion around Antonioni's works, and describing Antonioni's protagonists' aimless strolls through Italy's desolate streets and landscapes as "blind walks into emptiness," the Soviet critic argues that such movement is a natural critical response to capitalist culture, a testament to its social and political disintegration, and as such would be foreign to films produced in socialist states. He finds an opposite, desirable spatial paradigm in the military map, with its unambiguous sense of direction. Dobin writes, "Let's imagine a map of military operations. . . . Arrows mean attacks and defeats, operations that are successful and not. And through this map of military actions big arrows are drawn. They show the result of all ideas and contra-ideas, all intentions and contra-intentions."[41] One socialist counterexample to Antonioni's films that earned Dobin's praise is Kalik's *Man Follows the Sun*. Dobin saw in the film a nearly perfect balance between random episodic wanderings and the "big arrows" of the film's narrative trajectory, with the former sublimated into the latter's clear—one might say "straight"—line of the boy's enthusiastic walk toward the sun.

I Walk the Streets of Moscow is not mentioned in Dobin's article, possibly because the film was released at about the same time that his text went to print. But it is not hard to see that Danelia's film operates within the exact same spatial paradigms that Dobin perceives as being central to the cinematic developments of his era, dedramatizing the film's story, as well as culturally ingrained narratives of everyday life, through bodily movements "in the direction of transient experiences." And while Danelia's dedramatization through such movements is of a different nature than Antonioni's, it was precisely the film's "lack of a unified dramatic act"—to quote Yurenev again—that troubled Soviet commentators. One French critic, notably, reviewing *I Walk the Streets of Moscow* on the pages of *Cahiers du Cinéma* in 1965, grasped the nature of the film's urban strolls in a language that is comically evocative of Dobin's. He noted, as if in surprise, that there was nothing *military* in the protagonists' walks, suggesting furthermore that the film could be set anywhere in the Western world, in "Milan, Modène, or Marseille."[42] From this French point of view, the film defied precisely what Dobin thought was necessary for a properly—inherently—socialist narrative construction. If *I Walk the Streets of Moscow* does not strike viewers today as exceptional in its formal language and the extent of its dedramatization—especially in comparison with the practitioners of loose and absent narratives that figured in Dobin's text (including, in addition to Antonioni, Germaine Dulac and Jean Epstein)—it is perhaps because the film elevates the momentous sensory and itinerant experience of urban spaces itself to the level of narrative. It is a story of spatially defined encounters and experiences, organized not through principles of "iron constructions" but through the flexibility, transience, and movement that Danelia imagined was essential to the newly emerging spatiality of post-Stalinist architecture.

Danelia's lack of interest in the totality of vision—the kind that Dobin's military map would provide—is diagrammed from the beginning of the film, when we see Moscow, for just one time, from a disembodied aerial view that opens up a broad outline of the city's terrain (figure 3.7a). After making

Fig. 3.7a–b City from above and below. From *I Walk the Streets of Moscow*, 1964.

a 360-degree turn, the camera begins its descent toward the ground, moving closer with each subsequent shot. It focuses from high up on a lonely automobile, moves nearer to hover over the Moscow River, and then shifts to lingering shots of cars and commuters on whose legs and feet it pauses, before descending further to the subway below (figure 3.7b). The diversity of these feet—their shoes and shapes, and the speed and direction of the steps—is explicitly opposed to the totalized view of the city offered initially from on high, putting the emphasis instead on the material, sensory experience of each individual, the multitudinousness of which would be impossible to sublimate into a straight, narrative line.[43]

If Tati did see *I Walk the Streets of Moscow* when it debuted in France, he would have recognized the homology between Danelia's project and his own precisely because of the Soviet film's investment in the sensory experience of space and movement as a potential engine for reimagining everyday life. But in contrast to Danelia, who envisioned contemporary architecture in a fertile

The Architecture of Movement 111

dialogue with the freely walking body, Tati—in films stretching from *Mon Oncle* to the nascent *Playtime*—was preoccupied with the mechanizing and homogenizing force of new urban development on the bodily experience of the city. The homage in reverse that the opening of *Playtime* provides suggests both the shared concerns and the opposing outlooks of the two filmmakers. Tati's pessimism, of course, would prove to be warranted. Danelia's hopeful view of the city and belief in new possibilities for the subjective experience of space were, by the late 1960s, invalidated by the practical realities of the Soviet Union—precisely what the situationists had claimed was occurring in France already a decade before. The pivotal moment in this turn of events would occur just a year after Tati's film premiered, with the move of Soviet troops into Prague in 1968. By that point, Khrushchev's concrete and glass structures—and, by extension, the Palace of Young Pioneers—had become as emblematic of cultural stasis as Stalin's monumental towers.

Danelia, too, must have understood the futility of his imagination. His 1979 "sad comedy" *Autumn Marathon* (*Osennii marafon*), produced in the midst of the stagnation period that followed the Soviet Thaw, is permeated by nostalgia and is fully devoid of the earlier optimism. Its protagonist is trapped in the banalities of everyday life and an unhappy marriage. He resides in the already deteriorating and cluttered new apartment building, which is part of an architectural composition that looks more like a desolate landscape than a dynamic, stimulating space. And the city of the film—Leningrad—does not seem to harbor any energy for innovation or inspiration. The occasional focus on its sites, textures, and surfaces emphasizes the city's obsolete beauty rather than its potential for generating socially (or individually) productive movements and encounters. Most important, hurried running dominates the protagonist's urban passages as he attempts to get to yet another destination on time, never being absorbed in the here and now of any one place. The leisurely and graceful curves that drew us into *I Walk the Streets of Moscow* from its opening seconds are nowhere to be found.

Notes

1. François Penz, "Architecture in the Films of Jacques Tati," 64.
2. Tati's *Playtime*, while widely seen today as a masterpiece of world cinema, was a complete failure upon its release, nearly bankrupting the director. One of the earliest recognitions of Tati's achievements in *Playtime* was, of all places, at the Moscow Film Festival in 1969, where it received the festival's Silver Prize.
3. See, for instance, Sushko, *Marina Vladi*. In this biography of Marina Vladi, a French actress and a partner of the famous Soviet bard Vladimir Vysotskii, Sushko briefly mentions not only the

popularity in France of *I Walk the Streets of Moscow*, but a desire, on the part of Vladi's sister, to remake the film, with the same Soviet actors now walking the streets of Paris.

4. Rostislav Yurenev, "Odin den' iunykh," 26.

5. Bleiman and Vartanov, "O fil'me sporiat: fil'm obozreniie ili fil'm razdumie," 4.

6. Rosenbaum, "Tati's Democracy," 39. In a similar vein, Michel Chion paraphrases *Playtime's* story thus: "The lines on the ground are indicated implicitly by the geometry of the modern decor, and the characters who respect them at first gradually learn to move forward diagonally. They begin to act like the dogs in *Mon Oncle* which get excited by a particular smell and so pull their masters ahead. They ignore, in every sense of the word, the arrows and directions inscribed on the ground." Chion stresses precisely the subjective sensory experience of movement that the logic of modern architecture sidelines and represses in Tati's films (Chion, *The Films of Jacques Tati*, 114).

7. Yurenev, "Odin den' iunykh," 27. Emphasis mine.

8. Tasalov, "Nekotorye problemy razvitiia sovremennoi arkhitektury," 51.

9. The Palace of Young Pioneers is mentioned as one of the excluded scenes in the archival materials on the production of Danelia's film. See "Delo fil'ma 'Ia shagaiu po Moskve,'" 17.

10. The most prominent building of this kind to be erected during the Thaw period was the Kremlin Palace of Congresses (Kremliovskii dvorets s'ezdov), in which the same principles of new architectural environments were integrated, thus introducing ideas of sensory, mobile, and dialogical interactions with the environment into the very heart of Soviet political space. One critic, A. Stupin, described the building in the following way: "In the organization of the interior, we can also see a new approach. At its root is the principle of opening the interior spaces toward the outside. The spaces of the palace appear to merge with the surrounding exterior spaces. When people walk through the lobby, go up and down the stairs and soundless escalators, they sense not that they are inside a building but rather that they are walking on the grounds of the Kremlin; in front of them, through broad window apertures, the grand Kremlin panorama opens up. In the same way, one can see from anywhere outside the interior life of the palace" (Stupin, "Dvorets narodnykh forumov," 16).

11. Kosmatov, "Kompozitsia shirokogo kadra," 115. Kosmatov evokes terms already familiar to us from Soviet discussions of panoramic cinema, namely that the sheer size of the wide screen forces viewers to perceive the representation in parts—"architecturally," as I've argued in chapter 1. This necessitates an increase in the duration of each shot, to allow viewers time to survey the entirety of the screen.

12. There were a variety of systems that allowed for the production of films for a wide screen, with an aspect ratio of at least 1.85:1. In Soviet discussions, *shirokoekrannyi fil'm* refers to the equivalent of the US CinemaScope—a technology using an anamorphic lens that allowed for a compression of larger space onto a regular 35mm film, which is then projected onto a wide screen. The term *shirokoformatnyi fil'm* means that it was produced on an actual 70mm film. In my discussion, I leave aside the technological differences in the production to discuss the organization of space when projected onto an actual wide screen.

13. Kosmatov, "Kompozitsia shirokogo kadra," 117.

14. The architectural composition of the Palace of the Young Pioneers aspired to generate a dialogue—an exchange—among nature, the built environment, and children's bodies, but some of its rhetoric did not fit easily into such aspirations. The exterior of the main building was decorated, for instance, with a three-part mural, the title of which—*Man's Conquest of Nature: Of Earth, Water, Sky*—does not suggest an equal interaction between people and the environment. According to one critic, the mural, because of its large scale, served as an "active organizational principle" for the entire park surrounding the palace. This principle of conquest stands in direct conflict with the architectural principle of interaction, which escaped the attention of those reviewing the complex. See Pekareva, "Dvorets pionerov v Moskve," 58.

15. Reid, "Khrushchev's Children's Paradise," 166. Emphasis mine.
16. Paperny, *Architecture in the Age of Stalin*, 32.
17. Ibid.
18. Tverskoi, "Zametki o sovremennom goroskom ansamble," 40.
19. Ikonnikov, "Organizatsiia prostranstva i estetichekaia vyrazitel'nost' arkhitektury," 63.
20. Vertov, reprinted in *Kino-Eye: The Writings of Dziga Vertov*, ed. Annette Michelson, 17.
21. In a recent analysis, Malcolm Turvey has argued that the mechanical should not serve as an opposition to the organic in *Man with a Movie Camera*. Following Kant's *Critique of Judgment*, which defines the living organism as a whole for which individual parts are "both cause and effect of each other," Turvey argues that Vertov shows all elements of Soviet society (be it people, machines, city streets, or other objects) interacting purposefully with one another, as an "organic continuum," moving intentionally toward one common purpose: "Almost every part of this society, to paraphrase Kant, is both cause and effect of every other part" (Turvey, "Vertov: Between the Organism and the Machine," 9).
22. Emma Widdis also challenges the understanding of Vertov's practice as rooted in the celebration of the mechanical superiority of the camera, writing: "Although the movements of the cameraman are not always seen, they are a constant subtext of the film." That is, no matter how omnipotent and inhumanly mobile, the camera views are always rooted in the physical experiences of an actual human body of the camera operator (Widdis, *Visions of a New Land*, 74). I agree with Widdis's understanding of Vertov's practice, but there is a clear distinction between his organization and representation of human mobility and Danelia's: The transmission of embodied experiences of Vertov's cameraman to the screen comes about through an elaborate editing process that fundamentally reformulates these experiences; Vadim Yusov's camera in *I Walk the Streets of Moscow*, by contrast, seeks to keep the original experience of a unified body intact—even if only up to a point.
23. Bazin, "The Evolution of the Language of Cinema," 28.
24. It would be enlightening to examine to what extent the appearance of a Soviet child roaming the streets on screen is indebted to children's representations in European films of the postwar period, many of which were very favorably received among Soviet critics. Writing in 1961 about François Truffaut's *400 Blows*, for instance, critic N. Zorkaia drew attention to the young protagonist's urban explorations as a form of liberation from the stultification of everyday bourgeois living. She writes, "You can feel like a real person only when you free yourself from the circle of nonsense, foolishness, mechanical order. You can swiftly run down from Montmartre, and the whole of Paris will open in front of you. . . . You can stop by a small attraction, where a magical centripetal force will press you against a wall, spinning you around, pulling you up off the floor" (Zorkaia, "Tak zhit' nel'zia!" 136–37).
25. Vadim Yusov's work in Tarkovskii's *The Steamroller and the Violin* was highly praised. One reviewer in particular drew attention to the cameraman's ability to find poetry in the most banal surfaces and situations. The film on the whole was well received for precisely the fact that it showed, for adults, the world as perceived through the eyes of a child. See, for instance, Smelkov, "Katok i skripka." A few urban shots of *The Steamroller* are mirrored closely in *I Walk the Streets of Moscow*. *The Steamroller*, however, generated fierce criticism as well, as documented in Robert Bird's *Andrei Tarkovsky: The Elements of Cinema*, 30–33.
26. Critical understanding of children's urban roaming can be extended to the behavior of Tati's protagonist Monsieur Hulot (played by Tati himself). His earlier film *Mon Oncle* prioritizes children (with whom Hulot prefers to spend time) and their uninhibited behavior over the geometry of the adult world. Soviet film critic Aleksei Arbuzov described *Mon Oncle* through just this lens, as a work "above all, about freedom, about the situation of a big man-child in the world of alienation, among successes of the so-called civilization. A 'child' because Tati's protagonist possesses a certain primary wholeness" (Arbuzov, "S soveshchatel'nym golosom," 126).

27. A selective discussion of these childhood films can be found in Plisetskii, "Otkrytie mira," and Obraztsova, "Pervye shagi." Obraztsova draws a parallel between Tarkovskii's *Steamroller* and Albert Lamorisse's *Red Balloon* (France, 1956), to which Kalik's film also bears correspondences.

28. Strikingly, the plot of *Fairy Tale* is built around aged magicians' desire to become young again, which they do by collecting the time that lazy children waste every day. The film playfully encapsulates the Soviet preoccupation with time efficiency, as discussed in chapter 1, and provides an interesting parallel to the aimlessness of Danelia's protagonists, which, as noted, did not fare well with critics.

29. Bulgakova, "Cine-Weathers: Soviet Thaw Cinema in the International Context," 468–70.

30. Danelia, *Chito-grito*, 211.

31. Debord, *The Society of the Spectacle*, 121. Italics in the original.

32. In this emphasis on play and the critique of urban environment, one can make a connection between Tati and the situationists, though as David Bellos argues, the relation "is not a question of direct influence or of inspiration," and any meeting between Debord and Tati would have been highly unlikely. He notes, however, that Debord greatly admired Tati's films, suggesting further that "the striking confluence of the Situationists' understanding and of Tati's observation of social realities suggests that they were both in touch with the deeper currents of French national anxieties" (Bellos, *Jacques Tati*, 270). For another detailed discussion of the relationship between Tati and the Situationist International, see Marie, "Jacques Tati's *Play Time* as New Babylon."

33. Debord, "Report on the Construction of Situations," 22.

34. Debord, "Theory of the Dérive," 62.

35. For more on the situationists' spatial concepts and practices, see McDonough, "Situationist Space."

36. Debord, "Report on the Construction of Situations," 35.

37. Ibid., 36.

38. It is significant that such an architecturally driven vertical tilt undergoes an evaluation in Soviet cinema of the period. For instance, it structures the gaze of the French visitors to the Soviet capital in the 1960 film discussed in the Introduction, *Leon Garros Searches for His Friend*. As they are about to enter Hotel Ukraine—one of the main Stalinist skyscrapers defining Moscow's skyline—they survey it vertically and in awe, as a positive representation of Soviet power. In Danelia's film, by contrast, this tilt betrays a slight sarcasm, as well as a sense of a withering away of the urban experiences associated with Stalinist architecture.

39. In addition to his protagonist Monsieur Hulot, Tati builds *Playtime* around a group of US tourists visiting Paris. In their wanderings through the city (or rather what appears to be the same few streets with nearly identical buildings made of glass and steel), they never get to see the historical sights of Paris. The reflection of the Eiffel Tower in the constantly swinging glass door of a building is the only such view we get. Danelia's tourists do see architectural landmarks of the city, but their disengaged experience of the landmarks is in fact not so different from that of Tati's US tourists in Paris.

40. Dobin, "Teoreticheskie zapiski," 59.

41. Ibid., 61.

42. Comolli, "Passés les cigognes," 83.

43. This camera descent at the beginning of the film also can be understood in terms proposed by Michel de Certeau, who examines pedestrian movement through the city as a practice of "tactile apprehension and kinesthetic appropriation" that not only makes use of but actually *makes* urban space. Walking for him escapes and undermines the totalizing vision of the urban environment— most emphatically exemplified in the views from above that modern skyscrapers afford—which he argues is grounded in a separation of the body from the grasp of the street (De Certeau, *The Practice of Everyday Life*, 97).

4
A WALK THROUGH THE RUINS: LARISA SHEPITKO'S *WINGS*

A DIALOGICAL INTERACTION between body and space; an unfolding of the built environment through bodily motion; the body's becoming like space: These are the visual tropes that have dominated our discussion of the films in the previous two chapters. In their radical portrayals of the body–space relations, Mikhail Kalatozov's *The Unsent Letter* and *I Am Cuba* and Georgii Danelia's *I Walk the Streets of Moscow* displayed a certain level of utopian imagining, in which participants functioned less as specific, psychologically nuanced characters than as poetic, and in that way abstract, figures. We can remember once more the critique of Kalatozov and Urusevskii's productions, which bemoaned their protagonists' lack of depth; or we can think of the anonymous women dancing in Danelia's feature about whom we don't know anything. It is as if the depth and particularity of these figures had to be flattened in order for the intricate relation between body and space to emerge. But at what point does it become essential to think about this relation with a specific, psychologically grounded individual in mind? And what would one find if this individual were a woman and our understanding of her movement through and her perception of space were inseparable from her position as a gendered subject? What would an encounter between such an individual's interiority and her environment encompass? And what problems of a specifically cinematic nature would emerge in the representation of such encounters?

Indeed, if we begin to press the question of *who* is being represented, the blissful unity of body and space can quickly turn problematic, as is the case, for instance, with the opening sequence of *I Walk the Streets of Moscow*. While the young woman dances forward, consumed by her own reflection and motions, seeming to be intimately connected with her surroundings, she remains unaware that she is the object of multiple male gazes: that of a man in sunglasses sitting behind the glass wall of the terminal; that of Nikolai, who has just arrived at the airport and is outside our field of vision; and that of the camera-eye of Vadim Yusov filming this sequence. A man on screen, a man off screen, and the man on the "other" side of the screen, all fixing her in an axis of looks that becomes a counterpoint to her subjectively guided, liberating movements.[1] The camera, the modern architectural façade, and even the space off screen operate here as frames that secure the young woman into a certain position. Her body, her freedom of movement and spatial embrace become the property of the male gaze, which constricts from all directions the seemingly unbound space through which she dances.[2] But this does not become a problem within the film. The rigid separation of gender positions on which this imagery is built remains simply so—natural, one could say—and does not play a role in the film's exploration of walking as a practice of remaking of urban space.

This kind of separation *does*, however, become a problem in Larisa Shepitko's 1966 feature *Wings*. Shepitko, who quickly achieved national and international acclaim with the release of her 1963 diploma work *Heat* (*Znoi*), was vocal about the constraints and isolation of being a woman within what she understood to be a male profession—a concern that she maintained throughout her short career.[3] In *Wings*, she brings to the forefront of the film's formal and narrative operations the type of cinematic construction of women that Danelia fluidly naturalizes in his opening shots. *Wings*'s protagonist—a former war pilot, the awkward, inward-looking Nadezhda (Nadia) Petrukhina—cannot avoid being framed as an object, an image, in her everyday life.[4] She appears in the film as a motionless body measured by male hands; as a mute, framed face on a local television channel; as an inhibited figure standing in a café, stared at by a group of men; and in a photograph nailed to a wall in the local museum. All these sequences present her as circumscribed and restrained in space, unable to move freely, and, in the case of the photograph, referred to as "dead" despite Nadia's actual living body sitting right next to it.

The separation of gender positions becomes even more acute during Nadia's extended walks through the historic city of Sevastopol (where the film was made)—a setting that frequently accommodates the protagonist's body by means of its architectural frames, which the camera likewise replicates with its tight, enclosing framing. Neither architecture nor the camera helps to generate the kind of uninhibited bodily motion discussed in the previous chapter. Nevertheless Shepitko, like Danelia and others, feels compelled to send her protagonist wandering through the streets, thus nurturing further the appeal of the urban stroller—a Soviet flaneur—as an essential figure for reimagining contemporary city life. She chooses for this position the most difficult candidate: a middle-aged woman, deeply wounded by turns of the Soviet history, too rigid in her thinking, too enclosed in her own body, and utterly alienated from the culture within which she lives. Yet it is precisely this choice that allows Shepitko to profoundly complicate the function of the city wanderer within the Soviet environment: Issues of gender, history, and the practices of representation become entwined in the course of Nadia's walks. Her mobilization as a *subject* in the city, envisioned as a process of dynamic integration of her figure into the surrounding space, unfolds within an exploration of women's position in relation to the ever-present urban and cinematic frames. The result is an opening up of both body *and* space, each becoming amplified while inflecting the other. As Nadia's interiority—her desires, memory, and sensory self—is revealed while being projected onto the exterior environment, the latter itself is rendered heterogeneous, layered, and unfixed.

Heterogeneous and *unfixed* are precisely the kind of terms that critics have used to describe the inherent affinity between cinema and the city. Film scholar Ackbar Abbas, for instance, reflecting on the writings of Italo Calvino, Paul Virilio, and Walter Benjamin, concludes that "it is exactly the instability of the cinematic image that allows it to evoke the city in all its errancy in ways that stable images cannot."[5] His understanding is that the city, which is not fully graspable and representable (the picture we have of it is "always slightly out of date"), is related to cinema because of its own ungraspable nature. Both are rooted permanently in transience, mobility, and change. For Shepitko, such an affinity has to be qualified and developed critically—relayed, most importantly, through specific subjects who inhabit the city on film. She starts with a different—indeed opposite—kind of affinity, one based on the dominance of analogous urban and camera framing devices, which excessively *stabilize* and fix the female body, and with it the city image itself. It is only when these frames are neutralized or negated that the instability of urban space is evoked, enabling an experience of the city's "errancies"—complicating its visual fabric and making tangible diverse histories harbored within it. As this chapter will argue, Shepitko achieves such an experience of the city through the figure of her female urban stroller, a figure whose very existence necessitates a reorganization of filmic space, one that unsettles framed images through the mobility of cinematic voice and gaze.

Urban Screens and Frames

A roundtable discussion of *Wings*, published in *Iskusstvo kino* immediately after the film's release, revealed an emotionally charged reception stretching across the critical spectrum. Some praised the film for its "realism without compromise" and others accused it of antirealism and foresaw possible moral damage to socialist ideals.[6] Uniting these positions, however, was a shared focus on issues of history and generational shifts, with most critics agreeing that the primary conflict in the film is the protagonist's entrapment in her past—her inability, or perhaps unwillingness, to adjust to the cultural changes of the present.

Indeed, Nadia—a respected director of a professional school whose photograph is exhibited at a local history museum to honor her participation as a pilot in World War II—appears to exist in a social and emotional vacuum, fully estranged from her environment two decades after the war's end.[7] Neither motherhood nor her intimate relationship with the director of the museum help to assuage her utter inner discomfort, the outer expression of which takes the form of her tight, enclosed gait and curt, painfully formulaic manner of speech. The film follows a series of episodes from Nadia's life—her conflicts with students, encounters with her daughter, lengthy walks through the city, and recurring visits to the local flight school—most of which are presented as experiences of loneliness, embarrassment, and misunderstanding. The only relief comes in the nostalgic shots of the sky that recur throughout the film, or, occasionally, during her walks through provincial Sevastopol. The film ends on an ambiguous note: Nadia, while at the airfield of the flight school, sits down at the controls of an airplane and, to the surprise of the students on the ground who had been offering to give her "a ride," flies off. The final shots consist of skewed perspectives of the sky and the earth as seen from the freely moving airplane—images that could be understood variously as moments of Nadia's finally achieved happiness, glimpses from a final suicidal ride, or both.[8]

Wings is meticulous in constructing its protagonist's isolation as a result of her falling out of synchrony with history. Nadia's outdated Soviet style—her clothes, way of speaking, and strict professional dedication—is fully incongruent with the looser, flamboyant, laid-back manner of her daughter and her friends, and of the young journalist who interviews her midway through the film. But even in her role as a representative of a different generation, Nadia stands out primarily as a woman; the film is overpopulated by men, including men of her own age who seem at ease with the current state of affairs, having found their own sense of cultural integration. The historical rupture that dominates Nadia's experience is specifically that of a woman and is presented in the film above all as a spatial disconnection. It figures most saliently in Nadia's inability to embrace the here and now of her experiences, to find the pleasure and meaning that she obviously seeks in her urban strolls. Though wishing to be part of public life, she seems nevertheless always removed and joyless. The camera rarely shows the city from her point of view, focusing instead on her tightly framed body as she moves through the streets.

These elements did not escape the attention of critics at the time. During a 1966 roundtable discussion of *Wings*, one critic, Vera Shitova, incisively argued that the best way to understand Shepitko's film was to judge it not by its story line, but rather by what "is left over" from this—the film's "artistic leftover," as she called it (*ostatok iskusstva*), which was resistant to the kind of narrative questioning that the roundtable participants primarily engaged in. Drawing attention to scenes such as Nadia's walks and her imaginative escapes into the past and the sky, as well as to the material qualities of the film's images and mise-en-scène, Shitova identified in them a concretization of Nadia's "life perception"—as elements, in other words, that have to be judged aesthetically, as filmic embodiments of Nadia's renewed ability to "see, hear, and sense," which ultimately means to "be."[9] But, we can add, *Wings* focuses not only on the course of Nadia's sensory restoration, as Shitova astutely observed, but also on the specific capacity of film to convey such sensory *presence* of women in the urban environment.

Wings begins with just such a profoundly self-reflexive sequence, which throws the viewer into a *medias res* not of action, but of a metaphor of film production. Shepitko draws attention here to the richness and multiplicity of cinema as a sensory apparatus, but also contrasts the richness with the impoverished sensory experience of Nadia herself. The sequence, considered as a preface to the film as a whole, establishes the parameters of Shepitko's project: not only to examine the causes and effects of the protagonist's displacement from her environment, but, even more, to rethink how the senses of cinema participate in this process.

From its first seconds, the prologue invites us to engage in a formal exercise in cinematic perception. The opening static shot of a bustling city street—people walking, entering businesses, chatting—transpires in absolute silence and offers little to indicate the nature of its origin (figure 4.1a). It could be footage from a silent documentary, or someone's memory flashback, or a dream. More than anything, it betrays the indeterminacy and instability at the root of cinematic recording. As the establishing shot of the feature, it is sorely lacking in any concrete coordinates to situate the image in time and place. Soon, however, the silence is replaced by apparently nondiegetic music, and then by a different, seemingly diegetic rhythmic noise resembling a ticking clock. This latter sound has no particular correspondence with the street events and does not seem to originate there, and because no other space is offered to view, it seems eerily close, as if emanating from within our—that is, the viewers'—space. Yet before long, the source of this sound is identified. An austere-looking man enters the screen from the left, walking straight toward the camera, with his steps producing the ticking sound. His forceful motion toward and very near to the

Fig. 4.1a–b Window onto the street. From *Wings*, 1966.

camera, into the uttermost foreground of the screen space, makes it appear for a second as though he is about to step over into the spectators' space. But it is at this moment that the camera pulls back, revealing the previously off-screen area, and clarifying the sono-spatial uncertainties that have prevailed so far during the sequence. We realize that the camera has been filming from inside what appears to be a tailor shop, with the silent street *behind* a large windowpane (figure 4.1b). Because the frame of the opening shot matched exactly the frame of the window, the presence of the latter was obscured. But as soon as the unambiguous frame relations and the origin of the sound (or the reason for its absence) are established, a clear diegetic space emerges, forming stable positions for the camera, the viewer, and the figures on screen.[10]

The camera shifts now away from the window, tracking the tailor as he walks inside a dressing room and begins to measure the upper body of a woman—Nadia—waiting there (figure 4.2a). In the shots that follow, the back of her body is so close to the lens that the dark fabric of her jacket fills almost the entire space of the screen, as if to become undifferentiated from its surface (figure 4.2b). The tailor's hands and his measuring tape move even closer into the foreground. He touches and sizes Nadia, positioning the tape in various ways while pronouncing the numbers he sees. With the specific contours of Nadia's body remaining for the most part off screen, the tailor's measurements of the dark surface seem to visually refer not only to her body, but to the screen itself, manipulating one against the other, while the rest of the tailor's own body remains invisible, as if operating from somewhere close to the camera. Finally, he pronounces Nadia to be the standard size, the credits that have been running end, and the movie begins.

Shepitko introduces Nadia, the sole protagonist of the film, in the most circumscribed way, hidden behind multiple frames—the screen, the dressing room, the mirror—and far removed from the unframed life of the street in the opening shot. Her face and body remain mostly fragmented and obstructed, and her voice is almost entirely absent throughout the sequence. By contrast, the tailor—who will subsequently disappear from the film—actively occupies the screen in these first minutes. We encounter his whole figure as he walks toward the camera; he moves, looks, touches, talks, and listens throughout the sequence; he not only traverses the various spaces we see, but necessitates, with his very emergence and movement, the opening of spaces that were previously not available for our visual consumption. His actions extend in every imaginable direction, utilizing spaces within and outside his physical reach, but Nadia's barely exceed the confines of her body, as though she exists in an "existential enclosure" that keeps the surrounding space beyond her reach and inaccessible to her movement.[11] The tailor's entrance, furthermore, brings

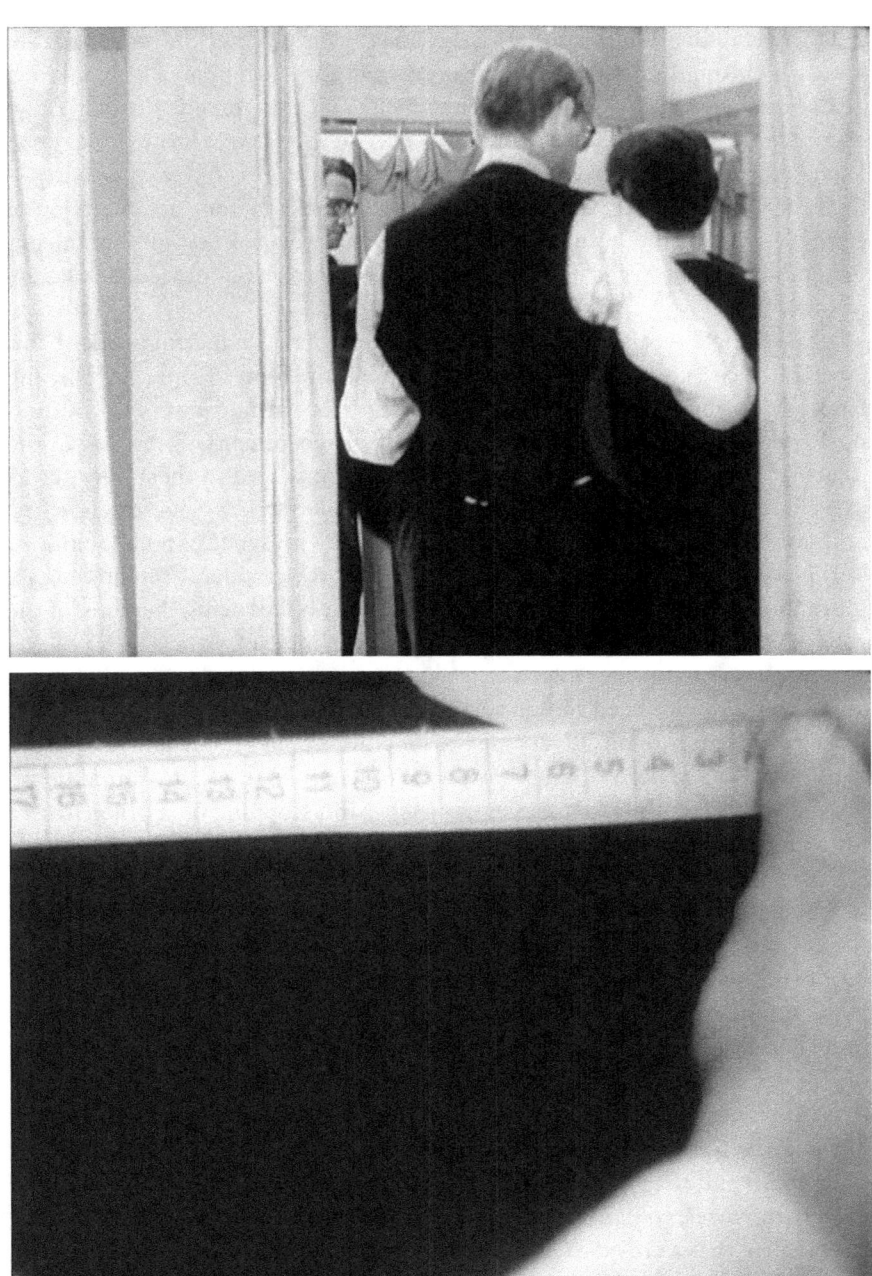

Fig. 4.2a–b Fitting Nadia into her clothes and onto the screen. From *Wings*, 1966.

unity, readability, and stability to the image, eliminating the uncertainties with which the film began. This visual integration culminates in his fixing, or standardizing, of Nadia's body, whereby he seems to impede the expansion even of her clothes beyond the diegetic space of the screen. If the prologue of *Wings* is Shepitko's metaphor for the processes of filmmaking and viewing—the tailor as filmmaker, we imagine—she is very clear about the operation of gender within them. It is indeed by ways of gender determination that the initial, indeterminate recordings of the city street transform into a constructed, narrative film.

The critical terms set by this prologue, with its formal framework of cinematic devices, continue to operate throughout the film, shaping and shifting Nadia's position within her environment and motivating viewers to continuously reevaluate her place vis-à-vis screened space. Shepitko's interest in the figure of a female walker acquires significance in regard to these very terms as well. Nadia's passage through Sevastopol's public spaces—its streets, cafés, and restaurants—is constantly interrupted by the presence of men looking at her. The woman on the street and the woman on the cinematic screen thus acquire the same status—not simply of being there, but of being there under the gaze of others, and thus as composed and framed images.

Just a few sequences after the prologue, we follow Nadia into the street, after she has announced to her neighbor that she plans to eat in restaurants "every day from now on," to escape the loneliness of her home and take in the urban air. We see her walking down a crowded street, looking around deliberately, throwing direct glances at passersby, and stopping on a bridge to enjoy a panoramic view of the city. But what begins as a pleasurable and unconstrained walk turns quickly into a string of awkward and stifling encounters in which she becomes the target of men's gazes. First she is stared down and turned away from a restaurant by the manager because she is not accompanied by a man; then she is stopped at a café window by yet another man looking at her from the inside and beckoning her to come in (figure 4.3a); and then she finds herself in the café surrounded by an exclusively male crowd, including one of her students, who keeps looking at her intimidatingly. It is significant that in this very same café, emptied of all customers, Nadia finds a moment of joy near the film's end as she reminisces with the female café manager about their youth and the two women begin to sing, and, propelled by the sound of their own voices, to dance. Their burst of pleasure comes to a sudden halt as they realize that a crowd of men is staring at them through the windows. The sequence ends in absolute silence and stillness as the two groups, divided by gender and the glass panes, glare at each other in awkwardness and amazement (figure 4.3b and figure 4.3c). Windows thus function within the film not

Fig. 4.3a–c Urban screens, divided by gender. From *Wings*, 1966.

Fig. 4.3a–c (*Continued*)

as regenerative elements of new architectural environments, not as modernist sites of connection between inside and out, private and public, as was the case in Danelia's film, but rather as devices for partitioning men and women on opposite sides of the screen and on opposite sides of urban experience. And even when Nadia looks back at her male counterparts, she is invariably the one who appears uncomfortable, projecting her sense of reification under the gaze of men. Seeking her own experiences in the city, she remains the object of someone else's.

The Flight of the Flaneur

Wings, however, signals early on that such a framed and stultifying relation to space is not the only one that Nadia knows. Her past as a pilot during World War II enters the present of the film by means of dreamy images of a perpetually moving sky that completely defy the kind of framing of her body prevalent in the representations of her current life. Explicitly replacing the trope of window frames, through which Nadia pensively gazes outside, these images express the act of her remembering or daydreaming. Although they omit her actual body, they communicate an intensely embodied, haptic, and subjective experience of space—one that is fluid and free of gravity, measuring coordinates, or any other restraining and objectifying devices. Lasting only a few moments each, they end in the reestablishment of the window frames, returning Nadia to the enclosures of her contemporary peacetime life. Brief and fleeting, these sequences suggest that Nadia's nostalgia is not just for the past but also for a specific spatial experience—for the fullness of being she was able to sense by moving freely through, and feeling one with, space. It is this experience that the film attempts to reconstruct in Nadia's urban walks—walking thus understood as a substitute for flying.

It is worth turning here briefly to the rich critical discourse related to a particular type of urban walker: the flaneur. The very viability of this figure has repeatedly been linked to a specific position within the urban environment, namely, one of invisibility and anonymity, of *not* being framed and turned into the object of another's gaze. This position is central to *Wings* and also carries the significance for film practice more generally, in that the flaneur's preoccupation with recording urban phenomena can be understood as a wish "to become an almost transparent and quasi-invisible medium of the perceptible world," as a kind of film camera.[12] *Wings* both engages and challenges such an analogy by insisting that women do not acquire such a position naturally.

Since its discursive emergence in the nineteenth century, the figure of the flaneur has faced multiple critical evaluations, including by feminists, who maintained that female urban strollers had largely escaped the attention of modernist writers. From Charles Baudelaire to Walter Benjamin, writers described flanerie as a practice of an urban dweller—a man—who, at his own pace and leisure, would stroll aimlessly and without any limits through the streets, taking in the fleeting phenomena of city life. Conceived explicitly as a product of the processes of rapid urban growth under industrial capitalism, the flaneur simultaneously turned into a *producer* of modern culture, one whose mobile perception picked up the disconnected surface fragments of the world and transformed them, through subjective mediation, into reflective texts and images.[13] The perceptual capacity of the flaneur became a privileged form of representing modern life, a way of giving sense to what had become transient and disjointed. An immersed participant in the life of the street, the flaneur could elevate himself above its crowds, could remain a detached, anonymous, and omniscient observer, unrestrained by any particular social assumptions and expectations about his behavior. Baudelaire described this state of being thus: "To be away from home and yet to feel oneself everywhere at home; to see the world, to be at the centre of the world, and yet to remain hidden from the world."[14]

Women, by and large, have been left out of this stage in the history of perception. Although men experienced—and constructed the experience of—modernity, women struggled to gain access to a mode of perception that would allow them a primary, and highly individual, connection to the life of the city.[15] Anke Gleber, writing on Weimar culture of the 1920s in particular, observes that female walkers rarely entered the discourse on flanerie, appearing at best on its margins and lacking a proper linguistic signification. Indeed, the public image of a single woman walking down the street was most readily associated with prostitution.[16] Instances of female urban strolls were almost always described as task-oriented and remained in the realm of "proper" public activities, such as department-store shopping; women's walking, unlike men's, was never depicted as purposeless, free, and focused on sensory encounters with the street, and it was never disconnected from the objectifying male gaze.[17] As Gleber argues, "The question 'To whom do the streets "belong"?' pertains more to women than to men. Whether the streets belong to the leisured or the working class of society, to its dandies or demonstrators, pedestrians or flaneurs, the free and unimpeded movement of women undergoes additional peril. The street has never 'belonged' to women. They cannot walk it freely without also experiencing public judgments or conventions that dictate their images, effectively rendering them objects of the gaze."[18]

To be sure, a flaneur of *any* gender cannot be seamlessly accommodated into the Soviet cultural discourse. His association with anonymity, subjective modes of perception, and fragmentation of modern metropolitan life contradicts Soviet ideals of communal, transparent experiences and the integrated wholeness of the socialist city. Nevertheless, this figure did take hesitant roots in the Soviet cinema of the 1960s, if we consider *Wings* together with the films of the previous chapter.[19] The reasons it did could be numerous, stretching from the widespread projects of urban renewal at the time and the heightened interest in street and public life that accompanied them, to an emerging sense that it was possible not only to perceive the street "at one's own pace," but also to narrate and mediate these perceptions, generating individual accounts of the city. And although the genealogy of Nadia's desire for mobile spatial experiences is linked in the film to her past as a pilot, Shepitko's precise explorations of the gendered structure of urban walks put her protagonist in the context of other, specifically cinematic, walkers of the period.

It is important to note furthermore that urban strollers became a regular feature in contemporaneous European films, which did not escape the attention of Soviet critics and filmgoers: Vittorio de Sica's *Bicycle Thieves* (1948), Michelangelo Antonioni's *La Notte* (1961), and Agnes Varda's *Cleo from 5 to 7* (1962), among others. A number of West European productions exposed Soviet audiences to a variety of nearly documentary recordings of urban life, which were nevertheless understood as highly subjective perceptions of these films' peripatetic figures.[20] Such films provided a set of parameters for understanding the possibilities of urban walks and perceptions, within which specifically Soviet experiences could be imagined. *Cleo from 5 to 7* and *La Notte*, in particular, presented a shift in postwar European cinema in their focus on a *female* urban stroller, suggesting that the cinematic screen had become an important site for exploring women's "right to the city" precisely because of its capacity to produce a gendered framework for viewing and moving similar to what one experiences while strolling down the street.

In this regard, *La Notte* deserves special attention. Although Shepitko did not acknowledge any explicit influence of Antonioni on her work, *Wings* offers a number of striking visual parallels to the Italian feature, suggesting the Soviet director's interest in the particular steps of Antonioni's female walker.[21] (Even though not all of Antonioni's films were released to wider audiences, Soviet critics frequently engaged in detailed discussions of his work throughout the 1960s, indicating that there were other venues for seeing the films.[22]) Among the broader narrative elements the two films share are the long walks taken by both Nadia and Antonioni's protagonist, Lidia; the process of introspection with which these walks become associated; the way textures, structures, and events in the surrounding cityscapes acquire meaning related to the protagonists' pasts, including their respective walks through overgrown fields on the outskirts of each film's urban center. Furthermore, there are parallels in specific visual details, including the presence of similar-looking airfields, airplanes, and rockets that evoke the memories of the protagonists' youth; the momentary but intent focus of the camera on a cobblestone street across which the women walk (figure 4.4a and figure 4.4b) and the appearance of Lidia and Nadia at corners of blocky contemporary buildings (figure 4.5a and figure 4.5b).

But perhaps the most captivating correspondence between Antonioni's work and *Wings* is the duality of Lidia's position within Milan's landscape. An author of her own urban itinerary and experience, she walks deliberately with an unbounded desire to connect to the angular, inhuman spaces of postwar Italian urbanism—to sense them not only through her mobile visual perception, but through direct touch, quite literally peeling away the layers of architectural surfaces (and as a result departing from the flaneur of Benjamin's description, who operates under the motto of "look but don't touch"[23]). At the same time, though, Lidia's status as a woman in this act of flanerie is repeatedly questioned. Her forty-minute-long passage from Milan's center to its desolate outskirts is punctuated by numerous encounters with men, staged as moments of intense, deliberate looking and assessment, to which she responds forcefully by returning—as an equal—their gazes (figure 4.6). Lidia's sense of "feeling at home in the city," her getting in touch with urban space to counteract "the alienation of the time," inevitably becomes a balancing act that requires her to diffuse this pervasive male gazing.[24]

Fig. 4.4a–b The materiality of the street. From *La Notte*, 1961 (a), and *Wings*, 1966 (b).

Fig. 4.5a–b Women against urban walls. From *La Notte*, 1961 (a), and *Wings*, 1966 (b).

Fig. 4.6 Lidia initiating and returning the male gaze. From *La Notte*, 1961.

However radically different her historical, cultural, and personal contexts are from Nadia's, Lidia can be understood as a cinematic prototype for Shepitko's protagonist. Her ability to "get in touch" with her surroundings while simultaneously making this process one of introspection, as becomes evident toward the end of Antonioni's film, is what Nadia seeks as well. And it is ultimately during the last segment of Nadia's walk, toward the end of *Wings*, that she appears capable of matching Lidia's accomplishment. This accomplishment occurs immediately after the episode of Nadia singing and dancing in the café, when she returns to the street and continues her apparently aimless walking, but now with a smile on her face, an added flamboyance to her movement, and an explicit urge to touch, which has been essentially absent in the film up to this point. She spontaneously grabs a small plate from the table of a street vendor, examines it with curiosity, and then puts it back (figure 4.7a). Shepitko insists on the meaningfulness of this action by having the vendor herself repeat it, clearly struggling to understand Nadia's motivation for giving her tactile attention to this insignificant object. Nadia's desire to extend her own self into the street—the acute presence of her own sensory experience in distinct contrast to the film's prologue—culminates when it begins to rain. We see her stretching her fruit-filled hands out toward the falling water (figure 4.7b), as her eyes, deeply and thoughtfully, observe the path and texture of the cobblestone road reaching nearly to the horizon.

This moment marks a transition to the most revealing sequence of the film—Nadia's memory of her time with her beloved Mitya during World War

Fig. 4.7a–b Nadia opening up to the street. From *Wings*, 1966.

II—in which her sensory presence overwhelms the cinematic image, but her body itself, as image, never appears. With this, Shepitko completely departs from Antonioni, who persists in shaping Lidia's passage through Milan by keeping her body the focus of his camera's gaze throughout. The balance of male and female flanerie that Antonioni represents within his frames occurs in *Wings* only through a critical reorganization of the cinematic space as a whole.

Acoustic Passages

Nadia's memory of Mitya generates the most striking shift within the film as the screened space becomes engulfed in the sounds of her voice and indivisible from her unseen body. Before looking at this sequence in detail, though, we need to acknowledge the manner in which the voice, and sound more generally, complicates the relation between body and space throughout *Wings*, formally and narratively. Several episodes in the film emphasize that the cinematic location of voices can fundamentally differ, and even be at odds with, the location and movement of bodies, thus critically employing what film historian Michel Chion has called the *acousmêtric* dimension of voice—that is, its possible disconnection from its origin, "its" body. Chion argues that such a voice acquires a new potency in relationship to what is shown on screen, an ability "to be everywhere, to see all, to know all, and to have complete power."[25] It exists in the borderlands of the interior and the exterior of the image, passing through what film spectators see, yet not letting them pinpoint its location, operating thus in "a place that has no name, but which the cinema forever brings into play."[26] The disembodiment of the voice occurs in *Wings* at several moments. Even if minute and insignificant, and not fully complying with the parameters of Chion's *acousmêtre*, they nevertheless set the stage for its complex imbrication when Nadia begins to envision her past.

One such moment, for instance, occurs early in the film, in Nadia's room, immediately after Pasha, her current companion, departs. As soon as he is gone, the camera zooms in on Nadia's face and shows her barely moving lips whispering "Pasha"—so quietly, we imagine, as to be impossible to hear except in the immediate proximity of her body. The camera then cuts to show a heavy, solid entrance door, as if to emphasize that the sound of her voice could not be transmitted beyond the room's boundaries. Yet a few seconds later Pasha returns, asking whether she has just called him. Although this sequence is meant to suggest the depth of their emotional involvement (indeed, an identical sound experiment fails later when Nadia attempts it with her daughter), it also draws our attention to the ability of a voice to permeate and occupy space in a way that a body cannot. While Nadia remains transfixed in a chair in the middle of her room, surrounded by heavy, static objects and structures, her voice drifts around without regard for any architectural or cinematic frameworks and boundaries. It travels into the space off screen as an actual, material presence, and in reaching the male figure located there, it ultimately expands Nadia's ability to engage space far beyond the immediacy of her environment and the reach of her immobile body.

Another relevant sequence shows Nadia at the corner of a blocky building—reminiscent, as noted earlier, of a similar sequence in *La Notte*—where she comes to visit her daughter. As Nadia stands next to the large, concrete wall, we notice the figure of a young girl entering the screen far in the background and a voice calling "Mama" simultaneously permeates the scene. The immediate assumption is that the voice belongs to the girl. The synchronicity of the voice and the child's body language invites us to understand it as such, even if we already know that Nadia's daughter must be older than this girl. But as soon as this shot is replaced with the next, our assumption is voided, as we see a young woman, who *is* Nadia's daughter and who, it turns out, had just called from the space off screen. We are forced to read the sequence backward in order to correct our initial understanding of the dynamics of the previous shot. (The orchestration of this sequence is so precise that it is hard to imagine Shepitko did not stage the perceptual confusion intentionally.) All these sequences systematically investigate the capacity of cinematic sound to engage cinematic space in ambiguous ways: to disrupt the unity and meaning of a shot, to destabilize a static environment within the frame, and to spread through space—not only the screened but also the theatrical space—and accordingly penetrate it everywhere.

We can in part understand Shepitko's fleeting but persistent experimentations with voice as a consequence of, and a reaction to, the period's developing sound technologies, above all the introduction of stereophonic sound systems to accompany panoramic and widescreen films. The original intent of stereophony was twofold: to increase the realistic impression of the cinematic image through a better spatial coordination of visual and aural information in the theatrical space and to intensify viewers' experience of physiological presence *within* the image through their actual acoustic envelopment. Although the project of generating an experience of cinema as an integrated spatial unity was at the core of these aims, Soviet critics and filmmakers began to push the critical potential of new sound technologies beyond these limits. The Soviet sound operator Lev Trachtenberg in particular expressed interest in the evocation of *dis*unity within a theatrical space, suggesting that "the movement of the sound, its place in space and its direction . . . [could] appear in juxtapositions and confrontations, in contrasts and rhythmical exchanges."[27] Advocating further for a certain friction between sound and image—what he described as a "contrapuntal arrangement (*kontrapunkt*) between different elements of spatially determined sound and the representation"—Trachtenberg imagined this to have a productive "dramaturgical significance," although he left open any specifics.[28] *Wings*, neither in widescreen format nor stereophonic sound, fleshes out the potential of such a friction between sound and image, and specifically between the imaged body and the disembodied voice. Indeed, Shepitko develops just the sort of "contrapuntal arrangement" proposed by Trachtenberg as an integral part of her rethinking of female subjectivity on screen.

To return to Chion, we can consider his suggestion that the disembodied cinematic voice operates from an unknown position in relation to the flaneur's own relationship to the urban environment and specifically to the flaneur's simultaneous immersion in the life of the street and observation of it as if from an indeterminate position: "to see the world, to be at the centre of the world," as we've already quoted Baudelaire, "and yet to remain hidden from the world." Like the flaneur, the disembodied cinematic voice exists within *and* outside the space it traverses; it is able to penetrate space while originating somewhere else. Furthermore, in the same way that the flaneur position has been unavailable to women, so too have critics noted a gender disparity with regard to the disembodied cinematic voice. Film scholar Kaja Silverman in particular has argued that classical Hollywood cinema almost never makes use of disembodied female voices, especially not as a voiceover that would narrate the story from outside the fiction presented on screen. A male voiceover, by contrast, occurs frequently in specific film forms and genres, in which it takes a position of external authority, "whose superior knowledge and diegetic detachment promise eventual justice."[29] Aligned with discursive power, heard but not seen, and thus immune to questioning or interrogation from the outside, the disembodied voice of men allows for an idealization of omnipotent male subjectivity.[30]

Silverman suggests that when a woman's disembodied voice does turn up in classical narrative films, it is only briefly, more as a voice-off (that is, a voice speaking from the space off screen) "whose" body is about to appear on screen, rather than as a true voiceover speaking from an indeterminable location and aligned with an unquestioned power and authority. Silverman writes, "To allow her to be heard without being seen would be . . . dangerous, since it would disrupt the specular regime upon which dominant cinema relies; it would put her beyond the reach of the male gaze (which stands in here for the cultural 'camera') and release her voice from the signifying obligations which that gaze enforces. It would liberate the female subject from the interrogation about her place, her time, and her desires which constantly resecures her."[31]

Shepitko's acoustic engagements—various forms of dissonance and desynchronization, practices of vocal disembodiment, and the obfuscation of the female speaker's body—should be put in line with the cinema of such feminist filmmakers as Yvonne Rainer and Bette Gordon whose sound experiments Silverman discusses, and *Wings*, in fact, precedes these women's relevant work. And although Shepitko does not engage a voiceover in the strict sense of Silverman's terms (the owner of such a voice would never appear on screen), the memory sequence marks a distinct shift in the representation of Nadia's body that, rather declaratively, puts her "beyond the reach of the male gaze."[32]

The sequence opens by exploiting once more the synchronicity of image and voice in order to thwart our understanding of what we see on the screen. An extreme long shot of a waving figure in a military uniform, surrounded by overgrown grass and trees, is accompanied by a voice—Nadia's—calling out "Mitya." The simultaneity of the waving hand and the calling voice suggests that the figure in the background is Nadia herself; but when this figure approaches, we see that it is a man—Mitya—making it clear that Nadia's calling came from the space off screen. What follows are five distinctly marked shots of Nadia's recollections of an encounter with Mitya during the war, as the two walk and talk on the unnamed ruins of a bygone civilization. Throughout, Nadia's body remains outside our field of vision; her youthful self does not make a single appearance in this sequence.

But this is not to say that she is not there. Her presence is abstractly imprinted through Mitya's gaze, as he frequently looks straight at the camera while talking to her, suggesting that she is immediately "behind" it. Even more obviously, she permeates the scene through her own gaze, for which the camera becomes a substitute, acting differently than it has for most of the film. It moves freely, somewhat nervously and erratically, and comes extremely close to the surfaces that surround the two figures, thus mediating Nadia's haptic vision (figure 4.8a and figure 4.8b). The sense of her being "right there," however, becomes especially powerful with the presence of her voice, as she and Mitya continue to converse throughout the sequence. Vibrant and deeply affective, of a tenor we have not yet heard, her voice resonates throughout the entire represented space, joining the subjective gaze of the camera and seeming to permeate each cell of the surrounding landscape. With this operation, Nadia in effect occupies the place "that has no name" or, to put it differently, she becomes ubiquitous, present in *all* spaces, transcending all spatial frames and boundaries. She is both within the diegesis, though off screen, speaking directly to Mitya, and on screen, enveloping Mitya with her voice and gaze from all directions. She also is on the other side of the screen, perceived to be behind the camera, and on our side, enveloping viewers in her voice just as

Fig. 4.8a–b Spatiality and tactility of remembering. From *Wings*, 1966.

she envelopes Mitya. Her visual absence is unsettling, even disorienting, precisely because her presence is so distinctly felt. The film's viewers want nothing more than to *see* this different Nadia—young and sensuous, full of desire and expressive abilities—and the camera feeds our desire by constantly shifting, reframing the image and opening up off-screen spaces where she supposedly "is," yet never revealing her vocal, speaking body.

The sequence completely reverses the prologue of *Wings* by making Nadia the agent of the film's sensual richness—its auditory, visual, and tactile means. For she, after all, is the actual point of the origin of the images we see, which emerge from her deepest, most cherished memories. The space of the ruins, the texture and materiality of which become a focus of conversation between Nadia and Mitya, is unthinkable here apart from her body. This space, in fact, becomes a mirror image of Nadia, as she envisions herself within this sequence not as a contoured, framed figure, but as an aural, spatial, and mobile configuration, in which her interiority, her subjectivity, assumes an external and boundless shape.[33] In its conflation of body and space, the sequence is a grounded materialization of the dreamy, mobile sky images discussed earlier. The voice itself performs a function similar to the experience of flying—it is fluid and dispersed, free of gravity, and untethered from any measuring coordinates or constraining frames and objectifying devices.

Memory, in the City

This sequence reflects on the film's overarching issue of walking. In a peculiar sense, what transpires here is an act of flanerie. Having stumbled upon the ruins, Nadia and Mitya walk through them, attentively observing the textures of the enduring surfaces and stepping into the furrowed tracks of the former inhabitants. The difference, of course, is that this space has nothing to do with the modern metropolis (or its provincial cousin) that gave rise to the flaneur; it is not characterized by crowds or arcades or urban speed of any kind, but rather is introduced more as a myth, outside any specific history or society. But within the film, it is in this sequence alone that the acts of walking and perception are presented in explicitly affective terms, with an emphasis on both the erotic nature of the walkers' wanderings and the spatial nature of Nadia's desires.[34] After all, Nadia looks back at her intimate encounter with Mitya as an act of walking—as a memory in which she is able to attain precisely that which evades her in her present strolls through Sevastopol. It is only here, in this nonplace, that she becomes a true flaneur, an uninhibited, mobile, and tactile observer; indeed, she is "almost transparent and quasi-invisible," mediating to us her experience of this space from an unlocatable, indeterminate position.[35]

The appearance of this mythical place invites us ultimately to consider the actual topography of Nadia's walks, both within her memory and in the real spaces of Sevastopol—not least because Nadia's experience of historical disconnectedness is depicted within the city, whose urban design and elaborate commemorative program explicitly seek to forge a connection to history. A designated hero-city for its valiant fighting during World War II and home to the legendary Black Sea Fleet, Sevastopol was nearly annihilated by the Nazi Luftwaffe during the first days of the German invasion in June 1941. After the war, the city underwent an extensive process of reconstruction, which, as historian Karl D. Qualls has argued, was achieved through a delicate and often contested dialogue between Moscow and the city's local authorities, who "fought back against Moscow's triumphal socialist designs for the postwar city and instead crafted human-scale projects that both met the people's material needs and revived their sense of place."[36]

The result was a rebuilt city fully cleared of war ruins and aligned with architecture that paid great tribute to Sevastopol's past—not only to the recent war but also its pre-Soviet past, reaching back to its Greek roots and honoring its central role in the Crimean war of the mid-nineteenth century. As Qualls has described, commemoration of the city's past was of particular significance for postwar urban planning, meant to ensure that the tales of individual and collective heroism would leave a "permanent mark on Sevastopol's urban legacy."[37] Through the restoration of old memorial sites and the rapid development of new ones, including monuments and obelisks, museums and squares, important historical events of Sevastopol were inscribed into its public material fabric. Operating as an open-air museum, Sevastopol became a city of memory *par excellence*. Its memorial spaces provided not only an outlet for grief and remembrance for the city's older inhabitants, but also an opportunity for the many newcomers and younger generations to identify with its history and develop a sense of local and national community.

It is surprising, then, that in a film relaying an individual experience of historical rupture and an attempt to cure it through urban walking, Shepitko makes almost no use of the city's commemorative spaces.[38] She shows no memorials, no squares, no street names that would directly elicit memories and experiences of the war, and the architecture that is shown most prominently here has no significance for individual pasts and memories. The columns of institutional buildings, for instance, next to which Nadia appears several times, solid and static in their historical monumentality, have no relation to her fragile and isolated state (figure 4.9a). Or similarly, a newly built neighborhood of Khrushchev-era apartment buildings is presented as simply blank in its historical connections—invariable, monotone, and faceless (figure 4.9b).

Fig. 4.9a–b The architecture of postwar Sevastopol. From *Wings*, 1966.

The most relevant public space is the city museum, which displays not only Sevastopol's history in general, but Nadia's own history in particular—exhibiting her wartime photograph (as well as Mitya's) and celebrating her military division. But Nadia remains detached from her own self as presented within the space of this structure; her image is framed and immobilized on the wall, and she insists on describing herself as a museum "object" (*eksponat*), like the taxidermic animals housed there as well. Dead space, dead objects, dead history: the museum replicates the static environment of the city, at least as experienced by Nadia, with none of the spaces conducive to individual memories and experience.[39] Immortalized as a hero in a public space, Nadia keeps the intimacy and the trauma of her wartime past deeply buried in the privacy of her enclosed body.[40]

But the space of the ruins, which brings history to movement and life, and where Nadia herself appears so vibrant and vital, also is an actual place in the vicinity of Sevastopol: the remnants of the medieval town of Chufut-Kale ("Judaic Fortress"), in the mountains just an hour northeast of Sevastopol. The town, which remains today one of the most important archaeological sites and a popular tourist destination in the region, dates to the sixth century, when it was first built as a fortress in the Crimean Peninsula. It continued to develop and flourish up to the mid-eighteenth century, becoming home to diverse ethnic populations, including Crimean Tatars and Jews. In the 1850s, the last group of Crimean Jews abandoned the town, after Russian law lifted the restrictions on where they were allowed to reside, and Chufut-Kale fell into ruins.[41] What was left behind is a basic stone infrastructure consisting of roads and gates, walls and cave interiors, a well, and a few buildings—an empty space, the history of which still speaks today through the material fragments of its stone surfaces. It is precisely these surfaces that become the point of conversation between Nadia and Mitya during their intimate walk, as they briefly imagine the life of the town's former inhabitants—reading their past as they wander through the ruins' material remains.

Yet Chufut-Kale enters the film not as a tourist site, and not even quite as a real place, but as an *image* of memory—unstable, embodied, and inherently subjective. It is never named or given a specific geographic location and is brought to the screen only through Nadia's contemplation of the cobblestones of a contemporary Sevastopol street, conflating the material and atmospheric essence of the two sites. By de-realizing the medieval ruins and superimposing them onto a Sevastopol street in this way, Shepitko explicitly moves the work of memory away from monuments of any kind, triggering, through Nadia's passage, the appearance of the past on the city's most prosaic material. We see the street in Sevastopol being emptied out, cleared of everything inessential as people and structures disappear from view, leaving in focus only the street's cobblestone surface. It is here, in this arbitrary location, that Nadia's walk begins to function as a mnemonic device, wherein she can evoke her own history through the "far-off times and places [that] interpenetrate the landscape and the present moment," to borrow the language of Benjamin's *Arcades Project*.[42] Furthermore, Shepitko presents this process of remembering as an act of a subjective spillover, as Nadia's body, stretching toward the street, releases what has been firmly contained within her, with her intimate past finding a transient place of its own within the urban present. Together with—or rather through—her voice (which explicitly projects outward as opposed to the gaze, which consumes and takes in what she sees), this past leaves the boundaries of her body and becomes spatialized. It is imagined to be dispersed in the textures and materials of urban foundations and, as a result, to extend across times and spaces.[43]

To understand more fully Shepitko's desire to spatialize private memory, it is useful to compare *Wings* with a set of films in which the figure of the flaneur and the residing of private memories in urban spaces are similarly problematized and specifically related to gender. These are the so-called rubble films of immediate postwar Germany, set in the ruins of German cities after the war's end and centered on the figure of *Heimkehrer*—men who have just returned home from military combat. Trapped in their traumatic war memories, these men are shown to be unable to integrate themselves productively into the country's reconstruction efforts. Indeed, they spend their time aimlessly wandering the streets and observing the spectacularly devastated cityscape, turning into flaneurs of the destroyed metropolis. As film scholar Jaimey Fisher has compellingly argued, these films present "private memory as juxtaposed to the public space of the city, such that [the characters'] memories become both panoramic and collective."[44] Fisher suggests that we can perceive this, for instance, in Wolfgang Staudte's *Murderers Are among Us* (1946), in which shots of Berlin—its "nonsubjective" panoramic views and sounds—prefigure the protagonist Mertens's traumatic recollection of a wartime massacre that haunts him. Although a direct flashback to that event does not occur until later in the film, his memory has been there all along, externalized and spatialized within the city and its views and sounds (and thus indivisible from collective history), waiting to be perceived by the flaneur, who is open to the overwhelming stimuli of this urban space harboring his traumatic past.

If such spatialization of private memories in the rubble films was a way to approach trauma in the immediate postwar period—before a more rigorous project of "coming to terms with the past" began—the containment of these memories also was a goal. Coming to terms with the past was accomplished, Fisher contends, with the help of women and their specific forms of mobility. Susanne, the female protagonist of Staudte's film—who, it is implied, returned to Berlin from a concentration camp—moves around the city with a clear sense of purpose and also is preoccupied with remaking her destroyed home. Her wartime memories and experiences do not interfere with her goal-oriented postwar life. Mertens's recovery from his traumas, from his flanerie, unfolds as a process of domestication, enabled largely by Susanne. He returns to his medical profession and, most important, to his private home, which she has diligently restored. As Fisher observes, from "inside the reconstructed private sphere . . . [Mertens] will no longer be so open to memory-triggering visual stimuli of the exploded urban panorama."[45]

Although *Murderers Are among Us* reconstructs the stability of everyday life by ridding its male protagonist of his wandering sickness—and resurrects in the process the boundaries between private and public, past and present (by means of iconic window frames, above all)—it never even questions whether its *female* protagonist might need to wander city streets in order to face her own memories, thus denying women's place within the nation's collective history. In this context, *Wings* seeks a reverse process, setting in motion what *Murderers* wants to evade or heal. Its protagonist walks until her memories are triggered out in the open, obfuscating in the process the barriers between private and public, past and present, and bringing the image of the ruins right into the center of the polished, reconstructed, postwar space. The medieval remnants called up by Nadia's passage acquire thus a multitude of meanings. They function not only as a site of her past encounter with Mitya, but also as the "other space" within the contemporary cityscape. Its substance is inseparable from views and sounds of Nadia's body, as well as the desires and experiences of her past, and it is perceived as a trace of inassimilable rupture in the fabric of the city, whose streets have been successfully cleared of the last war's ruins.[46]

We can discern in *Wings*—arguably for the first time in the context of Soviet cinema—a complex and developed image of a specifically Soviet female flaneur, of her historically and spatially determined endeavors and difficulties. In contrast to the city walker of Baudelaire's writings, for instance, who strives to make meaning out of fragmented and fleeting sensations of a European metropolis, Nadia walks in order to fragment and fill with fleeting sensations the planned and structured spaces of a socialist city, thus causing those spaces to be perceived as disparate and layered. Or to put it differently, it is precisely her walking that restores the instability and transience to Soviet urban space, making it more complex and thus conducive to individual and errant experiences.

And it is her mobile perception and sensory embrace of her environment that disturb the order not only of Soviet space but of Soviet history—pressing the collective tales of war heroism to give way to intimate memories, momentary experiences, and unhealed traumas. Indeed, if one of the central concerns of *Wings* hints at such an overarching issue as the calcified monumentalization of historical narratives and collective memory within Soviet environments (as exemplified in the pointed museum sequence), Shepitko finds it necessary to address it by confronting—through her flaneur—the equally calcified, rigid image of women in the public realm of the city. As she frees Nadia's figure from the boundaries of such an image, allowing her to become immersed in the street and encounter her past as a subject, she brings flux to both Soviet space and history, releasing them from their own tight and ordered frames.

Having started with stasis and stability of urban *and* filmic spaces, Shepitko acquires movement and transience for both, as she disassembles the realistic unity of cinematic representation in the memory sequence. The female body drives this process, as the wholeness of its image on screen gets dispersed into such basic cinematic components as voice, movement, and gaze. The multiplicity of the cinematic apparatus and its spaces come into play, transformed into flexible materials that are open to profoundly different configurations, while reconfiguring, in turn, the appearance of female subjectivity in the space of the movie theater. It is cinema's materiality—of an even more basic kind—that becomes similarly central to our understandings of the relationship between gender and space in the films of Kira Muratova, the subject of the next chapter.

Notes

1. The rigid, gendered structure of the gaze in Danelia's opening echoes directly what feminist critics have addressed in relation to classical narrative cinema. As Teresa de Lauretis, in her discussion of Laura Mulvey's seminal essay "Visual Pleasure and Narrative Cinema" (1975), writes, "The woman is framed by the look of the camera as an icon, an image, the object of the gaze, and thus, precisely, spectacle: that is to say, an image made to be looked at by the spectator(s) as well as the male character(s), whose look most often relays the look of the audience" (De Lauretis, *Technologies of Gender*, 99).

2. It is remarkable that although Danelia consistently entrusts women to perform a dynamic dialogue with their surroundings, he just as consistently positions a male figure right next to them, as a gazing subject. This is the case in the "dancing in the rain" sequence discussed at length in chapter 3 as well as in a few other sequences in the film.

3. Elem Klimov, *Larisa. Vospominaniia. Vystupleniia. Intev'iu. Kinostsenarii. Stat'i.*

4. Although *Wings* passed Soviet censorship and was released to a wider audience, it received a harsh reception by the group of viewers that it ostensibly presented—war veterans, among whom were many women. As one of them noted, "The film *Wings* cannot be released on the screens of this country, and especially on foreign screens, because its core idea is a defamation of Soviet women in general and Soviet pilots in particular" ("Delo fil'ma 'Kryl'ia,'" 69).

5. Ackbar Abbas, "Cinema, the City, and the Cinematic," 145.
6. "Kryl'ia: podrobnyi razgovor" (a roundtable discussion), 19, 18.
7. Shepitko's film reflects here on an important aspect of World War II history, namely the significant presence of women combat pilots in the Soviet Air Force during the war. As Reina Pennington has noted, the Soviet Union became the first country during the war to allow women to participate in extensive combat missions. But, as Pennington argues, although the Stalinist state had endorsed the active participation of women in the war effort, at war's end it also insisted that most of them be quickly discharged and banned from any further military service, drastically reverting the position of women to older gender stereotypes. See Pennington, *Wings, Women, and War*. As we see in Shepitko's film, the pilot school that Nadia frequents consists of men, including her former fellow combatant, which accentuates further the film's interest in gender, rather than generational, issues.
8. Such an opinion was supported especially by former pilots, who suggested that because airplane technology had changed so much since the war, the film's protagonist would not have been able to navigate the airplane without some training ("Delo fil'ma 'Kryl'ia,'" 59).
9. "Kryl'ia: podrobnyi razgovor," 20.
10. With a formal evocation of a window and a frame within the prologue, Shepitko generates an explicit dialogue with classical norms of film production, which applied to much Soviet cinema. Thomas Elsaesser and Malte Hagener, in their critical discussion of the concepts of window and frame in film theory, wrote, "Both models, frame and window, postulate the image as given and view the spectator as concentrating on how most fully to engage with the work and its structures, making wholeness and (assumed) coherence the focus of the analysis. If only by default, they tend to overlook the potentially contradictory processes of production (be they technological or institutional) that are also leaving traces on the films" (Elsaesser and Hagener, *Film Theory*, 16). Shepitko seeks to challenge just such postulates, demonstrating the process by which cinematic coherence comes into existence first by concealing and then by revealing the window or frame.
11. I borrow this phrase from the philosopher Iris M. Young, who, analyzing a specifically feminine spatiality, writes, "Feminine existence appears to posit an existential enclosure between herself and the space surrounding her, in such a way that the space which belongs to her and is available to her grasp and manipulation is constricted, and the space beyond is not available to her movement." Shepitko consistently constructs her protagonist's spatiality in such terms, creating a tangible "existential enclosure" beyond which Nadia cannot reach and which will be challenged throughout the film. See Young, "Throwing Like a Girl," 63.
12. Anke Gleber, *The Art of Taking a Walk*, 152.
13. Discussing Walter Benjamin's notes on flanerie as a methodology of his historical and sociological approach to reality, David Frisby addresses the dual position of the flaneur as a product and a producer of modernity: "The *flâneur*, and the activity of *flânerie*, is also associated in Benjamin's work not merely with observation and reading but also with *production*—the production of distinctive kinds of text. The *flâneur* may therefore not merely be an observer or even a decipherer, the *flâneur* can also be a producer, a producer of literary texts (including lyrical and prose poetry as in the case of Baudelaire), a producer of illustrative texts (including painting), a producer of narratives and reports, a producer of journalistic texts, a producer of sociological texts" (Frisby, "The *Flâneur* in Social Theory," 83, italics in the original).
14. Charles Baudelaire, "The Painter of Modern Life," 9.
15. One of the most influential expressions on this topic is Griselda Pollock's, who suggests, "there is not and could not be a female flâneuse" (Pollock, *Vision and Difference*, 71). Pollock's view, however, has been complicated and challenged. See, for instance, Leslie, "Ruin and Rubble in the Arcades."
16. As Susan Buck-Morss, for instance, writes, "Prostitution was indeed the female version of flanerie. Yet sexual difference makes visible the privileged position of males within public space. I

mean this: the flaneur was simply the name of a man who loitered; but all women who loitered risked being seen as whores, as the term 'street-walker' or 'tramp' applied to women makes clear" (Buck-Morss, "The Flaneur, the Sandwichman, and the Whore," 119).

17. See, for instance, Friedberg, *Window Shopping*, esp. 32–36.

18. Gleber, *The Art of Taking a Walk*, 175.

19. Another example worth mentioning here is the 1963 film *Two Sundays*, directed by Vladimir Shredel', in which a young woman from a small Siberian town arrives in Moscow for just one day, with no other agenda than to encounter the Soviet capital for the first time. Just as she begins her walk through the city, she stumbles over a man filming his surroundings with a camera, which he readily directs at her, integrating her immediately as an image within his recordings. As *Two Sundays* progresses, the young woman seems unable to escape the ubiquity of a fixing gaze: as soon as she leaves this first "man with a movie camera" behind, she runs into a group of journalists, also operating a camera. After they interview her within the glass walls of the Kremlin Palace of Congresses (a 1962 architectural landmark), her face is broadcast throughout the entire Soviet Union. The film makes it surprisingly clear, though apparently without critical intentions, that regardless of the surrounding architecture—the young woman in fact also visits the Palace of Young Pioneers—the gendered structure of urban sensations and experiences remains unchanged; it could be the same, indeed, in the midst of Stalinist skyscrapers.

20. Thus, a reviewer of Varda's *Cleo from 5 to 7* remarked, "This is a 'documentary Paris' which becomes a 'subjective Paris,' penetrated by anxiety" (Soloviova, "Kleo s 5 do 7," 114). Compare the reviewer's remark to Gleber's discussion of the flaneur: "He emerges as a pivotal historical figure within the modern debate on specularity, but one whose perspective exceeds the accumulation and analysis of 'objective' or visual 'facts'" (Gleber, *The Art of Taking a Walk*, 138).

21. In an interview for Bavarian television, in 1978, Shepitko expressed an affinity for the poetic visions of a number of foreign film directors, including Robert Bresson, Luis Buñuel, and early Akira Kurosawa. See Shepitko, Interview with Felicia von Nostiz.

22. Here is a short selection of Soviet critical discussions of Antonioni's work: Vaitsman, "Liniia razgranicheniia"; Varshavskii, "Ot pokoleniia k pokoleniiu"; Murian, "Gumanizm sotsialisticheskii i gumanizm abstraktnyi"; Korzhavin, "Poka byla liubov'"; and Rubanova, "Posle krasnoi pustyni: o nekotorykh itogakh Antonioni." Rubanova mentions in her discussion of Antonioni's work the films that had been shown publicly in Moscow, and *La Notte* is not one of them. Shepitko, nevertheless, could have seen it elsewhere—at VGIK (the State Institute of Cinematography), for instance, or during her travels abroad. *La Notte* is mentioned in nearly every Soviet analysis of Antonioni's cinema (including, extensively, in Rubanova's article), suggesting that the film was available for viewing, even if not for the general Soviet audience.

23. Quoted in Buck-Morss, "The Flaneur, the Sandwichman, and the Whore," 105.

24. Guiliana Bruno, *Atlas of Emotion*, 98.

25. Michel Chion, *The Voice in Cinema*, 24.

26. Ibid.

27. Trachtenberg, "Kogda zvuchit shirokii ekran," 99.

28. Ibid.

29. Kaja Silverman, *The Acoustic Mirror*, 162.

30. Silverman's analysis implies the possibility of comparing the function of the flaneur with that of a disembodied cinematic voice along gender lines. She suggests that the male discursive authority (and the ideal manifestation of his subjectivity) can be constructed through "any textual strategy which delineates the diegesis in terms of 'inner' and 'outer' spaces, and which locates male speech, hearing, and vision within the latter rather than the former" (ibid., 164).

31. Ibid.

32. Ibid., 165.

33. Shepitko's image of memory as explicitly spatialized relates directly to Paul Ricoeur's discussion of space and memory. He writes, "the memory of having inhabited some house in some town or that of having traveled in some part of the world are particularly eloquent and telling.... In memories of this type, corporeal space is immediately linked with the surrounding space of the environment" (Ricoeur, *Memory, History, Forgetting*, 148).

34. On the spatial nature of women's desires, see Jessica Benjamin, "A Desire of One's Own."

35. It is striking that in Aleksandr Askoldov's 1967 seminal film *Commissar*, the female protagonist, during the birth sequence, also envisions her revolutionary past in extremely spatialized terms. The protagonist's figure is not absent during the film's memory sequences, but rather alternates between distinct appearances and disappearances. Throughout, though, spatial tactility is essential to portraying the memory of her past experiences.

36. Karl D. Qualls, *From Ruins to Reconstruction*," 5.

37. Ibid., 29.

38. On the issue of memory in Soviet cinema of the 1960s more broadly, see Kaganovsky, "Postmemory, Countermemory." Kaganovsky discusses the gap between generations—those who participated in the war and those who came of age after it (as Shepitko herself did)—and argues that films of the 1960s exhibited a "working through of a trauma that was not [the filmmakers' generation's] own, that 'belonged' to the previous generation, but that nevertheless continued to haunt the present," 237.

39. To give full justice to the museum sequence, it must be noted that Nadia has her second memory flashback here, in which she witnesses, from inside her military airplane, Mitya's death as his airplane is shot down. The museum sequence immediately follows the sequence of her first memory flashback—the walk with Mitya through the ruins. Before the second memory sequence begins to unfold, Shepitko provides a pointed commentary on the museum's inability to communicate to its visitors the experiences of the past. From the dreadfully monotone voice of the museum guide, to the boxed expositions of historical objects, to the utter lack of interest shown by the visiting children, history appears here as a dead object. Nadia, however, makes an effort to approach the wartime photographs of Mitya and herself that hang on the wall (here, the viewers' desire to see the young Nadia is finally fulfilled), and, while looking at them, she envisions the moment of Mitya's death in the air. Although the film thus allows Nadia's memory to come alive inside the museum, the entirety of the sequence suggests that her ability to commune with her past occurs *despite* the entire museum culture, not because of it.

40. The extent to which the drive toward collective narratives of heroism permeated Soviet public discussions (an effort strongly expressed in the reconstruction of Sevastopol, as Qualls demonstrates in *From Ruins to Reconstruction*) can be felt in the reception of *Wings*, in the way several film viewers struggled to acknowledge the difficulties of overcoming war traumas. One respondent, for instance, noted that the depiction of a Soviet woman "with a difficult destiny" needed to be accompanied by "our Russian, Soviet optimism, especially if it is about a war hero—a Soviet female pilot. The heroism of female pilots is belittled through the display of artificial characters and the ideological emptiness of a psychiatrically ill patient" ("Delo fil'ma 'Kryl'ia,'" 69). Another suggested, "People themselves create their destiny.... The script writer presented a pathological case" (ibid., 58). And yet another: "I still feel the sensation of pessimism. The protagonist is unsettled.... This disorder impoverishes her character. The theme of personality degradation emerges" (ibid., 14).

41. On the history of Chufut-Kale, see Brook, *The Jews of Khazaria*, 24.

42. Benjamin, *The Arcades Project*, 419.

43. In this way, this scene responds directly to what Mary Ann Doane has described as a process of turning the body "inside out" through the off-screen voice. Doane, "The Voice in the Cinema," 41.

44. Fisher, "Wandering in/to the Rubble-Film," 472.

45. Ibid., 474.

46. The comparison between *Wings* and *Murderers Are among Us* makes even more sense if we think about Sevastopol's condition immediately after the war. With no more than 3 percent of its built structures remaining functional, the city's appearance was in essence like that of Berlin at the time: dominated by ruins, of the kind that became the acting space of German rubble films. If *Murderers* tries to clear away the rubble at the very moment in history when they were pervasive and unavoidable, *Wings* attempts to bring some of them back, in the form of the literal and metaphorical ruins of Chufut-Kale.

5
THE OBDURATE MATTER OF SPACE: KIRA MURATOVA'S *BRIEF ENCOUNTERS*

> I have a preference for the static, but I don't like to disturb the fabric of the screen. . . . I don't like to intrude into that fabric, I try to make the whole scene visible from one point of view. The same relates to my love for the static. I don't like running—what is called the dynamic in a direct sense. I love rhythm, but not sharpened, physical dynamics.
>
> Kira Muratova, "I'm Bored with All That Is Typical"

THE INTERIOR ENVIRONMENT that Kira Muratova creates in *Brief Encounters*, her first independently made film, is strange, to say the least. Overflowing with objects and textures of all kinds—heavily ornamented furniture, kitchenware, bookshelves, wallpaper, curtains, sculptural reliefs, pictures, and much more—her environments monopolize our attention, drawing us away from the people who inhabit and have shaped them. Sometimes these objects appear next to a human figure, doubling the focal point of the image; at other times they alone are presented in prolonged, nearly immobile shots reminiscent of still-life compositions. We can observe this, for instance, in the opening sequence, which ends with an extended, ten-second look at dirty dishes piled in a precarious state of balance in a sink (figure 5.1); or, later in the film, in the composition of a water pitcher and a pendulum clock's chain, whose nearly ephemeral stillness counteracts the two protagonists' futile conversation (figure 5.5b), or in the film's enduring final image of a table set perfectly for two but devoid of people (figure 5.13b).

Even more striking in these spaces are the walls: Their heavy, expansive materiality is repeatedly and adamantly stressed, even when they stand in the background. What is more significant, they dominate some of the most formal

Fig. 5.1 A static composition of dirty dishes. From *Brief Encounters*, 1967.

shots of the film, within which their accentuated flatness and texture often are primary elements. Thus, in the opening shots, the camera lingers for just a bit too long on a segment of an empty white wall, letting everything else, including the protagonist's head, shift to the periphery (figure 5.2a). Similarly, in a later sequence in a bedroom, the camera repeatedly pans over one segment of a wall before resting for a while on another, presenting it as a white, textured nothingness that dominates the frame (figure 5.2b). In yet another sequence, set inside newly built apartments, the white walls of the completely empty rooms become the single focus of the camera's—and the protagonists'—rather charged attention.

Through her insistence on trivial details, obscure fragments, and empty wall surfaces, Muratova subverts the expected hierarchy of what is significant, pulling forward what is usually behind, in between, overlooked. Her tendency to uncover such basic elements of interior space parallels her reductionist cinematic form—the propensity for extended still frames and a frequently shallow, almost planar staging. It is this kind of space that dominates the setting for *Brief Encounters*, whose story is equally spare, built around the seemingly unbridgeable differences between its male and its female protagonists. What

Fig. 5.2a–b The prominence of walls. From *Brief Encounters*, 1967.

stays with us is not the particular content of the repetitive, circular conversations of the film's leads, but rather their inability, on a deeper level, to find common ground; a harmonious balance is sought, but never achieved. The central male figure, played by Vladimir Vysotskii, summarizes the point appropriately, if ironically, at one point in the film: "We are from different tribes. . . . We won't understand each other [because] of our core disagreements." Muratova, however, does not rely on imposed social rules and roles to explain away these differences. Women in particular do not occupy traditional positions in *Brief Encounters*. Neither of the two female protagonists is a wife or a mother, one of them is a prominent city administrator, and both of them move freely between towns and villages, and public and private spaces without being confined to any specific environment. Nevertheless, space is the visual substance of the film, and it is central to the dynamic of irresolution that structures the film, as its matter and materiality persistently and emphatically come to dominate our attention. This chapter examines why it is so. If we understand *Brief Encounters*, in its narrative essentials, as a story of relations between men and women, then what is the meaning of the central place given to spatial matter within it? Can the director's fascination with objects and walls, often over and against the figures who use and inhabit them, be read through the lens of gender as a form of specifically feminist filmic project?[1]

With these questions, the discussion of gender shifts not only from the domain of social policies to the realm of material environment, but—as in the work of Larisa Shepitko—from the represented spaces to the practices of spatial representation. If the central concern of gender politics during the Khrushchev period was about women's broader integration into the nation's public and industrial life and their liberation from domestic duties, *Brief Encounters* takes a profoundly different position on what needs to be addressed and challenged.[2] It suggests that the question at hand is less about the particular spaces that women and men traverse, employ, and inhabit (again, both female protagonists move freely here between all kinds of public and private settings), than it is about *what* is perceived of these spaces, and how. Or, more precisely, is it about how our very encounter and engagement with space might be informed by gender, making palpable the different ways men and women experience and relate to their environments. One reason for such a shift can be found precisely in the centrality of spatial discourse to gender politics in the decade preceding Muratova's work, one that brought attention to a range of problems—from the need to create more public facilities such as children's centers and cafeterias to take the traditional burden off women, to, especially, the reorganization of private spaces so as to allow women to contribute more effectively to society. Lacking in these discussions was a sense of awareness that "woman" was operating here as an object within the conservative, patriarchal structures of Soviet institutions, given no agency to explore how she related to these spaces, what effect they had on her as a subject, and what place she saw for herself in the production of the built environment.

Brief Encounters examines these questions through the exploration of film's form and materiality. It is in the frequent reduction of shots to still-life compositions, or in the evocation of flatness and, as I will argue, the film screen itself that Muratova finds the necessary language to think about gender and space. The feminism of her filmmaking, furthermore, manifests itself in the negation of cinematic spatialities of the period—not just the traditional, classical-style film that uses spaces as backgrounds and containers for action, but also the dynamic, mobile forms of, for instance, panoramic film. As the epigraph to this chapter suggests, movement and dynamism—the concepts that substantially framed Soviet cinematic discourse in the decade leading to the production of *Brief Encounters*—are the things that Muratova explicitly "doesn't like." Instead, her contemplation of gender activates, perhaps necessarily, a very different practice of spatial representation, one in which obscure, random fragments and shallow, immobile surfaces become sites that critically visualize the relationship of the female body to space.

Still Life

Although *Brief Encounters* was released in the year marking the fiftieth anniversary of the Russian Revolution and is set in Odessa, whose "Potemkin steps" were forever immortalized by Sergei Eisenstein as a cinematic symbol of revolutionary struggle, Muratova's film addresses neither topic. Indeed, though political issues are a constant presence in *Brief Encounters*, they are dealt with only anemically and without any apparent concern for their resolution. Instead, private affairs prevail, assembled as a nonchronological sequence of present moments and flashbacks, seen from the perspectives of Valentina, the main protagonist (played by Muratova herself), and the other primary female character, Nadia (played by a rising star of the time, Nina Ruslanova). Repeated flashbacks of these women's brief encounters with Maxim, a flamboyant and elusive geologist, take up fully half the film's running time, and through them we come to learn of his intimate involvement with both women. Maxim has alternately visited Valentina in the city and courted Nadia while in the countryside, where she works in a cafeteria. Attempting to establish a stronger tie, Nadia finds Maxim's address in the city, which is in fact Valentina's apartment, where Nadia thus arrives at the film's opening and from which, having come to terms with Maxim's and Valentina's relationship, she departs at the end. But even as these private encounters overshadow political questions throughout the film, they are themselves arguably of only secondary concern for the filmmaker. Rather, it is her camera's unceasing attention to the spaces in which the film's affairs take place—and to the objects and surfaces that fill them—that dominates our experience of *Brief Encounters*. In addition to Valentina's apartment, where about half the film is set, these spaces include the streets and businesses of the city, Valentina's office, the construction site of a new apartment complex and the still-empty interiors within it, and areas at and around the countryside cafeteria where Nadia worked in the past, before she arrived in the city, and which are thus seen in flashback.[3]

It is in this latter setting that we first encounter Maxim, who emerges gradually from the depth of the landscape, while Nadia watches from the cafeteria's veranda. Seen initially in an extreme long shot, Maxim quickly approaches the foreground, coming into full view two shots later when he steps onto the porch and remains there until the end of the sequence. Set as if on a proscenium, the veranda features a prominent threshold, which separates not only interior from exterior (that is, the built environment from its surrounding landscape), but also the deep space of the landscape traversed by Maxim from the shallow area occupied by Nadia. And although Maxim crosses this threshold with ease, Nadia remains conspicuously on its shallow side—her body aligned with the porch's columns and balanced on its banister edges, yet never moving over into the space beyond. For her, the landscape remains something to look at, not to traverse (figure 5.3).

Something to look at, indeed: after Maxim's initial appearance out of the landscape's depths, the hills and fields assume the form of a painterly backdrop rather than any kind of immersive, all-embracing environment. An extensive trench cuts into the landscape and leads away from the foreground scene, inviting our gaze to follow it into deep space; at the same time, it contrasts with the pointedly planar surfaces that extend on either side. No matter how open, unlimited, and "right there"—right behind the veranda's threshold—this landscape is, it nevertheless feels removed, separated from both our space as viewers and the space of the film's characters. And this separation is made even more noticeable by the multiple banisters of the veranda that frame our view of it.

Thus, the landscape is fundamentally different from the spaces discussed in this book so far, especially the engulfing grand vistas that figured, among others, in panoramic film. This latter space is alluded to in the initial moment of Maxim's appearance but is immediately dispensed with—first framed as an image, and then replaced with the shallow area, assembled theatrically in the foreground of the mise-en-scène. The house, the veranda, and ultimately a simple bland wall serve to counter the illusory depth of the other side—a spatial distinction that is strikingly similar to one that art historian Griselda Pollock

Fig. 5.3 Threshold separating the veranda and landscape. From *Brief Encounters*, 1967.

identified in women's impressionist paintings of the nineteenth century. Pollock argues that the persistent occurrence of barriers in these images, such as balconies, verandas, and embankments, suggests a need on the part of women artists not only to separate public and private (or simply personal) spaces, but also to produce "on a single canvas two spatial systems," in which the feminine was aligned with a more compressed, shallow, and immediate environment and contrasted with what she understands as a masculine space, which is deep, three-dimensional, and distanced.[4] Muratova's sequence generates a similar formal distinction of spaces here, but by comparison with the impressionist paintings of Pollock's analysis, she intensifies even more the compression and flatness of the environment, directing our attention just as much toward these material and representational features as toward her human protagonists.

One element within this spatial economy of the veranda summarizes this distinction perhaps most obviously, while being shown only obliquely. It is a food advertisement poster on the wall that appears repeatedly throughout the sequence, but always only in partial views (figure 5.4a and figure 5.4b). Looking like a still-life composition, it explicitly contrasts with the surrounding landscape: Instead of nature, it shows small household items; instead of depth, simple flatness; and instead of wholeness, a fragmentation. And although Maxim perpetually comes and goes throughout the film, leaving the shallow

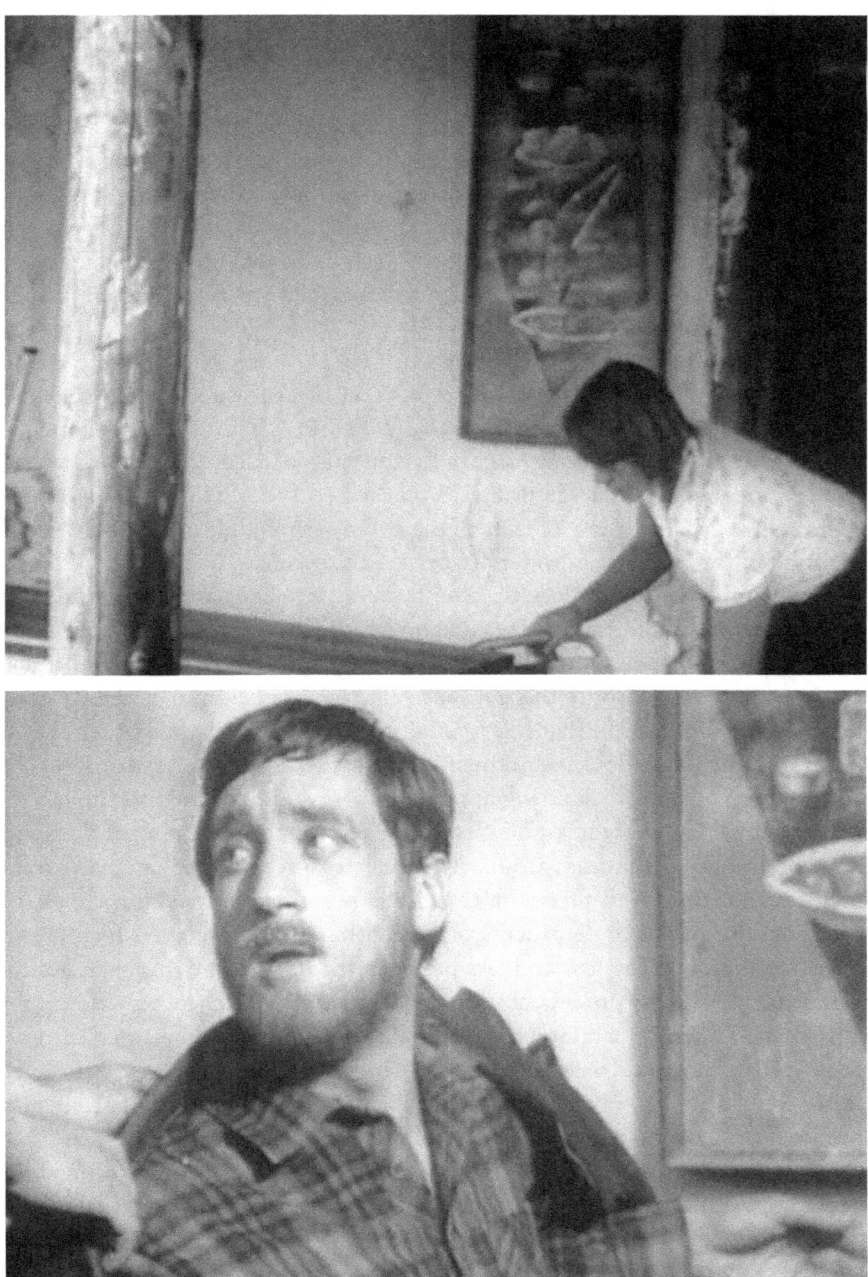

Fig. 5.4a–b Partial views of a food advertisement poster. *From Brief Encounters*, 1967.

space for free, noninhibiting nature, women in the film remain predominantly within the vicinity of the environment embodied in this poster—not necessarily a domestic setting, but one that is limited in depth and motion, and fragmented. The presentation of still life–like images, of both direct and oblique kind, becomes for Muratova nothing less than a method for creating two spatial systems within one sequence or often one shot, moving from a regular, realistic setting to what we might call an aesthetic space, which discards the usual hierarchies among people, objects, and the environment (such as foreground and background, or container and contained), asking instead for their equal consideration.

To observe such a movement at work we can look more closely at the sequence that culminates in the composition of the water pitcher and the chain of the pendulum clock on the wall of Valentina's bedroom. The sequence begins with this room looking essentially normal—a three-dimensional space, lived in and used. While Valentina sits on the bed and Maxim moves around, the camera reveals diverse objects of the room—a pendulum clock, a framed painting of the seashore, a water pitcher on a side table—which first come in to view simply as part of a noticeable but regular decor and then gradually monopolize our attention (figure 5.5a and figure 5.5b). As the camera progressively reduces both the amount of visible space and the depth of its dimensions, getting closer and closer to the wall, the same objects begin to emerge prominently, as a composition that offers an alternative focus for the sequence and organizes our way of looking at the mise-en-scène as a whole. The stillness of the pitcher and the clock string appears now in stark contrast to the movement of the large, embracing figures; the objects' lightness opposes the solid mass of the human bodies; and all of them relate to yet another expansive fragment of the white wall receiving their shadows. The composition elicits, in other words, an elaborate process of perception of lines, shapes, forms, and masses, differentiating less and less between the dead and living matter. The extent to which this process absorbs our attention (which otherwise might have drifted off, not sustained by the repetitive conversation between the two protagonists) becomes particularly staggering as the camera moves to the next shot—outside, in the open, with movement and depth now present again, and an almost liberating return to a regular, loosened-up environment.

Muratova's turn to still-life compositions at the beginning of her film career is striking, as there is little in the Soviet cinema of the period that would obviously prefigure her interest in it. In general, this genre was far from the center of Soviet cultural life in the 1950s and 1960s, probably because the "dead nature" at its core had little to contribute to the most burning questions in the cultural politics of the period—although some academic work on this

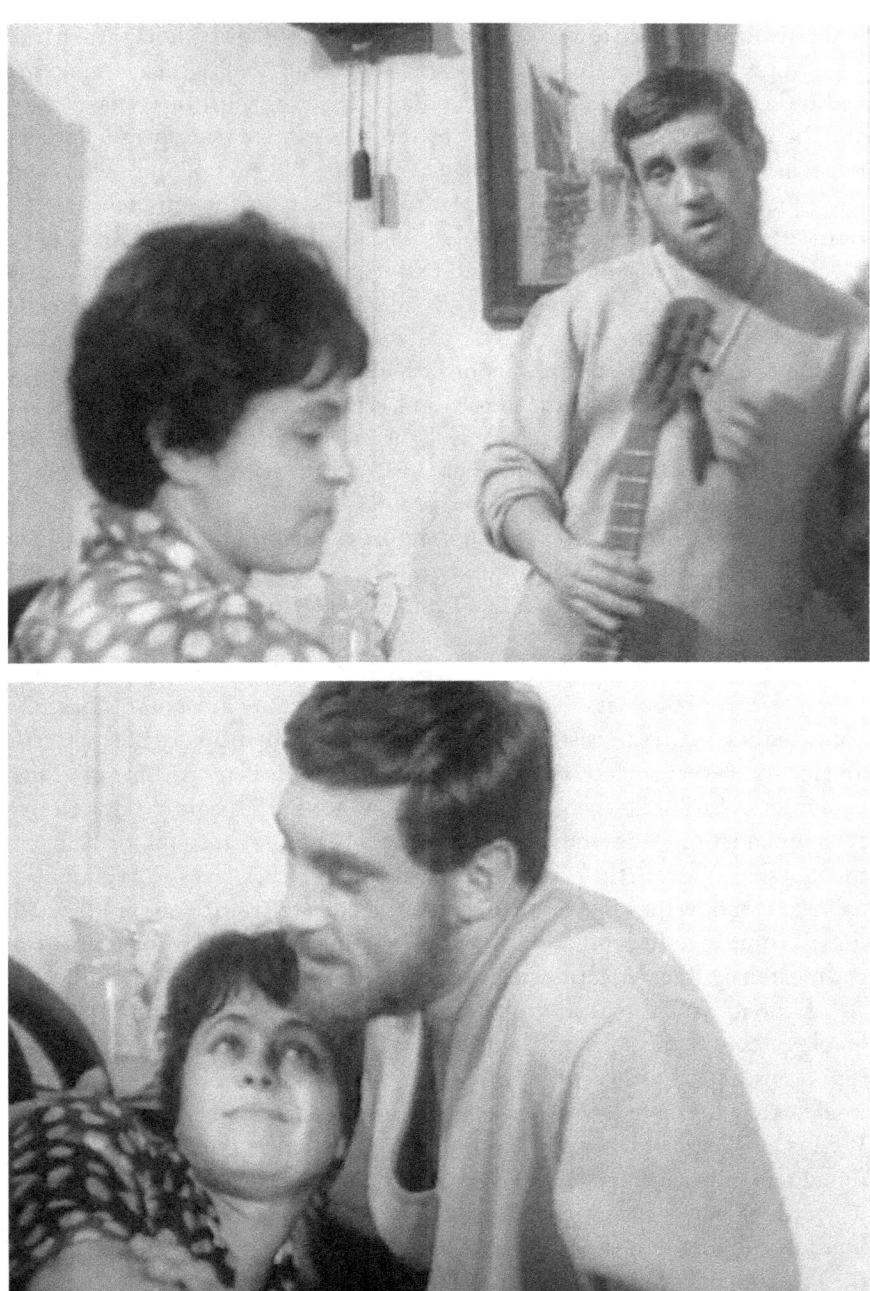

Fig. 5.5a–b The persistence of decorative objects. From *Brief Encounters*, 1967.

painterly form, written toward the end of the 1960s, will provide a useful parallel to Muratova's film aesthetics. But even though still life as an academic genre had little traction, discussions of everyday interior objects, their materiality, and their formal organization within private spaces were widespread. Popular journals were filled with a broad range of still life–like photographs whose intense focus on minute details is similar to Muratova's, although their integration within broader history and ideology is very different from her work.

Consider, for instance, figure 5.6 and its accompanying text from a 1959 issue of *Dekorativnoe iskusstvo SSSR* (*Decorative Arts of the USSR*): "A big, colorful ceramic vase or pitcher and a small metal or glass ashtray are placed on a side table with pull-out drawers or little doors. On the wall above them, a painting is hung, framed in the same wood as the table.... The painting should hang not centrally above the table but slightly to the side. The vase, too, should stand not in the middle but to the right or left of the painting, in order to balance visually the whole compositional group."[5]

As might be evident from the quotation, the purpose of the journal, which was published regularly during the Khrushchev years and beyond, was to offer its readers practical advice on how to create a modern, comfortable, domestic environment, one well suited to the new apartment buildings sprouting up in urban centers at the time. Curtains, carpets, tablecloths, dishes, furniture, and purely decorative objects: Nothing escaped the designer's eye of the journal's contributors, as they persistently drew their readers' attention to the materials and forms of every surface and object that could find its place within Soviet private interiors. What is most remarkable today about the journal's descriptive recommendations is their unmatched scrupulosity. They account for each element of the objects in the image—materials and textures, sizes and volumes—as well as for how the objects are to be positioned in relation to one another. All details come together compositionally, generating a balanced whole, with even the most insignificant features receiving a coherent placement.

Although such texts and photographs do not appear to us today to be ideology-bound, offering as they do seemingly impartial views on the production of aesthetically pleasing homes, at the time this was far from the case. The models they presented—reminiscent of midcentury modernist design in the West—were part of Khrushchev's broader campaign to guide Soviet citizens in matters of taste, introducing them to modern and simple furnishings and decorations that systematically departed from the excessive ornamentalism of Stalinist decades and the petit-bourgeois consciousness associated with it in the subsequent criticism.[6] Khrushchev's agenda, scholars have argued, unfolded in the most intrusive and dogmatic ways. Cultural anthropologist Victor Buchli, for instance, has noted that the campaign "employed normative notions of

Fig. 5.6 Well-balanced interior design. From *Dekorativnoe iskusstvo SSSR*.

good and bad taste along with household advice to regulate behaviour that would lead towards the realization of *byt* [everyday life] reformist socialist goals."[7] The scrupulosity and attention to detail evident in the narratives that accompanied the photographs matched well the political efforts to manage the organization of life behind private walls, making these images the most explicit and encompassing representations of the period's ideology.[8]

The meaning of such photographs is complicated further by the manner in which gender was implicated in the discussions of the new home, which reveal a profound determination not only to influence the public's taste for interior decorations, but also to manage methodically the domestic life of women. Although one could argue that such endeavors were initiated in good faith—in the service of women, as part of a political and feminist drive to ease their domestic chores and integrate them more strongly into the nation's public and economic life—they nevertheless served ultimately to further alienate women precisely from the realm that could provide a space for self-expression. In her discussion of Soviet kitchen design during this period, art historian Susan E. Reid has described the problem thus: "Press reports in the late 1950s indicate that there was a campaign to expand and systematize formal training in domestic science, and to professionalize a domain formerly left to female amateurs in the home: in other words, to foster a shift away from spontaneous, unregulated practices, based on women's traditions, towards conscious, codified, 'scientific' ones, informed by medical, pedagogical and other experts."[9] If we return once more to figure 5.06, we can imagine that the woman, though formally absent, is offered a place within the economy of this image that is as precise and calculated as that of the objects present within it, producing together a perfect, transparent, and rational order where nothing is left to chance.

It is not clear how much attention Muratova paid to these photographs and the discussions surrounding them, although the cultural profusion of the campaign would made them difficult to ignore. One cannot fail to notice in *Brief Encounters*, however (despite a similarly intense focus on the most insignificant details of interior environment), a *lack* of the kind of compositional style advocated on the pages of *Dekorativnoe iskusstvo*. The objects and spaces we find in Valentina's home defy any unity of stylistic description. They can be excessive and austere, ordered and messy at the same time and linked to diverse design histories and places, as if revealing the filmmaker's need to separate this home's interior from a particular historical period or ideology. These spaces avoid being representations of anything, persisting rather in their obdurate materiality and defying any scientific, rational method that would describe them appropriately. Lacking the explanatory transparency that the popular photographs possess, they appear simply significant, but of what is unclear.[10] And they establish a relationship with human figures—mostly female, but sometimes male—that is far from obvious. It is the relationship itself that is elicited here, with both human figures and the environment calling attention to each other through a continual dialogue among forms, volumes, and surfaces.

It is perhaps not accidental that one significant attempt at theorizing the genre of still life—a work produced by a woman artist and art historian, Irina Bolotina, at about the same time that *Brief Encounters* was made—offers a number of parallels to Muratova's visual principles.[11] Bolotina initiated a formalist analysis of the genre (in contrast to a more expected humanist or Marxist-Leninist interpretation, of which there were also some), arguing for a certain "purity" of still life, its autonomy from any "programs" of political or ethical order, as well as from narrative trajectories; the latter, if present at all, appear as something unnecessary and "external" to the actual painting.[12] She writes, "The protagonists here are painted in close-up, so that the gaze can touch them, can evaluate first and foremost their actual material qualities—the relief and texture of the surfaces, the details—as well as their interaction with the environment, their life in the environment. The measurement of the composition in a still life is directed toward the measurement of a small household item, which gives still life a greater sense of intimacy than other genres."[13]

Putting the experience of perception (a process that is phenomenological at its core) at the center of her discussion, Bolotina goes on to describe still life as a key to any painting because it teaches ways of perceiving visual form as such, without the distraction of transient, external stories and ideologies.[14] Perception for her is an ability to evaluate "material qualities" of represented objects through immediacy, tactility, and the evocation of the insignificant—the very elements that are associated in Muratova's film with female spatiality. And it is the focus on the *process* of perception—on looking and sensing at the level of the smallest, most insignificant material fragment—and the absolving of narrative trajectories that comes with it that connect the conceptualization of still life by both women; and this conceptualization separates them from the photographs of *Dekorativnoe iskusstvo*, which sought to guide the perception of such materiality into the larger order of external stories and ideologies.[15]

In the most evocative analysis of still life to date, art historian Norman Bryson similarly argues that the ejection of narrative is one of the genre's major hallmarks, describing it as "the world minus its narratives or, better, the world minus its capacity for generating narrative interest."[16] Bryson takes this assumption further by connecting still life to "rhopography" (as opposed to megalography, or the depiction of "great" things)—an argument that is not discussed in Bolotina's work but one that is essential to Muratova's aesthetic logic. In his book, aptly titled *Looking at the Overlooked*, Bryson explains rhopography in still life thus: "Rhopography (from *rhopos*, trivial objects, small wares, trifles) is the depiction of those things which lack importance, the unassuming material base of life that "importance" constantly overlooks. The categories of megalography and rhopography are intertwined. The concept of importance can arise only by separating itself from what it declares to be trivial and insignificant; importance generates "waste," what is sometimes called the preterite, that which is excluded or passed over. Still life takes on the exploration of what "importance" tramples underfoot. It attends to the world ignored by the human impulse to create greatness."[17]

Brief Encounters is filled with details of *rhopos*, and even explicit waste: not only dirty and broken plates that the camera does not fail to notice, but, more strikingly, the actual space of the living room, the walls of which at one point are completely covered with repurposed newspapers. The grand ideology—we can still get a quick glimpse of it in textual fragments on the wall—turns itself into trash, used-up material that, in fact, *makes* the interior space in this particular sequence (figure 5.7).

But Muratova's rhopographic program stretches further. The multiplication of trivial objects as the film progresses has the peculiar effect of an

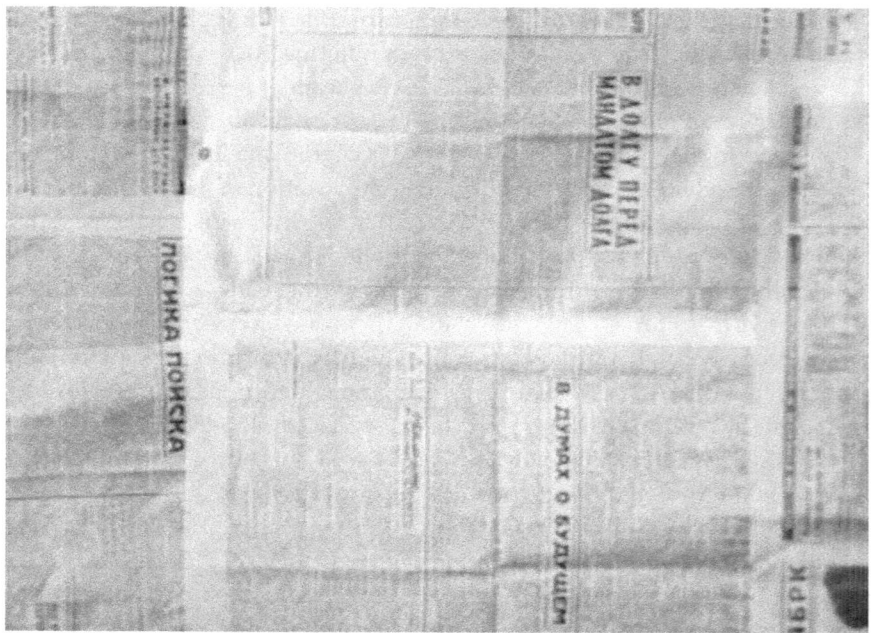

Fig. 5.7 Leftovers of ideology on the interior wall. From *Brief Encounters*, 1967.

Fig. 5.8 The renewal of space through multiplication of objects and surfaces. From *Brief Encounters*, 1967.

epistemological questioning of what, actually, can be known of this interior space, especially in the face of the film's incessant attention to its specific details. In contrast to a proper still-life painting that offers a singular space for examination, Muratova's environment appears to endlessly renew itself, as the camera zeroes in on new objects, places, and surfaces from sequence to sequence, sometimes making rooms we have seen before nearly unrecognizable. We can compare, for instance, the two sequences in Valentina's bedroom—the first with the water pitcher composition (figure 5.5a) and the other with Maxim and Valentina at the mirror (figure 5.8; both sequences might indeed be taking place within the same contiguous fictive time, judging from the protagonists' clothes). They appear so different in scale and configuration, and with such an extreme prominence of different objects in each, that one can only wonder how they were not noticed before. Similarly, at the end of another sequence, we are taken by surprise when encountering the large sculptural relief on a wardrobe (figure 5.10a and figure 5.10b), even though we have visited this room a few times before and must have glimpsed it, even if fleetingly. For all the "greater intimacy" with which the camera lets us contemplate the interiority of

Valentina's house, the house remains something of a fragmented labyrinth. Its parts constantly exceed the whole, which, in turn, resists a mental reconstruction and mapping, remaining relatively fluid and formless despite the camera's constant production of a compositional form. "Overlooking," furthermore, turns into a structural expectation in the process of perception. By the end of the film we have come to understand that while studying something intensely, we inevitably miss something else; because of this, the very immediate proximity of the environment never becomes fully familiar.

Flatness and Screen

Among the most ambiguous visual elements of *Brief Encounters* are the walls and the prominence of their presence, texture, and planarity. Their representation, too, agrees with the visual form of still life: They are shown in close-ups and in stillness, eliciting tactile perception while leaving the narrative aside; only now, the actual composition central to the genre is displaced to the periphery or eliminated altogether, and our attention is directed to what would usually appear in the background of a still life's visible space. If Bryson describes still life's rhopography as an exceptional focus on domestic, trivial objects, then Muratova takes the focus on the unimportant one step further, emphasizing that which has no primary significance, even within the traditions of the genre. The tactile intimacy of still life, the haptic gaze—which, as Emma Widdis has argued, Muratova searches for in her aesthetics in general—acquires here a particular tone.[18] The camera takes our gaze right up to a solid wall for no apparent reason; even as we have a sense of incredible proximity to the wall, we remain obdurately apart from it. Feeling, with our gaze, the texture of its surface does not bring us closer to either appropriating or knowing this space. The result is an encounter but not an understanding; instead, there is a continuous urge to ask why we (and frequently the film's protagonists) are made to stare at, and nearly touch, these wall surfaces. This is perhaps most evident in the shot of Maxim singing in bed in which the wall's white, textured surface behind his head dominates the frame, but, despite its immediacy, seems to block viewers' access to the image (figure 5.9). Such surfaces, as we shall see, are central to Muratova's conceptualization of not only interior but also filmic space, and to her explorations of the relationship between women and the built environment.

Muratova's interest in shallow spaces and planar surfaces—together with her refusal to employ excessive mobility of the camera, or what she calls in this chapter's epigraph "physical dynamics"[19]—suggests a complex restraint in the use of cinematic means. Hers is not simply a rejection of contemporaneous achievements in technology, but a blunter leap backward, intentional or

Fig. 5.9 Viewers face the textured, heavy wall that seems to block entrance into the image. From *Brief Encounters*, 1967.

not, toward the practices of early cinema, in which such shallow, often planar spaces served as a stage for cinematic action. As film scholar Antonia Lant has argued, early film was significantly preoccupied with a spatial contradiction at its own core—one between the absolute flatness of its own medium ("insubstantial, without texture or material") and its ability to represent full, lifelike, and volumetric space.[20] Lant demonstrates that the figure of Egyptian bas-reliefs provided an especially rich ground through which to address early film's developing spatiality. In fact, these reliefs themselves were considered in the contemporaneous art historical discourse in cinematic terms: an art form that actualized a separation of the figure from the background, initiating thus a process of the "animation of the surface."[21] If they were featured in the films at the beginning of the twentieth century as part of a multilayered process of uncovering and conquering of space by cinematic means, they all but disappeared with the emergence of classical narrative form and its insistence on the illusion of three-dimensional realism.[22]

Muratova resuscitates this contradiction by frequently engaging the flatness of the wall as a simple, two-dimensional surface that counterbalances volumetric figures and movement around it. One staging of such a contradiction takes place in a prolonged sequence in Valentina's house in which, fortuitously echoing Lant's argument, the aforementioned appearance of an oversized sculptural relief takes place. Set in the living room, the sequence focuses on Valentina's visitor Zinaida, who, after having circled around the room, pauses in a corner, right against one side of a wardrobe. As she continues the conversation from this rather awkward position, the frontal close-up of her head contrasts with the profile of a head in relief protruding dominantly from the adjacent wardrobe (figure 5.10a). Not only do the two almost equally sized heads vaguely resemble each other (critics have noted Muratova's propensity toward unmotivated isomorphy of forms), but they also resonate in terms of their positions relative to their respective backgrounds.[23] The relief is, precisely, a relief, existing on the threshold of two- and three-dimensionality, contiguous with the flat surface from which it emerges and yet also present volumetrically, sculpturally, and all-too-explicitly within the surrounding space. But Zinaida's figure, too, while unequivocally three-dimensional, is made to appear as if *of* the wall of the wardrobe by the explicit frame of the lines within which she moves; her figure completes the separation from the surface that was initiated by the relief, thus fully enacting an "animation of the surface."

But this is not all. As this shot is replaced with the next, and Zinaida turns slightly to stand with the walls of the room now in the background, another likeness emerges: the pattern of the wallpaper covering the living room looks like an abstracted form of the relief itself and of Zinaida—their general shapes replicating each other (figure 5.10b). These shots invite us to perceive the three forms regressively: moving from the volumetric, mobile figure of Zinaida to the partial three-dimensionality of the relief to the flat, still surface of the wall, whose abstract repetitive pattern has no claim to perspective or depth.

A comparable argument can be made about the sequence of Maxim singing in the bedroom, which relays a similar tripartite structure: an expansive white wall supporting an obtrusive headboard, which in turn supports Maxim's head (figure 5.9). The oval shape of his head is integrated so perfectly into the center of the board's ornamental curves that it looks like an animated element of the headboard's relieflike form resting against the wall's flat surface. And the same occurs again in the sequence of Nadia's exploration of the newly built apartments' empty spaces. As she solitarily enters the room, she moves right away to its large wall, first gently touching it and then slightly pressing herself onto it, as if wanting to merge with its surface (figure 5.11a). The light streaming onto her body from an invisible window creates a prominent shadow—another form of relief?—that responds to the motions of her body. In all these sequences, Muratova seeks to restore a tension similar to the one present in early cinema, only in reverse. Instead of contemplating how to represent realist space in the face of film's inherent flatness, she is focused on reviving this flatness precisely at a moment in history when film (especially with the development of cinematic panoramas) professed to conquer—and possess—space more than ever before.

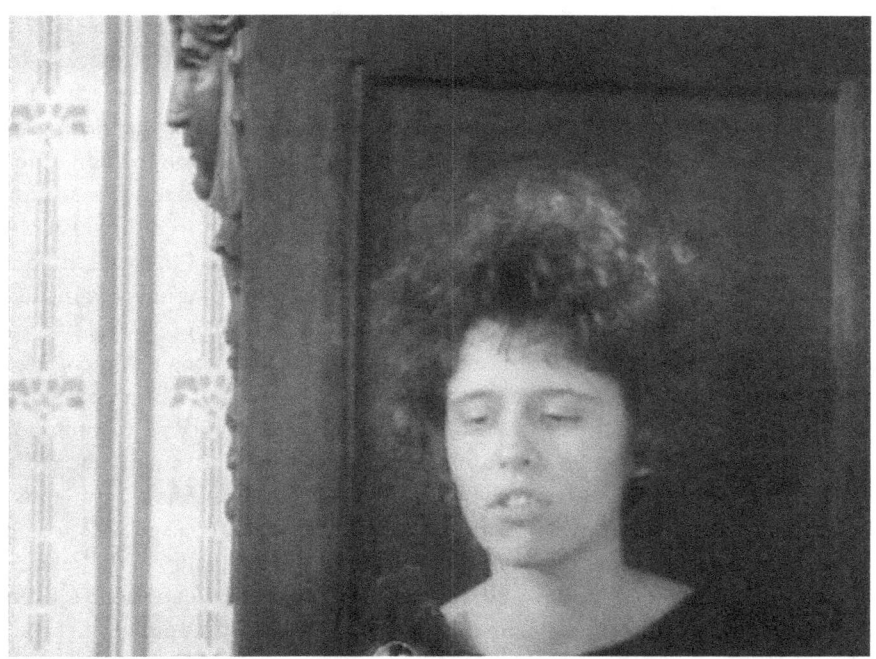

Fig. 5.10a–b From volumetric fullness to static flatness. From *Brief Encounters*, 1967.

Muratova's formal preoccupation with the materiality and flatness of the wall finds a significant parallel in the architectural discourse of the period. In a discussion of the kind of monumental art that interacts most effectively with new architecture—which engaged, as discussed in chapter 3, basic forms and transparent materials—critic S. Zemtsov drew special attention to contemporary developments in the art of murals. In the past, he argued, interior murals in public buildings tended toward illusionism, creating a three-dimensional space with painted skies and landscapes that dematerialized the wall, in fact "destroyed" it. The need for such illusionism, however, completely vanished with the proliferation of glass-curtain walls, which allow views to real-life exterior vistas. For Zemtsov, "Contemporary architecture does not recognize illusionism. It operates with real volumes and real spaces.... Contemporary painting does not need the destruction of the walls' materiality.... Contemporary architecture is built to a certain extent on contrasts: a transparent, glass exterior separation is counteracted by the solid interior wall. And a mural must substantiate this wall by every means."[24] One of the major goals of wall art, he thus suggests, is to make the materiality and two-dimensionality of the surface from which it emerges visible and amenable to senses and experience. Even more striking, he finds the best historical model for Soviet monumental art in the reliefs of ancient Egypt, precisely because they "emphasized well the materiality of geometrically simple forms and volumes, which is necessary for the character of contemporary architecture."[25]

In *Brief Encounters*, Muratova follows a similar logic—generating representation that would emphasize the materiality and two-dimensionality of the surface from which it emerges, counteracting its own illusionism. Thus we can make a shift here from walls as a basic, structural element of a dwelling to walls as an analog for the screen itself. The idea and form of the screen, indeed, appear to be of utter significance to Muratova's thinking about film.[26] Returning once more to this chapter's epigraph, most striking are the director's words on, precisely, the film screen: "I don't like to disturb the fabric of the screen," and repeated again, "I don't like to intrude into that fabric." Not just the screen, but its fabric (*tkan'*). Muratova seeks to preserve—indeed, to heighten—the screen's materiality, the presence of the thing whose sole purpose is to disappear in the service of representation, to be effaced in order to generate a copy of real, functional space. Muratova again reverses here the spatial logic of early cinema, seeking to give substance to something that is "insubstantial," to repeat Lant's description. She also inverts the developments of panoramic film, which sought to create an ever more complex apparatus in order to conceal the screen's own presence. Its elaborate materiality had to be removed from perception—rendered rhopographic, one could say—in order to impose the grandiosity of

Soviet space, and time, on the viewers.[27] But Muratova's reversal raises the question of why, and how, one would want to preserve the *matter* of the screen when it, by necessity, interferes with and distorts the projected image.

It is in relationship to this question that we can begin to understand Muratova's project more specifically in gendered terms. She undertakes a kind of all-inclusive excavation of elemental materiality that constitutes space—domestic and cinematic—and places this process within a woman's house, where contested encounters of gender are recurrently played out, and the possibility of a just balance is never realized. Thus, if the problem of gender is to be related to the problem of space in *Brief Encounters*, it has to happen on the level of the material constitution of the environment and its perception. One way to understand this relation, I propose, is through the concept of *chora*—a term that reaches back to Plato but has been richly appropriated in contemporary feminist writing, especially, for the purposes of this analysis, by Luce Irigaray.

In the most general terms, for both Plato and Irigaray, *chora* designates a kind of receptacle—a space—that is necessary for visible, identifiable material forms to emerge, but which, in the process, has to efface its own presence. Architectural philosopher Elizabeth Grosz, in her interpretation of *chora* in Plato's *Timaeus*, relevantly refers to it as a "screen": "Neither something nor yet nothing, *chora* is the condition for the genesis of the material world, the screen onto which is projected the image of the changeless Forms, the space onto which the Form's duplicate or copy is cast, providing the point of entry, as it were, into material existence. The material object is not simply produced by the Form(s), but also resembles the original, a copy whose powers of verisimilitude depend upon the neutrality, the blandness, the lack of specific attributes of its 'nursemaid.'"[28]

Although it would be reductive to fully equate the cinematic screen with the concept of *chora*, there is nevertheless a significant correspondence between the two: namely, the insubstantial and immaterial surface, whose lack of qualities, "its neutrality and blandness," allows perfect copies to come into being. More significant, Grosz arrives at this conclusive statement after isolating a striking analogy in Plato's writing. On the one hand, *chora* is a qualityless channel that is necessary for the emergence of all material things from ideal forms; on the other, it is the maternal body as a "nameless, formless incubation," the purpose of which is, similarly, to bring matter into the world.[29] It is this nearly seamless conversion of *chora* from a general receptacle to a female body that opens a space for feminist analysis.

In her 1984 work *An Ethics of Sexual Difference*, Irigaray questions whether it is possible to sustain any sociopolitical advances in women's rights without laying "foundations different from those on which the world of men is constructed."[30] The balance between genders, in other words, cannot be changed only on the basis of written laws. What needs to be changed is the very way we understand the foundations of culture, of which space and time are the principal constituents.[31] Although Irigaray is not explicitly concerned with the built environment, her analysis, as Grosz noted, proceeds through metaphors of dwelling and habitation.

Dwelling begins with the maternal body—an original place from which human life emerges, to which it remains indebted, and which continues to be significant in the course of life. Men, Irigaray suggests, while incapable of separating themselves from this original place, simultaneously deny its significance for the production of their discourse and their culture. This denial necessitates "the endless construction of a number of substitutes for his prenatal home ... [a]gain and again, taking from the feminine the tissue and texture of spatiality."[32] In this rather violent rhetoric of the production of space, we find a suggestion that material traces of the female body/space live on, appropriated without acknowledgment, dispossessed from the original owner, and ceaselessly operating as "guardians" that delineate and form male identity.

Women, according to Irigaray's logic, thus *are* space, but they themselves don't *have* one. Made to operate as an elemental, but invisible and unrecognized, framework for men and their identity—as, precisely, *chora*—they have no chance to relate, independently and meaningfully, to their own bodies and to explore and establish their own spatiality. "The maternal-feminine remains the *place separated from 'its' own place*, deprived of 'its' place."[33] The estrangement from their own bodies is also an estrangement from the surrounding environment, which fails to function for women as a meaningful envelope to help shape their being. Without having a space of their own, women are left in a constant state of homelessness, of wandering, while driven to inhabit "wrong envelopes" created by themselves and by men. Irigaray's rhetoric relates indirectly to the spatial and gender discourse of the Soviet Union in the 1950s and 1960s, which actively sought to organize domestic (feminine) spaces anew, but ultimately only to reinstate them as cultural "foundations on which the world of men is constructed."[34]

To uncover, to make sensuous, intelligible, and meaningful that which is usually expelled, repressed, or overlooked: we see that at work in the shots of empty walls between the objects they support, in the fabric of the film screen on which the diversity of visual forms appears.[35] The tendency of *Brief Encounters* to dig up the material forms of origins—to substantiate *chora*—stretches from dwellings and filmic spaces to the female body as well. Nowhere are all these elements folded into each other as simply and explicitly as in the sequence

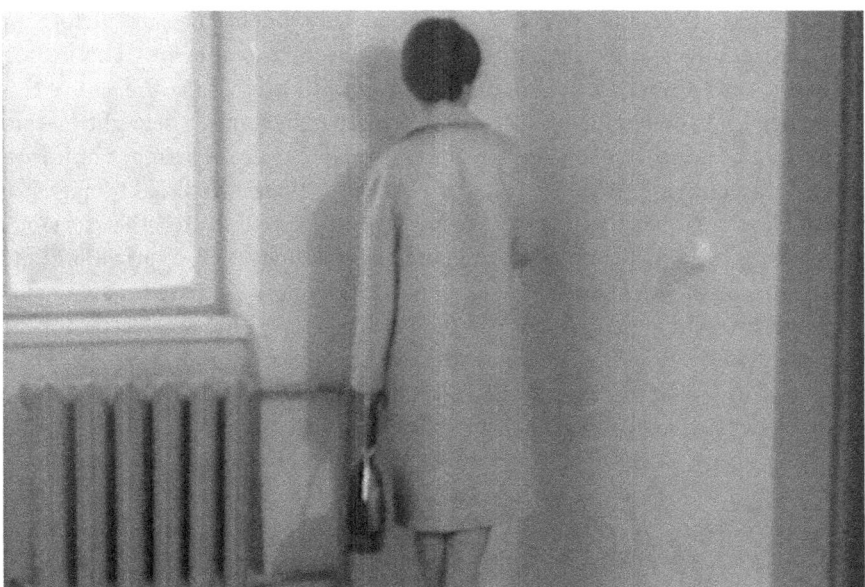

Fig. 5.11a–b Women's charged encounters with empty white walls. From *Brief Encounters*, 1967.

showing the empty apartments, through which both female protagonists pass with an almost metaphysical sense of awe (figure 5.11a and figure 5.11b).[36] The spacious white room, filled only with light, that Nadia enters embodies a kind of pure space: a dwelling before it becomes one; a cinema, at the moment of film's emergence; and a place that encourages a reciprocity between its own materiality and that of the female body. Let us elaborate on these. The space is staged cinematically: When Nadia enters, she immediately approaches the wall onto which the light is projected from an invisible window. As she moves along the wall, first touching, then gently pressing herself against it, her body forms a shadow—an imprint of herself that animates the surface. The projection serves here more to illuminate precisely the fabric of the screen/wall rather than to allow another, illusionary space to emerge. It is Nadia's soft touch, too, that draws our attention to it—a touch that is nonimmersive, nonpossessive, one that does not disturb but announces, makes the surface come into being. And conversely, her intuitive urge to imprint herself onto this primary space can be understood as a way of sensing her own body through an exercise of cinematic self-reproduction.[37]

Valentina, strikingly, performs a very similar passage. First, she touches the wall, which now leaves an imprint on *her* body (the wet paint that marks her fingers will later be transferred onto Zinaida's leg during another random moment of touch); and later, she contemplatively touches her face before extending her fingers toward the running water, as the camera painstakingly follows her hand's slow motion along the white wall. It is also at the end of this sequence that the female body, for the first time, becomes a straightforward point of a conversation. As both women are leaving the apartment building, Nadia suddenly asks Valentina if she (Valentina) perhaps should have children. Having gotten no definitive response, she goes on to tell the story of a fifty-year-old woman giving birth to triplets. The suggestion clearly alludes to Nadia's sense of Valentina's homelessness (despite her elaborate home), which has been brought up in various ways before that point in the film. And thus she brings up pregnancy and motherhood, speaking of the original female space— with triplets, in fact, an excess of it—as if to suggest that in order to have a true home, Valentina needs to get in touch with her own space.[38] This conversation happens immediately after the women's charged encounters with the pure, material nothingness of the white walls.[39]

The relationship between the built environment, the cinematic screen, and the female body grows even more prominent in Muratova's next film, the 1972 *Long Goodbyes*, to which I turn here briefly. In this film with strong Freudian overtones, motherhood is a contentious issue, as the long goodbyes of the title speak of a son's endless process of separation from his mother—of his desperate attempts to vacate the small, dark room in which the two of them live (and which invites an easy analogy to a womb). Occasionally, this room, filled with an unspeakable number of random objects, transforms into a protocinematic space. In one sequence, for instance, the son turns on a projector to look at slides of strangely artificial images of plants and animals. In another, the mother gazes at slides documenting extended meetings between her son and his estranged father, of which she had not been aware. Projected onto the entrance door and the adjacent wall, the slides become animated when people walk through the door or pass through the tunnel of projected light. That is, their movement in the actual space of the room is perceived as movement within the space of the images (figure 5.12a and figure 5.12b).

This process is uncanny, not only because of the perfection of this bodily integration that is able to make still images move, but also because the matter that functions as screen—the door, the wall, and especially the bodies—remains present in all their unassimilated materiality. The matter of these "screens," in fact, is illuminated even more in the process of projection, continuing to persist, to be present, while allowing "copies" to emerge. Even as this matter serves as the basis for projection, it simultaneously conflicts with it, altering its content. And although both mother and son occasionally fulfill this function as the screen, it is especially the mother who is drawn into this position. Looking at the photographs of her son and his father, she approaches and touches them, the dark silhouette of her upper body imprinted into the world from which she has conspicuously been eliminated (figure 5.12b; the dark circle in the lower half of the screen is the figure of the mother). As an all-too-visible screen, she is reinstated as *matter* in the world of the son and the father—as, precisely, inerasable "tissue and texture of spatiality," in which both men agreeably reside.[40] If *chora*—as a female body and as a women's position in the production of phallocentric space and culture—is a qualityless, erasable screen, as Grosz terms it, then Muratova seeks to lend it the most substantiated, grounded expression possible, for which the cinematic screen serves as a material and metaphoric analogy.

In the concluding chapter of *Looking at the Overlooked*, Bryson argues that the genre of still life needs to be understood through the relationship of gender to the domestic space; its strangeness is the male artist's foreignness to, and fascination with, the spaces and objects of the feminine environment. He reads this relationship through Freud's concept of the *unheimlich* (uncanny), which directly relates to the maternal body, "the former *Heim* [home] of all human beings, . . . the place where each of us lived once upon a time and in the beginning."[41] The process of separation from the maternal body, as Bryson discusses it via psychoanalysis, is never complete. A man's emergence as an

Fig. 5.12a–b Walls as cinematic screen. From *Long Goodbyes*, 1971.

autonomous subject is eternally plagued by the desire to return to the primary place of origin, to the enclosed, immersive space provided by the mother. To master this threat to masculine subjectivity, men claim as theirs "another kind of space, away from that cocoon and its fascinations; a space that is definitively and assuredly *outside*, behind a protective barrier, a space where the process of identification with the masculine can begin and succeed."[42] Still life embodies this kind of space for the male artist, in which formal representation of the domestic environment (its extreme aestheticization, above all) betrays both the nostalgia for the lost space of the mother and an extraordinary desire to rebuild it in terms compatible with masculine identity. Bryson identifies a fundamental difference between the still-life paintings of male and female artists. If, for the former, the space of still life remains estranged and nonparticipatory, "incapable of being occupied from the inside," for the latter, the aesthetic and the domestic do not conflict, "the hand which balances the formal composition is also able to reach out and make tea."[43]

In the emphasis on the repression of the maternal body and its resurfacing within another, external space as an unacknowledged but inerasable presence, Bryson's analysis of the *unheimlich* in relation to still life supports in many ways Irigaray's discussion of *chora*. But what distinguishes Irigaray is her departure from the mystification of the space of the maternal-feminine and a philosophical and pragmatic questioning of its just reintegration into cultural discourse and its spatiality. Muratova's work is concerned with a similar questioning. Her spaces and still-lifes, emerging from a female point of view and experiences, betray perhaps a fascination with—but not nostalgia for or a mystification of—domesticity: They are full of hands, indeed, to reach out and make tea. They have no drive to be elevated to the representational world compatible with masculinity—that is, rational and whole, ordered, without excess—but rather, as I have argued, tend to disintegrate into material fragments that defy meaning, conceptualization, and mapping. Muratova's film relegates us to the level of these fragments, back corners, and in-between surfaces and asks us to keep them in mind, or within touch, as we attempt to reconstruct this space—of the house, and of the entire story—in its totality. They remain assertive and visible, simultaneously generating and resisting the whole. And it is through the perception of *this* difference—between part and whole, matter and form—that *Brief Encounters* initiates a process of thinking about space and *sexual* difference.

The film ends with a nearly static shot of a still-life composition. What precedes it is a sequence showing the detailed process of its production. And what surrounds it contextually is a flux of departures and arrivals: Maxim is expected to appear at any moment to celebrate, conciliatorily, Valentina's birthday; Valentina just left because of work obligations; and Nadia, reconciled to the

Fig. 5.13a–b Empty space at the heart of the final composition. From *Brief Encounters*, 1967.

situation, is finally leaving the house as well, though it is not clear to where exactly. Before her final exit, she meticulously sets the table for two, in anticipation of the couple's meal. Plates, silverware, glasses, bottles, and a plate of fruit: They fill the naked geometry with which the shot began with a sense of a perfect order and a feminine "touch." Having finished with the table, Nadia puts on her boots, grabs an orange from the fruit plate, and leaves, while the camera, accompanied by an upbeat, punctuating music, surveys the room in one last long, circular take. It reveals, as always, old and new objects while striding by the walls with the now familiar wallpaper; it passes by the window while catching a last glimpse of Nadia walking outside—integrating her body into the rhythm of its own movement and making her virtually a fleeting, ephemeral part of the interior composition. It returns its view then back to the table, where it pauses until the film's very end, equating the screen once more with a flattened image, with objects appearing suspended *on* it as much as placed *within* it (figure 5.13a and figure 5.13b).

The viewer has plenty of time to dwell on this last composition, having just observed the process of its making—completed by a woman whose traces are all but gone from this final mise-en-scène. Its neat symmetry offers a hopeful picture of Valentina and Maxim's balanced future, but this balance remains of a different nature for us, the viewers, than it will be for the two protagonists. This is because this balance rests on the presence of absence—on the orange that is gone from the plate but has left a distinct void right below the center of the image (figure 5.13a). This empty, negative space that has no substance—and even more explicitly, no shadow—carries nevertheless an indexical trace of Nadia's gesture, impregnated with the last touch she made in the creation of this space. But this trace is neither tangible nor visible, nor is it knowable as such. It is waiting to be overlooked, to persist outside the order of signification for any potential visitor, including Valentina and Maxim, who would see in this arrangement of oranges a complete set. It is only the film's viewers, with their newly trained perception for details, who are invited to touch this emptiness with their gaze and to "evaluate it for its material qualities," to which Nadia's figure will remain indispensable. As a result, this blind spot can be seen not only as part of a concluding shot of the finished story, but also the kernel of a new beginning: the invisible yet primary focus in the organization of space that would allow us to reconsider the meaning of a gendered, balanced, and social whole.

Notes

1. The issue of Muratova's feminist film practice—within both Soviet and international contexts of the 1960s—has been addressed before. See especially Lilya Kaganovsky, "Ways of Seeing."

Kaganovsky discusses the film's nonlinear structure, its explicit breakup with cinematic conventions of female representation, and its articulation of "desire as a circulation around the always missing piece" (490) as hallmarks of the Soviet counter, and feminist, cinema of the 1960s. Susan Larsen addresses the issue of the gaze in Muratova's film, arguing that the film's structure disables viewers' identification with the male gaze (Larsen, "Korotkie vstrechi/Brief Encounters").

2. For wide-ranging discussions of Khrushchev's policies on women, as well as the organization of women's life and their experiences of it, see Ilič, Reid, and Attwood, *Women in the Khrushchev Era*.

3. On Muratova's relationship to Odessa, where she was sent after her studies at the All-Union State Institute of Cinematography (VGIK), see Abdulaeva, *Kira Muratova: Iskusstvo kino* [Kira Muratova: The Art of Cinema], 203–8.

4. Pollock, *Vision and Difference*, 81.

5. Baiar, "Dekorativnye predmety v kvartire," 46.

6. Indeed, the introduction to the 1966 book *The Culture of the Lived Interior* explicitly stated, "the program of the Communist Party of the USSR allocates a great role to the arts in the affairs of social transformation and the building of communism, opening for it grandiose perspectives—to spiritualize the work of the people, to decorate their everyday life, to introduce beauty in all areas of Soviet people's activities. The honorable and responsible role falls onto the decorative and applied arts, which are connected to the society's productive activity in the tightest and most immediate way, acting as a bridge between its material and spiritual world" (Kriukova, *Kultura zhilogo interiera*, 5).

7. Buchli, "Khrushchev, Modernism," 162.

8. Buchli reminds us of the significance the domestic realm occupied within the cultural shifts occurring immediately after the 1917 Revolution, when domesticity was associated generally with the prerevolutionary petit-bourgeois consciousness that had to be eradicated in order to build socialism. Much of this rhetoric, Buchli suggests, reemerged after Stalin's death: taste education began to play a central role in the modification of "bourgeois" behavior, in an attempt to realign the materiality of everyday life with the values of socialism (ibid., 161–76).

9. Reid, "The Khrushchev Kitchen," 299. The desire for efficiency, Reid demonstrates, was extensive and far-reaching. She writes further, "the aim was to eliminate disordered or irrational movement in the kitchen so that every movement was as efficient and productive as possible: to replace chaos, spontaneity and waste by modern efficiency and conscious order" (303). Christine Varga-Harris complicates the issue further by discussing the dynamics between the state, women, *and* men in regard to home design (Varga-Harris, "Homemaking and the Aesthetic and Moral Perimeters").

10. Muratova's material presentation of objects can be understood as staging a contradiction between narration and description, which is central to the still-life genre. If narration is associated with time progression and meaning, description is associated with a pause in the narrative time flow and the accumulation of details with no apparent meaning. See discussion of still life in regard to narration in Blanchard, "On Still Life." Descriptive representations are generally problematic for Soviet aesthetic practices, precisely because they make ideology and meaning nontransparent. This point of view can be seen for instance in the criticism of Alain Resnais and in Alain Robbe-Grillet's film *Last Year in Marienbad*, in which the Soviet critics saw the obsessive, detailed, and mechanical reconstruction of reality as working against the clarity of meaning, causing a "de-ideologization and refusal of reality" (Vaisfeld, "Ne obobshchaite konei," 109).

11. A collection of Bolotina's writings was published in Moscow in 1989; it does not date individual essays but states that she wrote them between 1967 and 1982. Her conceptualization of still life remains more or less the same from one text to another, allowing us to make an assumption that her ideas about the genre quoted here had been formed already in the 1960s. See Bolotina, *Problemy russkogo i sovetskogo natiurmorta*.

12. Bolotina, *Problemy russkogo i sovetskogo natiurmorta*, 17. Marxist-Leninist interpretations of the genre of still life can be found in Pruzhan and Pushkarev, *Natiurmort v russkoi i sovetskoi zhivopisi*.

13. Ibid., 18.

14. It is worth noting that a similar account of still life appears also in Soviet avant-garde discussions, specifically in Nikolai Tarabukin's 1923 essay "From Easel to the Machine," in which he writes, "At the same time [the French impressionists'] work was directed toward freeing painting from a content dependent upon ideology or subject matter, and from the 'literary story' which usually prevailed over form in traditional canvases" (Tarabukin, 136).

15. It is not surprising that Muratova's film was heavily criticized for lacking a "central idea," a "general line," and for its fragmentariness. See Kovarskii, "Chelovek i vremia," 50. See also the archival file on *Brief Encounters*, with accusations that Muratova lacks a clear ideological evaluation and suggestions that that she needs a more directly stated line of thought ("Delo fil'ma 'Korotkie vstrechi,'" 11).

16. Bryson, *Looking at the Overlooked*, 60.

17. Ibid., 61.

18. Widdis, "Muratova's Clothes, Muratova's Textures, Muratova's Skin." The focus of Widdis's argument is the tactility of the material environment in Muratova's cinema and the evocation of haptic perception in viewers, which she investigates in relationship to subjectivity and affect.

19. Muratova.

20. Lant, "Haptical Cinema," 45.

21. Ibid., 55.

22. We can find a comparable dynamics of flatness and depth in early Russian cinema, particularly in the films of Evgeny Bauer, where the perception of depth is achieved through an extreme layering of objects and surfaces, producing an illusion of "never-ending space." See DeBlasio, "Choreographing Space, Time, and 'Dikovinki.'"

23. Abdulaeva, *Kira Muratova*, 227–39. Abdulaeva discusses various manifestations of the multiplication and repetitions of forms in Muratova's œuvre, of people, words, gestures, and objects, the meaning of which, Abdulaeva suggests, cannot be systematized in any universal way. Although they invite interpretation, they sometimes are nothing more than a "semantic trick."

24. Zemtsov, "Poiski novogo v monumentalnom iskusstve," 24. Another, more general, discussion that addresses the issue of the walls in new housing constructions—which, freed from Stalinist decorative excesses, inevitably emphasized their own "flatness, texture, and color"—can be found in Volodin, "O nekotorykh osobennostiakh razvitiia sovetskoi arkhitektury na sovremennom etape," 8.

25. Zemtsov, "Poiski novogo v monumentalnom iskusstve," 24.

26. With her interest in the materiality of the screen, Muratova extends the tradition of Russian and Soviet filmmakers (as well as theater directors and theoreticians) interested in the distinct presence of the screen in film perception. Robert Bird, in his analysis of Andrei Tarkovsky's screen dynamics, discusses the Russian–Soviet genealogy of thinking of the screen "as a membrane that facilitates communication between visible and invisible realms" (Bird, *Andrei Tarkovsky*, 79).

27. Evsei Goldovskii discusses at length the technological possibilities of eliminating the visibility, the presence, of the screen in panoramic films. See Goldovskii, *Ot nemogo kino k panoramnomu*, 50–51.

28. Grosz, *Space, Time, and Perversion*, 115.

29. Ibid.

30. Irigaray, *An Ethics of Sexual Difference*, 6.

31. My analysis here focuses primarily on issues of space, but time too is distinctly problematized in the work of both Muratova and Shepitko. As Lilya Kaganovsky has thoroughly demonstrated,

the breakup of temporal linearity became a significant aspect of Soviet women's cinema: "Time no longer flows in one direction (always toward a clear utopian future), but is halted, frozen, rewound, fragmented, and erased" (Kaganovsky, "Ways of Seeing," 498). More broadly, Benjamin M. Sutcliffe discusses the fragmentariness of time as a hallmark of women's prose of the Thaw period, arguing that "women's temporality is fragmented, cyclical, and self-erasing" and also "ateleological." Compellingly, he connects this temporality to space by suggesting that it is "a temporal equivalent of the room of one's own whose absence Virginia Woolf laments" (Sutcliffe, *The Prose of Life*, 38, 39).

32. Irigaray, *An Ethics of Sexual Difference*, 11.

33. Ibid., 10, emphasis in the original.

34. Nowhere is the failure of Khrushchev's policies to substantiate any lasting changes in the position of women better described than in the writings of Tatiana Mamonova, one of the most prominent Soviet feminists of the post-Stalinist generation. As she noted, "it is not difficult to write into the constitution Articles 35 and 53 guaranteeing the equality of women; it is considerably more difficult to realize this in practice" (Mamonova, *Women and Russia*, xviii). .In her (and her fellow feminists') discussions of the position of women in the Soviet Union, and of women's consistent subjugation to the world of men, Mamonova shares a good deal with Irigaray's thinking, although speaking not from a theoretical, but from a purely practical and experiential point of view. On the history of Mamonova's feminist efforts, and the resistance to her truly feminist pursuits that began already in the 1960s, see Ruthchild, "Sisterhood and Socialism."

35. Zara Abdulaeva refers to a curious quote by Muratova, describing her encounter with costume designer Rustam Khamdaev, who apparently helped develop her fascination with exposing the invisible foundation of that which is exposed and visible to the eye: "When he told me that a necklace should not be filled with jewels but should allow the thread to be visible in some places, it was for me like a revelation, like an apple for Newton. . . . And I thought: this is it, how easy it is to show the construction of the world—that jewels, that is, are put together on a thread." Muratova herself describes this event as a milestone for her interest in costumes, and for decorations more generally. Although this meeting took place in 1976, this logic of "the construction of the world," as she puts it, is present already in her first films, although perhaps more tentatively (Abdulaeva, *Kira Muratova*, 209). Muratova gave a somewhat different account in a roundtable discussion, Polit.ru, July 29, 1999, available online at http://kira-muratova.narod.ru/into014.html. Emma Widdis also refers to this quote, to make an apt conclusion, which parallels mine, that "Her surfaces are there, one might suggest, in order to conjure up what they conceal" (Widdis, "Muratova's Clothes").

36. This sequence has an interesting precursor in Soviet cinema: Lev Kulidzhanov's widely popular and highly praised 1957 feature *The House I Live In* (*Dom v kotorom ia zhivu*). Set in Moscow in 1935, the film opens with a series of scenes showing people moving into a newly constructed apartment building and acting like Muratova's protagonists. They test the presence of water in the pipes and contemplate extensively the rooms' clean white walls. One of the protagonists, Lida, enters the room and looks radiantly at its walls, full of expectations for her future life with her husband, a geologist. As the film unfolds, we see this space turning into a personal prison: pleasant and clean, full of ornaments and decorations produced by Lida, it is of no interest to her husband, who is almost always absent, gone on geological expeditions. The initial emphasis on empty spaces, the dynamics between Lida and her husband, and the focus on the material objects that fill the room suggest a direct lineage to Muratova's film. But if Kulidzhanov's sequence did play a role in the creation of *Brief Encounters*, it would be as a critical point of departure, a place from which Muratova's interrogation of the materiality of space—the walls, the ornaments—would begin in relation to gender.

37. Muratova's interest in the materiality of the film screen offers a significant contribution to the discussions of the cinematic screen in relation to gender and feminist filmmaking. Judith Mayne has provided one of the earliest studies in this regard, examining the film screen as a potentially disruptive and ambiguous figure in classical Hollywood films. See Mayne, *The Woman at the Keyhole*.

38. Mikhail Iampolski has recently argued that Valentina's house embodies, above all, a place of absence (Iampolski, *Muratova: opyt kinoantropologii*), "a space where absence, emptiness, not-fullness manifest itself with a special power" (20). Iampolski connects this absence with the absent figure of Maxim, who never enters the house in the film's "present," and, more generally, with the sense of nonfreedom that the house communicates. He furthermore understands the sequences of wall touching as directly connected to the absence of Maxim: "the whole permanence [*prochnost'*] of the walls is generated by the fictitiousness [*mnimost'*] of a man within them" (26). Iampolski thus brings the materiality of space in relation to gender but seems to conceive of this materiality as a substitute for the absent man, and thus negative in its connotations. My argument is that the powerful presence of the material environment allows a reconsideration of the nonfictitiousness, the reality of women within it; the dialogical interaction between space and women is initiated *because* of the absent man.

39. It is noteworthy that in the sequence with the relief, the conversation likewise revolves around gender. As the camera studies Zinaida's relationship to the distinct spatial surfaces, she is completing a monologue about, essentially, her lack of place in the gendered (and classed) Soviet culture.

40. In its play with surface and depth, this sequence also complicates the landscape representation that occurred in *Brief Encounters*, in the discussed sequence of Maxim's first appearance. If, in *Brief Encounters*, Muratova seeks to deaden the landscape (and its three-dimensionality) by making it look flat, like a picture, in *Long Goodbyes* she enlivens it through the materiality of the surface onto which it is projected. In both cases, she denaturalizes nature, insisting that it too, like all other spaces, has to be understood together with the screens that give birth to it in cultural discourse.

41. Sigmund Freud, "The 'Uncanny,'" 245.

42. Bryson, *Looking at the Overlooked*, 172.

43. Ibid., 173, 165.

CONCLUSION: THE OTHERNESS OF SPACE

THE CINEMATIC SCRUTINY of space in Soviet culture of the 1950s and 1960s was rooted in an urgency to find new forms of social engagement. It was also propelled by a need to redefine the role of cinema in the wake of Stalin's death. Rethinking the language of cinema, Soviet filmmakers began to emphasize the production of the environment as a social and filmic problem, creating spatial experiences within theatrical walls that differed significantly from those of established socialist practices. These filmmakers reorganized the spaces of familiar cities, landscapes, and public and private interiors, opening them up to dialogical interactions with viewers and protagonists; they grounded these interactions in material specificities, individual histories, and embodied mobility; and they repeatedly suggested that spaces need not conform to the original intent of their production—that they are always incomplete and open to other uses, meanings, and functions.

The path this book has traced illustrates the increasingly complex understanding of spatial relations that motivated Soviet cinema during 1950s and 1960s. Beginning with the relatively familiar embrace of such broadly discussed issues as national unity and peripheral integration, the expansion of personal mobility, and architectural reinvention, filmmakers moved to activate new—or previously latent—modes of spatial thinking and engagement. Key categories in this reconceptualization of the social meaning of space include immersion, periphery, and—as expressed in this book's title—movement and materiality. Thaw-era cinema sought to advance the critical potential of these terms by continuously parsing their significance both individually and in relation to one another.

Though immersion entered into debates about panoramic cinema as an ideologically uncomplicated entertainment device, one that allowed viewers to experience the cohesion of the country's spaces and history within the walls of a theater, it turned in the films of Kalatozov and Urusevskii into a critical negation of this very idea. From bodily mimicry of the natural environment to the camera's production of space *as* a body, immersion in the two filmmakers' work disturbed established Soviet relations between subjects and their environment and broke apart structures of vision that sought to enforce spatial and ideological unity. Formally less imposing and on a smaller, more casual scale, immersion assumed a similar role in Danelia's work, disrupting established, teleologically driven structures of everyday life and imagining new modes of urban experience. Shepitko, too, explored the compelling power of immersion as a means of rethinking Soviet subjectivity and space but reconfigured its parameters through the specific lens of gender. In Muratova's work, finally, immersion is imaged as a "face-to-face" encounter: a relation that is tactile, dialogical, and affective, understood as an experience of being *with*, rather than dispersed *in*, space.

A similar trajectory—toward greater theoretical acuity and more differentiated critical activation—can be observed across Thaw-era cinema's engagement with our other guiding conceptual terms. Periphery, for instance, is first utilized in reference to the Soviet Union's geographically remote and geopolitically significant outer territories, then reimagined as the idea of an inaccessible, separate space that opens up alternate modes of perception and is reconceptualized finally as a form of base matter—or, to invoke this study's key categories, essential materiality—that shifts our understandings of the relationship between bodies (specifically, gendered bodies) and the spaces they inhabit. And although these filmmakers' concern with movement begins with sweeping traversals through the entirety of the Soviet empire, it ends with Muratova's focus on the static and insignificant objects of still-life tableaux. Needless to say, the stasis of such images has nothing to do with the immobility of Stalinist culture. Rather, stillness here becomes movement's dialectical negative: without it, movement cannot exist but in the focus on dynamics and change, it is perpetually overlooked. That the present book's analysis of all these terms culminates in an examination of work by, and about, women is not accidental. For the universality of any term, any concept, breaks apart when considered in relation to gender—which thus becomes a fundamental term for rethinking the legitimacy of any totalizing conception of the social organism.

Did this spatial experimentation end with the Soviet Thaw? Or did these films generate a mode of cinematic and political thinking that goes beyond the historical parameters of those decades? More specifically, can this form of social critique be transferred effectively from post-Stalinist socialism to post-Soviet Putinism, and if so, what political efficacy might a present-day Russian filmmaker find in such spatial interrogation? One revealing example of this continual interrogation, though to very different ends, is the work of contemporary filmmaker Andrei Zviagintsev, best known in the United States for his 2014 release *Leviathan*. As in the films examined in this book, space functions as a primary element—a consistently overwhelming presence—in Zviagintsev's work, one that is central to its narrative and formal power. In this, Zviagintsev's films both demonstrate the continual import of the spatial examinations undertaken by Thaw-era cinema and can productively refract our gaze back on this work. It is with such a refracted look back—one that unfolds a heretofore unremarked-upon ethical dimension to their investigations—that I wish to close.

If Muratova's *Brief Encounters* invited us to rethink the relationship between space, cinema, and gender, planting a different aesthetic framework for understanding social progress, then Zviagintsev's 2011 film *Elena* suggests that such efforts were for naught. The opening sequence of his film can be seen as a sardonic commentary on the futility of Muratova's cinematic imagination when transported into the context of contemporary Russia. *Elena* opens with a pristine and generous apartment interior filled with light and minimal decoration whose spaces come into view as a series of still-life images, which speak of the very wholeness and completion that Muratova painstakingly suspended in *Brief Encounters* (figure 6.1a). The sequence culminates in a shot of an elegantly set breakfast table at which a man and a woman are seated facing each other in perfect symmetry; there are no apparent gaps or empty spaces worthy of attention, and no excesses of any kind that would call into question the visual balance of the image (figure 6.1b). We quickly realize, however, that this balance is contingent on the couple's incontestable roles within a social and domestic hierarchy. He (Vladimir) is a wealthy, elderly "new Russian," impeccably groomed and dressed, and she (Elena) is his middle-aged wife of ten years, in a middle-aged body, who provides all the necessary services to maintain their residence's faultless spatial order, functioning as cook and housekeeper, sexual companion, and nurse.

All spatial "faults" within the film are displaced to the periphery of the environment it portrays, far into the outskirts of Moscow, where Elena's son lives with his family in an unsightly apartment building (figure 6.2). A leftover from the Soviet era, the structure is located within an ungainly industrial landscape. The filth and vulgarity that fill this space are carefully removed from the central Moscow inhabited by Vladimir and Elena, just as the

Fig. 6.1a–b The perfection of interior spaces and gendered symmetry. From *Elena*, 2011.

vacuous, dull faces of the suburban residents seem to be of a different human order than the sophistication and purposefulness expressed in each gesture of proper Muscovites. Zviagintsev paints an unforgiving image of post-Soviet Russia, rooted in class and gender divisions that are assiduously mapped onto the surrounding space. The dreams of a progressive city, or any dreams of societal progress, have no place here at all, and when Elena, in a moment of fury, suggests to Vladimir that the "have-nots" will be able to take the place of the "haves" at some point, she can only trigger in him (and us) a sarcastic smirk in response. But the have-nots, indeed, move in. After Elena murders her husband quickly and quietly as a means to secure financial support for her son, the latter's family relocates into the couple's living quarters, which they turn into their own home, with ease. The film ends nearly where it began—with a series of images showing the apartment's pristine spaces, the main difference being that a new group of people is settling in and appropriating its rooms, objects, and surfaces to new ends.

Fig. 6.2 Soviet architectural leftovers. From *Elena*, 2011.

Although we have already witnessed a complete breakdown of ethics in human relations up to this point in the film, including Vladimir's simple and perfectly executed murder, the ending of *Elena* conveys a particular sense of unease: We can only shudder as we listen to Elena's son discuss ways to divide the spacious rooms so that each family member can have a place of his or her own. His family, if not exactly likable, is surely in need, and so why, then, do we find this literal spatial appropriation and reconfiguration so dreadful? These last moments of the film make tangible what has been present all along: that the represented environment, especially the couple's home, acquires a place within the film that we want to see preserved.

In *Elena*, as well as in Zviagintsev's other widely acclaimed works *The Return* (2003) and *Leviathan* (2014), the filmmaker insists on representing space—whether nature or the built environment—as a dual condition, making it appear both as a direct effect of human relations and as something more, something that transcends its human inhabitants. We can sense this "more" through the extreme definition of Zviagintsev's digitally processed images, which disturbs, however slightly, our perception of what is shown on screen. We also can discern this "more" in the stillness and seemingly immutable permanence of his interiors, which are presented in long takes that make them appear to rise above the momentary specificity of their existence. And we also can perceive the "more" of Zviagintsev's spaces in the purity and even indifference of the vast landscapes that engulf the fictional scenery in *The Return* and *Leviathan*. As the disintegration of human fellowship and civility grows, and the degree and scope of violence intensify with each of Zviagintsev's successive films, these spaces continue to persist, to just *be there*, as beautiful and ungraspable matter. It is precisely the possibility of this matter's destruction, of human actors impinging on space (implied in the last sequences of *Elena*, or directly accomplished in the demolition of the protagonists' house in *Leviathan*) that I believe can trigger particular anxiety and discontent for viewers of Zviagintsev's films. But he also suggests the indestructibility of this matter: one of *Leviathan*'s last images draws our attention to an unclear, perhaps broken spot on the ceiling of the church that has just been erected by the local despot on the grounds of the demolished house. We cannot help but perceive this spot as an indeterminate vestige of the original construction. Although it cannot be grasped directly as such—there is no explicit material or visual connection between them—it has an otherworldly aspect within the kitschy glory of the church, opening the space up to another way of seeing.

What are these ways of seeing that Zviagintsev's films explore and inspire? Although his environments, like the cinematic spaces of the Thaw, are marked by strangeness and difference, by their own disunity and apparent reach beyond any narrative signification, their overall function and meaning are of a different kind. They tend to be removed from the immediacy of our— and the protagonists'—experiences, not made accessible through materiality, proximity, or touch. They are at a distance, both conceptually and physically, disallowing sensory immersion (one of the privileged positions for Zviagintsev's camera to look at a particular space is from an explicitly different space—from inside a different room, behind a threshold, and so forth). And although these spaces provide a place for human movements, murders, and all possible everyday practices, they also seem to remain unaffected by them in a tangible way. Even if Vladimir and Elena's apartment is filled with their belongings, it seems detached from the immediacy of their lives. Familiar, inhabited, and natural environments are permeated, then, by a sense of absolute otherness, an otherness that seeks nothing else than an acknowledgment and recognition of itself.

Zviagintsev thus takes the disunity and heterogeneity of space to an extreme level. He seeks "another" function of space not in alternative modes of use, appropriation, or immersion, but solely in otherness as such, in the manifestation of an inaccessibility that nevertheless demands from us a process of comprehension whose parameters are far from clear. His films suggest that no matter what a specific place is—untouched nature or an environment erected through injustice and violence—we can always begin to perceive, through his camera's cinematic gaze, its resolute and infinite otherness. It is in this process of perception, I want to suggest, that Zviagintsev sees the possibility of the sort of ethical relation that is so profoundly absent in the interactions of the people his films portray.

In this regard, we can understand the spaces in Zviagintsev's films through the work of philosopher Emmanuel Levinas, for whom the constitution of an ethical subject is rooted in a recognition of the other's infinite otherness, which is to say, an act of "grasping the ungraspable while nevertheless guaranteeing its status as ungraspable."[1] In rethinking the moment of encounter between self and other, Levinas reverses the grounds of traditional Western philosophy, in which the other can remain as such only momentarily, before being conceptualized within the operative categories of the encountering self—otherness thus being turned into something "same." To enter into an ethical relation for Levinas means above all to preserve the *infinitude* of otherness as such, to resist its appropriation as selfsame. According to Levinas, the social manifestation of such ethics is to be found in the human face, which, he writes, "resists possession, resists my powers. In its epiphany, in expression, the sensible, still graspable, turns into total resistance to the grasp."[2] In Zviagintsev's cinema, such resistance, as I've described, is found solely in space itself, which—as a surface expression of social existence—we can thus understand as an echo, or a mirror, of the human face. The process of perceiving this open and incomplete space, of infinitely grasping its inaccessibility, constitutes in Zviagintsev's work the only seed for political ethics.

Zviagintsev's opening up of space to an ethical vision not only advances the scrutiny of spatial relations that Thaw-era films undertook, but also retrospectively crystallizes less evident elements of these films' searches and practices. Space, in its essence, is a communal formation, where social forces, individual practices, competing ideologies, and cultural norms manifest themselves in material, physically tangible ways. Friction or conflict within this material manifestation results from the spatial engagement of an individual, or a group, that diverts from accepted conventions—something that Lefebvre understood to be a sign of social progress and to bear revolutionary potential. Soviet socialism envisioned the material organization of space to be harmonious, whole, and complete, without conflict, excess, or friction; only in that way could it function as the expression, the public face, of the country's ideological promise. The renewed focus on the individual in official Soviet discourse of the 1950s and 1960s was not to be in discord with that vision—harmony between the individual and the collective, as addressed in my introduction, was at the center of discussions of new, post-Stalinist socialist space.

But as this book has argued, Thaw-era cinema took as its task the activation of *disunities* of Soviet space on scales both large and small, and it did so primarily through individual bodies—those imaged on screen, watching in theaters, or made present by the cinematic apparatus itself. Thaw-era cinema invested these bodies—their ways of sensing, speaking, and moving—with a capacity to animate materials, sensations, and experiences that defied the conceptual clarity and harmony of Soviet ideology, and accordingly to make the heterogeneity of Soviet space active, visible, and tangible. This cinema thus understood space to be a communal formation—but, increasingly, one of irreconcilable differences rather than harmonious sublimations. It is through its relation to this persistent generation of difference, the appearance of something *other* within a communal space, that Zviagintsev's work sheds light on these earlier practices.

Spatial otherness such as I've identified in Zviagintsev's work assumes a range of forms in Thaw-era films, each produced through diverse human and cinematic actions: the spontaneous mobility of panoramic audiences producing an experience of space that exceeds cognitive or diagrammatic control; the elaborate camera movement of Kalatozov and Urusevskii's productions generating a nearly alien, sentient space that appears to take on a human gaze and body; the playful walking in Danelia's feature creating a newly sensory space; the specifically gendered perception of Shepitko's film activating a profoundly mnemonic space; and the static camera observations of Muratova's cinema bringing to light a gendered materiality of space that is otherwise unremarked. Through moving and seeing, touching and speaking, the subjects in these films not only sense and appropriate their environments but permeate and alter them, rendering the communal space a dynamic collection of its infinite others' sensory traces. And all these films insist on viewers' necessary grasping of this otherness that punctures the space, directly appealing to their minds and senses.

This otherness is more concrete than that of Zviagintsev's cinema. Its sources are easier to identify and its meanings more graspable, rooted in the established, "same," categories against which Levinas spoke. But it nevertheless contains an ethical potential similar to the one the philosopher describes. Presenting communal space as deeply charged with, and indeed inseparable from, the perceptions and movements of its inhabitants, the cinema of the Thaw years impels its viewers to approach their own environment through a similar perspective: as an ethical community in which we can actively seek to encounter the other, through its spatial traces, while simultaneously recognizing the infinite impossibility of this very prospect.

Notes

1. Levinas, "Transcendence and Height," 19.
2. Levinas, *Totality and Infinity: An Essay on Exteriority*, 197.

BIBLIOGRAPHY

Archival Abbreviations and Translations used in Bibliography

RGALI: Rossiiskii gosudarstvennyi arkhiv literatury i iskusstva (Russian State Archive of Literature and Art)

Fond: Funds, Record Group

Delo: file

Opis': inventory

Abbas, Ackbar. "Cinema, the City, and the Cinematic." In *Global Cities: Cinema, Architecture, and Urbanism in a Digital Age*, edited by Linda Krause and Patrice Petro, 142–56. New Brunswick, NJ: Rutgers University Press, 2003.

Abdulaeva, Zara. *Kira Muratova: Iskusstvo kino* [Kira Muratova: The Art of Cinema]. Moscow: Novoe Literaturnoe Obozrenie, 2008.

Aleksashina, V. "Promyshlennost' v gorode." *Sovetskaia arkhitektura* 17 (1965): 65–78.

Arbuzov, Aleksei. "S soveshchatel'nym golosom." *Iskusstvo kino*, no. 11 (1961): 121–28.

Baiar, O. "Dekorativnye predmety v kvartire." *Dekorativnoe iskusstvo SSSR*, 7, no. 20 (1959): 15–17.

Balsom, Erika. "Screening Rooms: The Movie Theatre in/and the Gallery." *Public*, no. 40 (Fall 2009): 24–39.

Barker, Jennifer. *The Tactile Eye: Touch and the Cinematic Experience*. Berkeley: University of California Press, 2009.

Baudelaire, Charles. "The Painter of Modern Life." In *The Painter of Modern Life and Other Essays*, translated and edited by Jonathan Mayne, 1–40. London: Phaidon, 1964.

Bazin, André. "The Evolution of the Language of Cinema." In *What Is Cinema?* translated by Hugh Gray, 23–40. Berkeley: University of California Press, 1967.

Beissinger, Mark R. *Scientific Management, Socialist Discipline, and Soviet Power*. Cambridge, MA: Harvard University Press, 1988.

Bellos, David. *Jacques Tati*. London: Harvill, 1999.

Belton, John. *Widescreen Cinema*. Cambridge, MA: Harvard University Press, 1992.

Benjamin, Jessica. "A Desire of One's Own: Psychoanalytic Feminism and Intersubjective Space." In *Feminist Studies/Critical Studies*, edited by Teresa de Lauretis, 78–101. Bloomington: Indiana University Press, 1986.

Benjamin, Walter. *The Arcades Project*. Translated by Howard Eiland and Kevin McLaughlin. Cambridge, MA: Belknap, 1999.

———. "The Lamp." In *Walter Benjamin: Selected Writings*. Vol. 2, pt. 2, *1931–1934*, edited by Michael W. Jennings, Howard Eiland, and Gary Smith, and translated by Edmund Ephcott and others, 691–93. Cambridge, MA: Belknap, 1999.

———. "Moscow." In *Walter Benjamin: Selected Writings*. Vol. 2, pt. 1, *1927–1930*, edited by Michael W. Jennings, Howard Eiland, and Gary Smith, and translated by Edmund Ephcott and others, 22–46. Cambridge, MA: Belknap, 1999.

———. "On the Mimetic Faculty." In *Walter Benjamin: Selected Writings*. Vol. 2, pt. 2, *1931–1934*, edited by Michael W. Jennings, Howard Eiland, and Gary Smith, and translated by Edmund Ephcott and others, 720–22. Cambridge, MA: Belknap, 1999.

———. "The Work of Art in the Age of Its Technological Reproducibility." In *Walter Benjamin: Selected Writings*. Vol. 4, *1938–1940*, edited by Howard Eiland and Michael W. Jennings, and translated by Edmund Ephcott and others, 251–83. Cambridge, MA: Belknap, 2003.

Beskin, O. "Iskusstvo dioramy." *Dekorativnoe iskusstvo SSSR*, no. 11 (1958): 13–16.

Bird, Robert. *Andrei Tarkovsky: The Elements of Cinema*. London: Reaktion, 2008.

Blanchard, Marc Eli. "On Still Life." *Yale French Studies*, no. 61 (1981): 276–98.

Bleiman, Mikhail and An. Vartanov. "O filme sporiat: film obozreniie ili film razdumie. Razgovor mezhdu An. Vartanovym i M. Bleiman." *Sovetskii ekran* 12, no. 180 (1964): 2–4.

Bogdanov, I. "Kamera v dvizhenii." *Iskusstvo kino*, no. 5 (1960): 117–24.

Bolotina, Irina. *Problemy russkogo i sovetskogo natiurmorta* [The Problems of Russian and Soviet Still Life]. Moscow: Sovetskii khudozhnik, 1989.

Bolotova, Alla. "Colonization of Nature in the Soviet Union: State Ideology, Public Discourse, and the Experience of Geologists." *Historical Social Research/Historische Sozialforschung* 29, no. 3 (2004): 104–23.

Bowlt, John E., ed. and trans. *Russian Art of the Avant-Garde: Theory and Criticism, 1902–1934*. New York: Thames and Hudson, 1988.

Brecht, Bertolt. *Collected Plays*. Edited by John Willett. London: Bloomsbury Methuen Drama, 2012.

Brook, Kevin Alan. *The Jews of Khazaria*. Lanham, MD: Rowman and Littlefield, 2006.

Bruno, Giuliana. *Atlas of Emotion: Journeys in Art, Architecture, and Film*. New York: Verso, 2002.

———. "Visual Studies: Four Takes on Spatial Turns." *Journal of the Society of Architectural Historians* 65, no. 1 (2006): 23–24.

Bryson, Norman. *Looking at the Overlooked: Four Essays on Still Life Painting*. London: Reaktion, 1990.

Buchli, Victor. "Khrushchev, Modernism, and the Fight against *Petit-bourgeois* Consciousness in the Soviet Home." *Journal of Design History* 10, no. 2 (1997): 161–76.

Buck-Morss, Susan. *The Dialectics of Seeing: Walter Benjamin and the Arcades Project*. Cambridge, MA: MIT Press, 1991.

———. *Dreamworld and Catastrophe: The Passing of Mass Utopia in East and West*. Cambridge, MA: MIT Press, 2002.

———. "The Flaneur, the Sandwichman, and the Whore: The Politics of Loitering." *New German Critique*, no. 39 (1986): 99–140.
Bulgakova, Oksana. "Cine-Weathers: Soviet Thaw Cinema in the International Context." In *The Thaw: Soviet Society and Culture during the 1950s and 1960s*, edited by Denis Kozlov and Eleonory Gilburd, 362–401. Toronto, ON: University of Toronto Press, 2013.
Bykhovskii, B. "'Itog i ostatok' ili balans renegata." *Voprosy filosofii*, no. 7 (1964): 112–22.
Caillois, Roger. "Mimicry and Legendary Psychasthenia." Translated by John Shepley. *October* 31 (Winter 1984): 16–32.
Cavendish, Philip. *The Men with the Movie Camera: The Poetics of Visual Style in Soviet Avant-Garde Cinema of the 1920s*. Oxford, UK: Berghahn, 2013.
Charney, Leo. "In a Moment: Film and the Philosophy of Modernity." In *Cinema and the Invention of Modern Life*, edited by Leo Charney and Vanessa Schwartz, 279–95. Berkeley: University of California Press, 1995.
Chion, Michel. *The Films of Jacques Tati*. Translated by Antonio D'Alfonso. Toronto, ON: Guernica, 1997.
———. *The Voice in Cinema*. Translated by Claudia Gorbman. New York: Columbia University Press, 1999.
Cohen, Stephen F. *The Victims Return: Survivors of the Gulag after Stalin*. London: I. B. Tauris, 2010.
Comolli, Jean-Louis. "Passés les cigognes." *Cahiers du Cinéma*, no. 164 (1965): 83–84.
Danelia, Georgii. *Chito-grito*. Moscow: Eksmo, 2009.
DeBlasio, Alyssa. "Choreographing Space, Time, and 'Dikovinki' in the Films of Evgenii Bauer." *Russian Review* 66, no. 4 (2007): 671–92.
Debord, Guy. ""Report on the Construction of Situations and on the International Situationist Tendency's Conditions of Organization and Action," In *Situationist International Anthology*, edited by Ken Knabb, 17–25. Berkeley, CA: Bureau of Public Secrets, 2006.
———. *The Society of the Spectacle*. Translated by Donald Nicholson-Smith. New York: Zone Books, 1995.
———. "Theory of the Dérive." In *Situationist International Anthology*, edited by Ken Knabb, 50–54. Berkeley, CA: Bureau of Public Secrets, 2006.
De Certeau, Michel. *The Practice of Everyday Life*. Translated by Stephen F. Rendall. Berkeley: University of California Press, 1984.
De Lauretis, Teresa. *Technologies of Gender*. Bloomington: Indiana University Press, 1987.
"Delo fil'ma 'Ia shagaiu po Moskve'" [File on the Film *I Walk the Streets of Moscow*]. Russian State Archive of Literature and Arts (RGALI), Fond 2944, opis' 4, delo 150.
"Delo fil'ma 'Korotkie vstrechi'" [File on the Film *Brief Encounters*]. Russian State Archive of Literature and Arts (RGALI), Fond 2944, opis' 4, delo 1104.
"Delo fil'ma 'Kryl'ia'" [File on the Film *Wings*]. Russian State Archive of Literature and Arts (RGALI), fond 2944, opis' 4, delo 820.
"Delo fil'ma 'Neotpravlennoe pis'mo'" [File on the Film *The Unsent Letter*]. Russian State Archive of Literature and Arts (RGALI), Fond 2453, opis' 1, delo 664.
Dickerman, Leah. "Camera Obscura: Socialist Realism in the Shadow of Photography." *October* 93 (Summer 2000): 138–53.
Doane, Mary Ann. *The Emergence of Cinematic Time*. Cambridge, MA: Harvard University Press, 2002.

———. "The Voice in the Cinema: The Articulation of Body and Space." *Yale French Studies*, no. 60 (1980): 33–50.
Dobin, Efim. "Teoreticheskie zapiski." *Iskusstvo kino*, no. 7 (1964): 59–75.
Dobrenko, Evgeny. "The Art of Social Navigation: The Cultural Topography of the Stalin Era." In *The Landscape of Stalinism: The Art and Ideology of Soviet Space*, edited by Evgeny Dobrenko and Eric Naiman, 163–200. Seattle: University of Washington Press, 2003.
Dombrovskii, Konstantin. "Novye khudozhestvennye sredstva." *Iskusstvo kino*, 3 (1958): 36–38.
Domínguez, Carlos Espinosa."The Mammoth That Wouldn't Die." In *Caviar with Rum: Cuba–USSR and the Post-Soviet Experience*, edited by Jacqueline Loss and José Manuel Prieto, 109–17. New York: Palgrave Macmillan, 2012.
Dyko, L. "Tvorcheskiie poiski Sergeia Urussevskogo," *Iskusstvo kino*, no. 7 (1961): 102–12.
Ebert, Roger. "I Am Cuba." rogerebert.com, accessed June 2, 2015. http://www.rogerebert.com/reviews/i-a-cuba-1995.
Efimova, Alla. "To Touch on the Raw: The Aesthetic Affections of Socialist Realism." *Art Journal* 56, no. 1 (Spring 1997): 72–80.
Eisenstein, Sergei. "Montage of Attractions, an Essay." In *The Film Sense*, edited and translated by Jay Leyda, 230–33. New York: Harcourt Brace Jovanovich, 1975.
Elsaesser, Thomas, and Malte Hagener. *Film Theory: An Introduction through the Senses*. New York: Routledge, 2010.
Epstein, Edward Jay. *The Rise and Fall of Diamonds: A Shattering of a Brilliant Illusion* (New York: Simon and Shuster, 1982.
Fedorova, Anastasia. "Vtoraia molodost' VDNKh." *Tribuna*, accessed August 2014. http://riatribuna.ru/news/2014/08/11/49381.
Filtzer, Donald. "From Mobilized to Free Labour: De-Stalinization and the Changing Legal Status of Workers." In *The Dilemmas of De-Stalinization: Negotiating Cultural and Social Change in the Khrushchev Era*, edited by Polly Jones, 154–69. London: Routledge, 2006.
Fisher, Jaimey. "Wandering in/to the Rubble-Film: Filmic Flânerie and the Exploded Urban Panorama after 1945." *German Quarterly* 78, no. 4 (2005): 461–80.
"Fond Romana Karmena" [The Fonds on Roman Karmen]. Russian State Archive for Literature and Arts (RGALI), Fond 2989, opis' 1, delo 16.
Freud, Sigmund. "The 'Uncanny.'" In *Standard Edition of the Complete Works of Sigmund Freud*. Vol. 17 (1917–1919), *An Infantile Neurosis and Other Works*, edited by James Strachey, 219–56. London: Hogarth, 1919.
Friedberg, Anne. *Window Shopping: Cinema and the Postmodern*. Berkeley: University of California Press, 1994.
Frisby, David. "The *Flâneur* in Social Theory." In *The Flâneur*, edited by Keith Tester, 81–110. London: Routledge, 1994.
Gilburd, Eleonory. "The Revival of Soviet Internationalism in the Mid to Late 1950s." In *The Thaw: Soviet Society and Culture during the 1950s and 1960s*, edited by Denis Kozlov and Eleonory Gilburd, 362–401. Toronto, ON: University of Toronto Press, 2013.
Gleber, Anke. *The Art of Taking a Walk: Flanerie, Literature, and Film in Weimar Culture*. Princeton, NJ: Princeton University Press, 1998.
Goldovskii, Evsei. *Ot nemogo kino k panoramnomu* [From Silent to Panoramic Cinema]. Moscow: Izdatel'stvo Akademii Nauk SSSR, 1961.
———."O sistemakh kinematografa budushchego." *Technika kino i televidenia* 6 (1960): 9–37.

———. *Problemy panoramnogo i shirokoekrannogo kinematografa* [Problems of Panoramic and Widescreen Cinematography]. Moscow: Gosudarstvennoe izdatel'stvo Iskusstvo, 1958.

Goodwin, James. *Eisenstein, Cinema, and History.* Champaign: University of Illinois Press, 1993.

Gorokhov, Viktor. "Zritel vkhodit v ekran." *Iskusstvo kino,* no. 3 (1958): 31–35.

Gorsuch, Anne E. "Time Travelers: Soviet Tourists to Eastern Europe." In *Turizm: The Russian and East European Tourist under Capitalism and Socialism,* edited by Anne E. Gorsuch and Diane P. Koenker, 205–26. Ithaca, NY: Cornell University Press, 2006.

Grosz, Elizabeth. *Space, Time, and Perversion: Essays on the Politics of Bodies.* New York: Routledge, 1995.

Gunning, Tom. "The Cinema of Attractions: Early Film, Its Spectator, and the Avant-Garde." *Wide Angle* 8, nos. 3–4 (1986): 63–70.

———. "Moving Away from the Index: Cinema and the Impression of Reality." In *Screen Dynamics,* edited by Gertrud Koch, Volker Pantenburg, and Simon Rothöhler, 42–60. Vienna: Synema, 2012.

Guthman, Edward. "Soviet Bird's-Eye View of Cuba." *San Francisco Chronicle,* April 14, 1995, C3.

Hansen, Miriam. "Benjamin and Cinema: Not a One-Way Street." *Critical Inquiry* 25, no. 2 (1999): 306–43.

Hanson, Philip. *The Rise and Fall of the Soviet Economy: An Economic History of the USSR from 1945.* London: Pearson, 2003.

Hixson, Walter L. *Parting the Curtain: Propaganda, Culture, and the Cold War, 1945–1961.* New York: St. Martin's Griffin, 1997.

Hornsby, Robert. *Protest, Reform, and Repression in Khrushchev's Soviet Union.* Cambridge: Cambridge University Press, 2013.

Huyssen, Andreas. *Present Pasts: Urban Palimpsests and the Politics of Memory.* Stanford, CA: Stanford University Press, 2003.

Iampolski, Mikhail. *Muratova: opyt kinoantropologii* [Muratova: The Experience of Cine-Anthropology]. Moscow: Seans, 2008.

Ikonnikov, Andrei. "Organizatsiia prostranstva i estetichekaia vyrazitel'nost' arkhitektury." *Arkhitektura SSSR,* no. 2 (1963): 42–65.

Ikonnikov, Andrei, and Georgii Stepanov, *Estetika sotsialisticheskogo goroda* [The Aesthetics of the Socialist City]. Moscow: Izdatel'stvo akademii khudozhestv SSSR, 1963.

Ilič, Melanie, Susan E. Reid, and Lynne Attwood, eds. *Women in the Khrushchev Era.* New York: Palgrave Macmillan, 2004.

Irigaray, Luce. *An Ethics of Sexual Difference.* Translated by Carolyn Burke and Gillian C. Gill. Ithaca, NY: Cornell University Press, 1993.

Ishchenko, Elena. "Konchai bazar." *Trud,* accessed August 21, 2014. http://www.trud.ru/article/12-08-2014/1316579_konchaj_bazar.html.

Izvilova, Irina. "Drugoe prostranstvo." In *Kinematograf ottepeli: k 100-letiiu mirovog kino* [The Cinema of the Thaw: Dedicated to the 100th Anniversary of World Cinema], edited by Vitalii Troianovskii, 77–98. Moscow: Materik, 1996.

Jakobson, Roman. "On a Generation That Squandered Its Poets." Reprinted in *Roman Jakobson: Language in Literature.* Edited by Krystyna Pomorska and Stephen Rudy, 273–300. Cambridge, MA: Harvard University Press, 1987.

Jameson, Fredric. "Periodizing the 60s." In *The Ideologies of Theory, Essays 1971–1986.* Vol. 2, *Syntax of History,* 178–208. Minneapolis: University of Minnesota Press, 1988.

Jones, Robert A. *The Soviet Concept of "Limited Sovereignty" from Lenin to Gorbachev: The Brezhnev Doctrine*. London: Macmillan, 1990.
Josephson, Paul, Nicolai Dronin, Ruben Mnatsakanian, Aleh Cherp, Dmitry Efremenko, and Vladislav Larin. *An Environmental History of Russia*. New York: Cambridge University Press, 2013.
Kaganovsky, Lilya. "Postmemory, Countermemory: Soviet Cinema of the 1960s." In *The Socialist Sixties: Crossing Borders in the Second World*, edited by Anne E. Gorsuch and Diane P. Konker, 236–50. Bloomington: Indiana University Press, 2013.
———. "Ways of Seeing: On Kira Muratova's *Brief Encounters* and Larisa Shepit'ko's *Wings*." *Russian Review* 71, no. 3 (2012): 482–99.
"Kakoi ekran luchsche?" *Iskusstvo kino*, no. 1 (1962): 87–92.
Kamenskii, A. "Khudozhnik Urusevsky." *Iskusstvo kino*, no. 2 (1968): 90–93.
Karmen, Roman. "S'emki na pylaiushchem ostrove," *Iskusstvo kino*, no. 6 (1961): 123–31 and *Iskusstvo kino*, no. 7 (1961): 125–32.
Kerzhentsev, Platon, writing in *Pravda*, August 5, 1923, 3. Quoted in Mark R. Beissinger, *Scientific Management, Socialist Discipline, and Soviet Power*, 54. Cambridge, MA: Harvard University Press, 1988.
Khrabrovtskii, Savelii. "Letter to the Central Committee of the Communist Party." In *Kinematograf ottepeli: dokumenty i svidetel'stva* [The Cinema of the Thaw: Documents and Testimonies], edited by Valerii Fomin, 24–26. Moscow: Materik, 1998.
Kibita, Natalia. *Soviet Economic Management under Khrushchev: The "Sovnarkhoz" Reform*. London: Routledge, 2013.
King, David. *The Commissar Vanishes: The Falsification of Photographs and Art in Stalin's Russia—Photographs from the David King Collection*. New York: Henry Holt, 1997.
Klimov, Elem. *Larisa. Vospominaniia. Vystupleniia. Intev'iu. Kinostsenarii. Stat'i: Kniga o Larise Shepitko* [Larisa: Recollections, Speeches, Interview, Film Scenarios, Essays: A Book about Larisa Shepitko]. Moscow: Iskusstvo, 1987.
Klimov, N. A. *Rabochii den' v obshchestve, stroiashchim communism* [Work Day in a Society Building Communism]. Moscow: Izdatel'stvo sotsial'no-ekonomicheskoi literatury, 1961.
Korzhavin, N. "Poka byla liubov'." *Iskusstvo kino*, no. 1 (1967): 88–97.
Kosmatov, Leonid. "Kompositsia shirokogo kadra." *Iskusstvo kino*, no. 2 (1959): 113–19.
Kotov, V. D. "Panoramnyi Teatr 'Mir.'" *Technika kino i televideniia* 5 (1958): 57–65.
Kovarskii, N. "Chelovek i vremia." *Iskusstvo kino*, no. 10 (1968): 49–57.
Kozlov, Denis and Eleonory Gilburd. "The Thaw as an Event in Russian History." In *The Thaw: Soviet Society and Culture during the 1950s and 1960s*, edited by Denis Kozlov and Eleonory Gilburd, 18–81. Toronto, ON: University of Toronto Press, 2013.
Kracauer, Siegfried. *Theory of Film: The Redemption of Physical Reality*. Princeton, NJ: Princeton University Press, 1997.
Kriukova, Irina, ed. *Kultura zhilogo interiera* [The Culture of the Lived Interior]. Moscow: Ministerstvo kultury SSSR, Institut istorii iskusstv, 1966.
Krukones, James H. "Peacefully Coexisting on a Wide Screen: Kinopanorama vs. Cinerama, 1952–1966." *Studies in Russian and Soviet Cinema* 4, no. 3 (2010): 283–305.
"Kryl'ia: podrobnyi razgovor." *Iskusstvo kino*, no. 10 (1966): 12–30.
Lant, Antonia. "Haptical Cinema." *October* 74 (Autumn 1995): 45–73.
Larsen, Susan. "Korotkie vstrechi/Brief Encounters." In *The Cinema of Russia and the Former Soviet Union*, edited by Bridgit Beumers, 119–27. London: Wallflower, 2007.

Lefebvre, Henri. *Key Writings*. Edited by Stuart Elden, Elizabeth Lebas, and Eleonore Kofman. London: Continuum, 2003.
———. *The Production of Space*. Translated by Donald Nicholson-Smith. Oxford, UK: Blackwell, 1991.
———. "L'urbanisme aujourd'hui: Mythes et réalités—Débat entre Henri Lefebvre, Jean Balladur, et Michel Écochard." In Henri Lefebvre, *Du rural à l'urbain* (Paris: Anthropos, 1970), 217–27. Quoted in Łukasz Stanek, *Henri Lefebvre on Space: Architecture, Urban Research, and the Production of Theory*. Minneapolis: University of Minnesota Press, 2011.
Lenin, Vladimir. "The Home and Foreign Policy of the Republic." In *Collected Works*. Vol. 33, August 1921–March 1923, 143–77. Moscow: Progress, 1973.
Leslie, Esther. "Ruin and Rubble in the Arcades." In *Walter Benjamin and the Arcades Project*, edited by Beatrice Hanssen, 87–112. London: Continuum, 2006.
Levin, Moshe. "Society, State, and Ideology during the First Five-Year Plan." In *Cultural Revolution in Russia, 1928–1931*, edited by Sheila Fitzpatrick, 41–78. Bloomington: Indiana University Press, 1978.
Levinas, Emmanuel. *Totality and Infinity: An Essay on Exteriority*. Translated by Alphonso Lingis. Dordrecht, Neth.: Kluwer, 1991.
———. "Transcendence and Height." In *Emmanuel Levinas: Basic Philosophical Writings*, edited by Adriaan T. Peperzak, Simon Critchley, and Robert Bernasconi, 11–31. Bloomington: Indiana University Press, 1996.
Liaskalo, V. "Ischerpany li vozmozhnosti kinopanoramy?" *Iskusstvo kino*, no. 1 (1961): 153–55.
Lukin, Ia. "Nekotory voprosy sinteza monumental'nogo iskusstva i arkhitektury." *Sovetskaia arkhitektura* 14 (1962): 111–20.
Mamonova, Tatiana, ed. *Women and Russia: Feminist Writing from the Soviet Union*. Translated by Rebecca Park and Catherine A. Fitzpatrick. Boston: Beacon, 1984.
Margolit, Evgenii. "Landscape, with Hero." In *Springtime for Soviet Cinema: Re/Viewing the 1960s*, edited by Alexander Prokhorov and translated by Dawn A. Seckler, 29–50. Pittsburgh, PA: Pittsburgh Russian Film Symposium, 2001.
Marie, Laurent. "Jacques Tati's *Play Time* as New Babylon." In *Cinema and the City: Film and Urban Societies in a Global Context*, edited by Marc Shiel and Tony Fitzmaurice, 257–69. Oxford: Wiley Blackwell, 2001.
Markel', Maia. "Dolzhen li operator videt'?" *Iskusstvo kino*, no. 10 (1961): 51–57.
Markov, Mark. "Nekotorye zakony vospriiatia iskusstva." *Iskusstvo kino*, no. 9 (1957): 90–104.
Marks, Laura. *The Skin of the Film: Intercultural Cinema, Embodiment, and the Senses*. Durham, NC: Duke University Press, 2000.
Martin, Terry. *The Affirmative Action Empire: Nations and Nationalism in the Soviet Union, 1923–1939*. Ithaca, NY: Cornell University Press, 2001.
Mayne, Judith. *The Woman at the Keyhole: Feminism and Women's Cinema*. Bloomington: Indiana University Press, 1990.
McCauley, Martin. *Khrushchev and the Development of Soviet Agriculture: The Virgin Land Programme, 1953–1964*. New York: Holmes and Meier, 1976.
McDonough, Thomas F. "Situationist Space." *October* 67 (Winter 1994): 58–77.
Metz, Christian. "On the Impression of Reality in the Cinema." In *Film Language: A Semiotics of the Cinema*, translated by Michael Taylor, 3–15. New York: Oxford University Press, 1974.

Michelson, Annette, ed. *Kino-Eye: The Writings of Dziga Vertov*. Translated by Kevin O'Brien. Berkeley: University of California Press, 1984.
Mikhailov, Nikolai Nikolaevich. *Moia Rossiia* [My Russia]. Moscow: Sovetskaia Rossiia, 1966.
Mikhalev, Nikolai. "Proekt rekonstruktsii VVTs priobriol konkretnye kontury." *RBK Daily*, accessed August 21, 2014. http://www.rbcdaily.ru/market/562949986552111.
Muratova, Kira. Interview with BBC Russian.com. "Kira Muratova: Mne skuchno vsio tipichnoe" [Kira Muratova: I'm Bored with All That Is Typical], Last accessed May 16, 2007. http://news.bbc.co.uk/hi/russian/talking_point/newsid_6661000/6661695.stm.
Murian, V. "Gumanizm sotsialisticheskii i gumanizm abstraktnyi." *Iskusstvo kino*, no. 11 (1965): 10–20.
Neporozhnii, P. "Elektrifikatsiia i gradostroitelstvo." *Sovetskaia arkhitektura* 15 (1963): 3–11.
Novakovskii, V. E., ed. *Vystavka Dostizhenii Narodnogo Khoziastva SSSR: Putevoditel' 1959* [The Exhibition of Achievements of the People's Economy: A 1959 Guide]. Moscow: Gosudarstvennoe nauchno-technicheskoe izdatel'stvo mashinostroitelnoi literatury, 1959.
"Novye filmy: 'Ia Kuba.'" *Iskusstvo kino*, no. 3 (1965): 24–37.
Obraztsova, A. "Pervye shagi." *Iskusstvo kino*, no. 8 (1961): 13–16.
Pantenburg, Volker. "1970 and Beyond: Experimental Cinema and Installation Art." In *Screen Dynamics: Mapping the Borders of Cinema*, edited by Gertrud Koch, Volker Pantenburg, and Simon Rothöler, 78–92. Vienna: SYNEMA, 2012.
Paperny, Vladimir. *Architecture in the Age of Stalin: Culture Two*. Translated by John Hill and Roann Barris. New York: Cambridge University Press, 2002.
Pekareva, N. "Dvorets pionerov v Moskve." *Arkhitektura SSSR*, no. 9 (1962): 50–62.
Pennington, Reina. *Wings, Women, and War: Soviet Airwomen in World War II Combat*. Lawrence: University Press of Kansas, 2001.
Penz, François. "Architecture in the Films of Jacques Tati." In *Cinema and Architecture: Méliès, Mallet-Stevens, Multimedia*, edited by François Penz and Maureen Thomas, 62–69. London: British Film Institute, 1997.
"Pervye panoramnye kinoteatry: zritelskiie otzyvy." *Sovetskii ekran* 6 (1958): 16.
Petrov, Petre. "The Freeze of Historicity in Thaw Cinema." *Kinokultura*, no. 8 (2005). http://www.kinokultura.com/articles/apr05-petrov.html.
Plisetskii, G. "Otkrytie mira." *Iskusstvo kino*, no. 1 (1961): 87–89.
Pollock, Griselda. *Vision and Difference: Feminism, Femininity, and Histories of Art*. London: Routledge, 1988.
Programme of the Communist Party of the Soviet Union. Adopted by the 22nd Congress of the C.P.S.U., October 1961. Moscow: Foreign Language Publishing, 1961.
Prokhorov, Alexander. "The Unknown New Wave: Soviet Cinema of the Sixties." In *Springtime for Soviet Cinema: Re/Viewing the 1960s*, edited by Alexander Prokhorov. Translated by Dawn A. Seckler, 7–28. Pittsburgh, PA: Pittsburgh Russian Film Symposium, 2001.
Pruzhan, I. N., and V. A. Pushkarev. *Natiurmort v Russkoi i sovetskoi zhivopisi* [*Still Life in Russian and Soviet Painting*]. Leningrad: Avrora, 1970.
Qualls, Karl D. *From Ruins to Reconstruction: Urban Identity in Soviet Sevastopol after World War II*. Ithaca, NY: Cornell University Press, 2009.
Rajagopalan, Sudha. *Indian Films in Soviet Cinemas: The Culture of Movie-going after Stalin*. Bloomington: Indiana University Press, 2009.

Reid, Susan. "The Khrushchev Kitchen: Domesticating the Scientific-Technological Revolution." *Journal of Contemporary History* 40, no. 2 (2005): 289–316.

———. "Khrushchev's Children's Paradise: The Pioneer Palace, Moscow, 1958–1962." In *Socialist Spaces: Sites of Everyday Life in the Eastern Bloc*, edited by David Crowley and Susan E. Reid, 141–80. Oxford, UK: Berg, 2002.

———. "Modernizing Socialist Realism in the Khrushchev Thaw: The Struggle for a Contemporary Style." In *The Dilemmas of De-Stalinization: Negotiating Cultural and Social Change in the Khrushchev Era*, edited by Polly Jones, 209–30. London: Routledge, 2006.

———. "Photography in the Thaw." *Art Journal* 53, no. 2 (1994): 33–39.

Ricoeur, Paul. *Memory, History, Forgetting*. Translated by Kathleen Blamey and David Pellauer. Chicago: University of Chicago Press, 2004.

Rosenbaum, Jonathan. "I Am Cuba." *Chicago Reader*, accessed June 2, 2015. http://www.chicagoreader.com/chicago/i-am-cuba/Film?oid=1057045.

———. "Tati's Democracy: An Interview and Introduction by Jonathan Rosenbaum." *Film Comment* 9 (1973): 36–41.

Ross, Kristin. "Lefebvre on the Situationists: An Interview." *October* 79 (Winter 1997): 69–83.

Rubanova, I. "Posle krasnoi pustyni: o nekotorykh itogakh Antonioni." *Voprosy kinoiskusstva* 10 (1967): 318–43.

Ruthchild, Rochelle. "Sisterhood and Socialism: The Soviet Feminist Movement." *Frontiers: A Journal of Women Studies* 7, no. 2 (1983): 4–12.

Ryklin, Michail. *Räume des Jubels* [Spaces of Jubilation]. Frankfurt am Main: Suhrkamp, 2003.

Scheffauer, Harman G. "The Vivifying of Space." In *Introduction to the Art of the Movies*, edited by Lewis Jacobs, 76–85. New York: Noonday, 1960. Cited in Anthony Vidler, "The Explosion of Space: Architecture and the Filmic Imaginary." *Assemblage*, no. 21 (1993): 44–59.

Sheptiko, Larisa. Interview with Felicia von Nostiz. https://www.youtube.com/watch?v=nZdVGxQaCm8, accessed May 12, 2015.

Shnaiderov, V. "O filmakh-puteshestviiakh." *Iskusstvo kino*, no. 10 (1960): 137–42.

Silverman, Kaja. *The Acoustic Mirror: The Female Voice in Psychoanalysis and Cinema*. Bloomington: Indiana University Press, 1988.

Situationist International. "Preliminary Problems in Constructing a Situation." In *Situationist International Anthology*, edited by Ken Knabb, 49–51. Berkeley, CA: Bureau of Public Secrets, 2006.

Smelkov, Yurii. "Katok i skripka." *Iskusstvo kino*, no. 8 (1961): 25–26.

Smith, Mark B. *Property of Communists: The Urban Housing Program from Stalin to Khrushchev*. DeKalb: Northern Illinois University Press, 2010.

Sobchak, Vivian. *The Address of the Eye: The Phenomenology of Film Experience*. Princeton, NJ: Princeton University Press, 1992.

Soja, Edward W. "Vom 'Zeitgeist' zum 'Raumgeist': New Twists on the Spatial Turn." In *Spatial Turn: Das Raumparadigma in den Kultur- und Sozialwissenschaften*, edited by Jörg Döring and Tristan Thielmann, 241–62. Bielefeld, DE: Transcript, 2008.

Soloviova, I. "Kleo s 5 do 7." *Iskusstvo kino*, no. 5 (1964): 114–16.

"Sovetskoe panoramnoe kino." *Technika kino i televideniia* 4 (1957): 92–93.

Soy Cuba, a mamute siberiano [*I Am Cuba, A Siberian Mammoth*]. DVD. Director Vincente Ferraz, 2005; Milestone Film and Video, 2005.

Stanek, Łukasz. *Henri Lefebvre on Space: Architecture, Urban Research, and the Production of Theory*. Minneapolis: University of Minnesota Press, 2011.

Stupin, A. "Dvorets narodnykh forumov." *Arkhitektura SSSR*, no. 4 (1962): 11–22.

Sushko, Yuri. *Marina Vladi, obaiatelnaia kolduniia* [Marina Vladi, a Charming "Witch"]. Moscow: Eksmo, 2012.

Sutcliffe, Benjamin. *The Prose of Life: Russian Women Writers from Khrushchev to Putin*. Madison: University of Wisconsin Press, 2009.

Tarabukin, Nikolai. "From Easel to the Machine." In *Modern Art and Modernism: A Critical Anthology*, edited by Francis Frascina and Charles Harrison, 135–42. New York: Harper and Row; London: Open University Press, 1986.

Tarkovskii, Andrei. "Zapechatlionnoe vremia." *Iskusstvo kino*, no. 4 (1967): 68–79.

Tasalov, V. "Nekotorye problemy razvitiia sovremennoi arkhitektury." *Arkhitektura SSSR*, no. 6 (1961): 50–53.

Taubman, William. *Khrushchev: The Man and His Era*. New York: W. W. Norton, 2003.

Trachtenberg, Leonid. "Kogda zvuchti shirokii ekran." *Iskusstvo kino*, no. 3 (1961): 98–101.

Turvey, Malcolm. "Vertov: Between the Organism and the Machine." *October* 121 (Summer 2007): 5–18.

Tverskoi, L. "Zametki o sovremennom goroskom ansamble." *Arkhitektura SSSR*, no. 2 (1960): 40–43.

Urusevskii, Sergei. "O forme." *Iskusstvo kino*, no. 2 (1966): 27–37.

Vaisfeld, I. "Ne obobshchaite konei: Zametki o sovremennom kinoiskusstve." *Iskusstvo kino*, no. 1 (1963): 108–13.

Vaitsman, Evgenii. "Liniia razgranicheniia." *Iskusstvo kino*, no. 4 (1963): 37–46.

Varga-Harris, Christine. "Homemaking and the Aesthetic and Moral Perimeters of the Soviet Home during the Khrushchev Era." *Journal of Social History* 41, no. 3 (2008): 561–89.

Varshavskii, Ia. "Ot pokoleniia k pokoleniiu." *Iskusstvo kino*, no. 6 (1965): 50–57.

Veklenko, A., and B. Belkin. "K voprosu o sistemakh kinematografa budushchego." *Tekhnika kino i televideniia* 6 (1960): 19–27.

Vidler, Anthony. "The Explosion of Space: Architecture and the Filmic Imaginary." *Assemblage*, no. 21 (1993): 44–59.

Vladimirova, Alena. "Park kultury, otdykha i sporta." *Moskovskaia Pravda*, September 11, 2014. http://www.mos.ru/press-center/smi/index.php?id_14=11297&m_4=Sep&y_4=2014&t_14=Sep2014.

Volodin, P. "O nekotorykh osobennostiakh razvitiia sovetskoi arkhitektury na sovremennom etape." *Sovetskaia arkhitektura* 16 (1964): 3–14.

Vysotskii, M. Z. *Shirokoekrannoe stereofonicheskoe kino* [Widescreen Stereophonic Cinema]. Moscow: Iskusstvo, 1957.

Widdis, Emma. "Muratova's Clothes, Muratova's Textures, Muratova's Skin." *Kinokultura*, no. 8 (April 2005). http://www.kinokultura.com/articles/apr05-widdis.html.

———. *Visions of a New Land: Soviet Film from the Revolution to the Second World War*. New Haven, CT: Yale University Press, 2003.

Wolff, Janet. "The Invisible *Flâneuse*: Women and the Literature of Modernity." In *The Problems of Modernity: Adorno and Benjamin*, edited by Andrew E. Benjamin, 141–56. London: Routledge, 1989.

Woll, Josephine. *The Cranes Are Flying: The Film Companion*. London: I. B. Tauris, 2003.

———. *Real Images: Soviet Cinema and the Thaw*. London: I. B. Tauris, 2000.

Yanowitch, Murray. "Soviet Patterns of Time Use and Concepts of Leisure." *Soviet Studies* 15, no. 1 (1963): 17–37.

Young, Iris M. "Throwing Like a Girl: A Phenomenology of Feminine Body Comportment, Motility, and Spatiality." In *The Thinking Muse: Feminism and Modern French Philosophy*, edited by Jeffner Allen and Iris Marion Young, 51–70. Bloomington: Indiana University Press, 1989.

Yurenev, Rostislav. "Odin den' iunykh." *Iskusstvo kino*, no. 4 (1964): 26–29.

"Zabota o cheloveke—osnova sovetskogo gradostroitel'stva." *Arkhitektura SSSR*, no. 6 (1960): 1–3.

Zavialov, Ivan. *Skorost', vremia i prostranstvo v sovremennoi voine* [Speed, Time, and Space in Contemporary War]. Moscow: Voennoe izdatel'stvo ministerstva oborony, 1965.

Zemtsov, S. "Poiski novogo v monumentalnom iskusstve." *Arkhitektura SSSR*, no. 4 (1962): 23–31.

Zlobin, A. "Poiski, nakhodki, utraty." *Iskusstvo kino*, no. 5 (1961): 106–8.

Zorkaia, N. "Tak zhit' nel'zia!" *Iskusstvo kino*, no. 1 (1961): 135–38.

FILMOGRAPHY

Alionka, directed by Boris Barnet, 1961.
Bez strakha i uprioka [With No Fear or Reproach], directed by Alexander Mitta, 1962.
Bicycle Thieves, directed by Vittorio de Sica, 1948.
Black God, White Devil, directed by Glauber Rocha, 1964.
Bronenosets Potemkin (The Battleship Potemkin], directed by Sergei Eisenstein, 1925.
Chelovek idiot za solntsem [Man Follows the Sun], directed by Mikhail Kalik, 1961.
Chelovek s kinoapparatom [Man With a Movie Camera], directed by Dziga Vertov, 1928.
Cheriomushki, directed by Gerbert Rappoport, 1963.
Cleo from 5 to 7, directed by Agnes Varda, 1962.
Devushka bez adresa [The Girl Without an Address], directed by Eldar Riazanov, 1957.
Dolgie provody [Long Goodbyes], directed by Kira Muratova, 1971.
Dom v kotorom ia zhivu [The House I Live In], directed by Lev Kulidzhanov, 1957.
Dva voskreseniia [Two Sundays], directed by Vladimir Shredel', 1963.
The 400 Blows, directed by François Truffaut, 1959.
Elena, directed by Andrei Zviagintsev, 2011.
Gorizont [Horizon], directed by Iosif Kheifits, 1961.
Gorod bol'shoi sud'by [The City of Great Fate], directed by Il'ia Kopalin, 1961.
Ia Kuba [I am Cuba], directed by Mikhail Kalatozov, 1964.
I am Cuba, a Siberian Mammoth, directed by Vicente Ferraz, 2005.
Ia shagaiu po Moskve [I Walk the Streets of Moscow], directed by Georgii Danelia, 1964.
Il'ia Muromets, directed by Aleksandr Ptushko, 1956.
Ivan Brovkin na tseline [Ivan Brovkin in the Virgin Lands], directed by Ivan Lukinskii, 1958.
Katok i skripka [The Steamroller and the Violin], directed by Andrei Tarkovskii, 1960.
Khozhdenie po mukam [A Long Ordeal], directed by Grigorii Roshal' and Mary Andzhaparidze, 1957–1959.
Kogda derev'ia byli bol'shimi [When the Trees Were Tall], directed by Lev Kulidzhanov, 1961.
Komissar [The Commissar], directed by Aleksandr Askoldov, 1967.
Korotkie vstrechi [Brief Encounters], directed by Kira Muratova, 1967.
Kryl'ia [Wings], directed by Larisa Shepitko, 1966.

Leon Garros ishchet druga [Leon Garros Searches for His Friend], directed by Marcello Pagliero, 1960.
Letiat Zhuravli [The Cranes Are Flying], directed by Mikhail Kalatozov, 1957.
Leviathan, directed by Andrei Zviagintsev, 2014.
Matros s "komety" [A Sailor from "Comet"], directed by Isidor Annenskii, 1958.
Mne dvadsat' [I Am Twenty], directed by Marlen Khutsiev, 1962.
Mon Oncle, directed by Jacques Tati, 1958.
Murderers Are among Us, directed by Wolfgang Staudte, 1946.
Nad Tissoi [Over Tissa], directed by Dmitrii Vasieliev, 1958.
Neotpravlennoe pis'mo [The Unsent Letter], directed by Mikhail Kalatozov, 1959.
La Notte, directed by Michelangelo Antonioni, 1961.
Osennii Marafon [Autumn Marathon], directed by Georgii Danelia, 1979.
Pervyi eshelon [The First Echelon], directed by Mikhail Kalatozov, 1955.
Playtime, directed by Jacques Tati, 1967.
Prikhodite zavtra [Come Tomorrow], directed by Aleksandr Pashkov, 1962.
Pylaiushchii Ostrov [Flaming Island], directed by Roman, Karmen, 1961.
The Red Balloon, directed by Albert Lamorisse, 1956.
Seriozha, directed by Georgii Danelia, 1962.
Shiroka strana moia [Wide Is My Country], directed by Roman Karmen, 1958.
Skazka o poteriannom vremeni [A Fairy Tale about Lost Time], directed by Alexander Ptushko, 1964.
The Soft Skin, directed by François Truffaut, 1964.
Sorok Pervyi [The Forty First], directed by Grigorii Chukhrai, 1956.
The Touch of Evil, directed by Orson Welles, 1958.
Tsirk [Circus], directed by Grigorii Aleksandrov, 1936.
The Umbrellas of Cherbourg, directed by Jacques Demy, 1964.
Vesna na Zarechnoi ulitse [Spring on Zarechnaia Street], directed by Feliks Mironer and Marlen Khutsiev, 1956.
Vzroslye deti [Adult Children], directed by Villen Azarov, 1961.
Zhili byli starik so starukhoi [Once Upon a Time There Lived an Old Man and an Old Woman], directed by Grigorii Chukhrai, 1964.

INDEX

Adult Children, 12
aerial views, 72-74, 73f2.8, 110-11, 111f3.7
aesthetics: in *Brief Encounters*, 177, 180n10; in *Elena*, 187; and gender, 21; in *I Am Cuba*, 50, 51, 74, 76-77, 80-81; in *I Walk the Streets of Moscow*, 106, 109; ideology in, 180n10; in kinopanorama, 33, 34-35, 36-38; movement in, 76-78, 77f2.9; in panoramic cinema, 20, 29-30; socialist, 34, 37-41, 106; in still lifes, 21, 158, 159-60, 163-64, 166; in *The Unsent Letter*, 51, 63, 81nn5-6, 82n21; in widescreen format, 94; in *Wings*, 120
airport terminals, 86, 87f3.2, 90, 91-92, 94-95
Alionka, 11
"animation of the surface," 167-68
Antonioni, Michelangelo, 109-10
Arbuzov, Aleksei, 114n26
Architecture in the Age of Stalin (Paperny), 96
architecture/built environment: and body-space relations, 116-17; children's perception of, 101-105; as cinematic material, 18-19; in economic revival plans, 5-6; embodied mapping of, 12; exterior spaces in, 170; glass in, 92-94, 170; in *I Am Cuba*, 74; in *I Walk the Streets of Moscow*, 91-96; materiality and flatness in, 170; and movement, 20-21, 88, 91-102, 109-12; otherness of, 189-90; Palace of Young Pioneers, 113n14; of panoramic cinema, 38-39, 45; in Sevastopol, 141; in Situationism, 105-109; in social transformation, 15-16; Soviet leftovers of, 189f6.2; surface pliability of, 74
attractions, cinema of, 30-34, 39
Autumn Marathon, 112
barriers, gendered, 144, 155-56, 175, 177
Bazin, André, 100
Belkin, B., 38
Bellos, David, 115n32
Benjamin, Walter, 63, 64-65, 76, 84n45
Beskin, O., 37
Bleiman, Mikhail, 89
bodies: collective, in *I Am Cuba*, 79; framing of, 122-24, 123f4.2; in *I Am Twenty*, 104-105; individual, in disunity, 191-92; mimicking landscape, 54-56, 55f2.1-59f2.4; in sense of movement, 95; in urban space, 88
bodies, female: as chora, 171-72, 174-75; framing of, 118, 124-26, 125-26f4.3, 145n1; in memory representation, 145; in still lifes, 154; and walls, 172-74, 173f5.11. *See also* gender; women
bodily movement: in cultural discourse, 96-97, 109-10; in *I Walk the Streets of Moscow*, 20-21, 88, 101, 110; through the built environment, 20-21, 88, 91-102, 109-12; of viewers, 36-37, 39; in widescreen format, 94
body-space relations: female, 154, 171-74; gender in, 117-18; in *I Am Cuba*, 67-68, 72, 75-76; in *I Walk the Streets of Moscow*, 116-17; sound in, 134-35; in *The Unsent Letter*, 65-66; in *Wings*, 139

207

Bolotina, Irina, 163
Bolotova, Alla, 82n14
Brief Encounters: aesthetics in, 177, 180n10; departures and arrivals in, 177-79; environment in, 150-53, *152fs*.2; flatness in, 150-51, 156, 166-74, *167fs*.9, *169fs*.10; gender and space in, 21, 153-55, 171, 183n38; objectification of women in, 142, 153-54; screens in, 170-71; still life in, 150-51, *151fs*.1, 154-60, *157fs*.4, 162-63, 164-66, 177-79, *178fs*.13; thresholds in, 155-56, *156fs*.3
Bruno, Giuliana, 18, 130n24
Bryson, Norman: *Looking at the Overlooked*, 163-64, 175-76
Buchli, Victor, 160, 162
Buck-Morss, Susan, 17, 64
built environment. *See* architecture/built environment
Bulgakova, Oksana, 104

Caillois, Roger: "Mimicry and Legendary Psychasthenia," 63-64
camera dynamics: in excitement, 75-76, 84n44; in *I Am Cuba*, 67-74, 75-76; in *I Walk the Streets of Moscow*, 100-101; mimesis in, 68; in perception, spatial, 51, 97; in representational practice, 50; in *The Unsent Letter*, 60, 83n24
capitalism, 70, 105-106, 109-10
cartography. *See* maps/mapping
centripetal hierarchy, 8-9, 51-55, 82n15
Certeau, Michel de, 115n43
children: in European films, 114n24, 114n26; and mimesis, 63, 64-66; at play, 101-104, *103fs*.5
Chion, Michael, 113n6, 134
chora, 171-72, 174-76, 177
Chufut-Kale (Jewish Fortress), 142-43
Cinerama (US), 30-33, *33f1*.3
Cinerama's Russian Adventure, *33f1*.3
Circular Panorama, 26-30, *27f1.1*, 35, 36, 38-39, 45-46. *See also* kinopanorama; panoramic cinema
Circus, 34-35
cities: cinematic representation of, 1-2, 12, 18; heterogeneity in, 118; materiality of, 106; memory in, 139-45; as playgrounds, 101-105, *103fs.5*; as social space, 106. *See also* urban space/environment
City of Great Fate, The, 1-2, *3fo.1*
Cleo from 5 to 7, 128-29
Come Tomorrow, 104
Commissar, 35
Communism. *See* ideology
composition: architectural, 93-94, 95, 96-97, 113n14; in cinematic realism, 37; in kinopanorama, 31; of mimetic passages, 56-57; static, 150-51, *151fs.1*, 154, 156-60, *157fs.4*, 165-66, 177-79; walls in, 166
Concini, Ennio de, 109
conflict: in communal space, 191; dwelling as, 15-17; in *I Walk the Streets of Moscow*, 89-90; in *The Long Goodbye*, 175; in panoramic cinema, 38-41; in *Wings*, 118-19
conquest, spatial, 8-10, 11, 13, 52-53
construction: in post-Stalinist USSR, 4-8; of VDNKh, 25-26. *See also* architecture/built environment
Cranes Are Flying, The, 49, 60
Cuba. *See I Am Cuba*
Cuban Missile Crisis, 84n47
cultural discourse, Soviet: bodily movement in, 96-97, 109-10; external space in, 177; flaneurs in, 128; realism in, 37; urban space in, 106
curves, 88-91, 101-102

Danelia, Georgii, 20-21, 92-94, 102, 112, 116-17, 145n2, 186. *See also I Walk the Streets of Moscow*
death: memory of, in *Wings*, 148n39; in mimetic passages, *61-62f2.5*, 61-63, 66-67
Debord, Guy, 105-106
dedramatization, 109-10
Dekorativnoe iskusstvo SSSR (Decorative Arts of the USSR), 160-62, *161fs.6*
Dickerman, Leah, 39-40
diegetic space and sound, 120-24, 137, 139
disruption: of hierarchical systems, 107-108, *108f3.6*; of mobility, 13-14
disunity: and sound, 135-36; in Soviet space, 190-92
Doane, Mary Anne, 43-45
Dobin, Efim, 109-10
Dombrovskii, Konstantin, 31

domestic space: and gender, 6, 171-72, 175-77; in interior design, 160-63, 161f5.6, 180nn8-9
dwelling, 15-17, 172, 174

economic revival plans, 4-8, 10
Eisenstein, Sergei, 33-34, 67, 154
Elena, 187-90, 188f6.1
empty spaces, 98, 100, 142, 168, 178f5.13, 179, 182n36, 187
environment: bodily assimilation into, 61-62f2.5, 61-64; in *Brief Encounters*, 150-53, 152f5.2; in *Elena*, 187-88; in everyday lives, 106; in *I Am Cuba*, 68-70; in narrative, 190; and spatial conquest, 8-9, 10; as still life, 155-56, 164-66; in *The Unsent Letter*, 52. See also architecture/built environment; urban space/environment
ethics, 189-90, 191
Ethics of Sexual Difference, An (Irigaray), 171-72
everyday life: immersion in, 186; mapping of, 12-14; narrative movement in, 110, 111-12; play in, 104; revolution in, 15-16; Situationism in, 106; taste education in, 161-63, 162f5.6, 180n6, 180n8
Exhibition of Achievements of the People's Economy (VDNKH), 25-26
existential enclosure, 122-24, 146n11
experience: embodied, 35-36, 97-101, 114n22; gender in, 124-26, 125-26f4.3; mimesis in, 66; in panoramic cinema, 35-41; physiological, 35-41, 50-51; point-of-view shots in, 72, 74; sensory, 111, 120, 128, 132-34, 133f4.7; space and time in, 107; of time, 44-45; transient, 109, 110; urban, 100, 124-26, 125-26f4.3
exploration, 9, 11, 13, 53, 90, 114n24
external/exterior spaces, 86, 90, 92-94, 93f3.3, 113n10, 155, 170, 177

Fairy Tale about Lost Time, 104, 115n28
female gaze, 129-30
Filtzer, Donald, 10
First Echelon, The, 11
Fisher, Jaimey, 143-44
Five-Year Plans, 17-18, 42, 52
flaneurs (urban strollers): anonymity of, 127, 128; and gender, 21, 127-30, 147n30; as prostitutes, 128, 146-47n16; sensory experience of, 132-34, 133f4.7; voice of, 136; in *Wings*, 117-18, 126-34, 144-45. See also walking
formalism, 50, 75
frames/framing: in film theory, 146n10; of gender, 117-18, 124-26, 125-26f4.3, 145n1; in *Wings*, 118-28, 121f4.1
functionalism, 6-7, 7fo.2, 16

gender: and barriers, 144, 155-56, 175, 177; and body-space relations, 117-18; in *Brief Encounters*, 21, 153-54, 171; and cinematic voice, 136; and domestic space, 6, 171-72, 175-77; in *Elena*, 188, 188f6.1; of flaneurs, 21, 127-30, 147n30; framing of, 117-18, 124-26, 125-26f4.3, 145n1; in historical rupture, 119; and immersion, 186; and interior design, 21, 162; and materiality, 183n38; in spatialization of memory, 143-44. See also bodies, female; women
Girl without an Address, 12
glass structures, 92-94, 170
Gleber, Anke, 128
global space, 84n47
Goldovskii, Evsei, 30, 36-37, 38-39, 48n37
Gordon, Bette, 137
Gorokhov, Victor, 35-36, 41
Gorsuch, Anne E., 9
Grosz, Elizabeth, 171
Gunning, Tom, 33

Hansen, Miriam, 84n44
harmony: and balance, 160; rhetoric of, 16
Heimkehrer (German war veterans), 143-44
heterogeneity: in cinema and city, 118; movement in, 96-97; of Soviet space, 190-92
hierarchies: centripetal, 8-9, 51-55, 82n15; disruption of, 107-108, 108f3.6; domestic, 187; in spatial transformation, 16
historical rupture in *Wings*, 119, 140-42, 141f4.9, 144
House I Live in, The, 182n36
housing, urban, 6-8, 8fo.3

I Am Cuba: aesthetics in, 50, 51, 74, 76-77, 80-81; body-space relations in, 67-68, 72, 75-76; cinema in, 76-78; collective bodies in, 79; guerillas in, 78-80, 79f2.11; hotel rooftop in, 69f2.6; mimicry in, 20, 51-52, 74; narrative in, 68, 70, 72, 74, 76-78; representational practice in, 50; space and time in, 50, 66-74; spatial logic in, 78-79

I Am Twenty, 104-105

I Walk the Streets of Moscow: architecture in, 91-96; body-space relations in, 116-17; lines and curves in, 88-91; modes of walking in, 99f3.4; narrative movement in, 110-12; *Playtime* compared to, 86-88; Situationism in, 107-109, 108f3.6; trope of walking in, 20-21; walking-in-the-rain sequence, 98-101, 99f3.4, 105, 106-107

Iampolski, Mikhail, 183n38

ideology: in aesthetics, 180n10; in *Brief Encounters*, 164-65, 164f5.7; and children's perceptions, 102; in criticism of *The Unsent Letter*, 81n6; disunity in, 191-92; in falsified images, 40; in interior design, 160-62, 161f5.6, 180n8; mimesis in, 65-66; in panoramic cinema, 29-30, 33-34, 36, 40-41; in perpetual displacement, 80-81; of space, 20; time in, 42; in urban planning, 7-8

Ikonnikov, Andrei, 4, 97

illusions, 32, 167, 169-71, 174

imagery: of dreams, 126-27; of memory, 142, 148n33; and sound, 135-36

imitation. *See* mimesis

immersion: environments in, 190; panoramic, 19, 20, 26-27, 28, 29, 38, 39; physiological, 65; in spatial relations, 185-86. *See also* integration

immobility: in architecture, 96; freedom from, 75-76, 98; and reality, 36-37

indexicality, 39-40, 41, 43

instability, 118, 120, 122, 144-45

integration: death as, 63; in panoramic cinema, 29, 37-38, 41-42, 44-45; screens in, 21, 174-75; sound in, 19; through urban walking, 118; of women, 153. *See also* immersion

interior design, 6-7, 7f0.2, 21, 160-62, 161f5.6, 180nn8-9

interior spaces, 113n10, 151-52, 155, 164-66, 165f5.8, 187-89, 188f6.1

internationalism, 9-10

Irigaray, Luce, 171-72, 177

isolation: gendered, 117-18, 119; spatial, 70-72, 71f2.7

Ivan Brovkin in the Virgin Lands, 11

Jacobson, Roman, 17-18
Jameson, Fredric, 80
Jones, Robert A., 10

Kaganovsky, Lilya, 179-80n1, 181-82n31
Kalatozov, Mikhail, 20, 49, 186. See also *I Am Cuba*; *Unsent Letter, The*
Kalik, Mikhail, 102
Karmen, Roman, 32-33, 84-85n49
Kerzhentsev, Platon, 42
Khutsiev, Marlen, 104-105
kinopanorama, 30-41
Kokoreva, Natalia, 60
Kremlin chimes, 108-109
Kremlin Palace of Congress, 113n10
Kulidzhanov, Lev, 104

La Notte, 128-32, 130-32f4.4-4.6, 134
landscape, 54-56, 55f2.1-59f2.4, 63, 67, 155-56, 156f5.3, 189-90
Lant, Antonia, 167
Lauretis, Teresa de, 145n1
Lefebvre, Henri, 14-17, 106
Leon Garros Searches for his Friend, 12-13, 115n38
Let's Go, 28f1.2
Leviathan, 187, 189-90
Levin, Moshe, 17
Levinas, Emmanuel, 190-91
logic, spatial, 78-79, 170-71
Long Goodbyes, 174-75, 176f5.12
Looking at the Overlooked (Bryson), 163-64, 175-76

male gaze, 116-17, 124-26, 128, 132f4.6, 136-37, 145n2
Mamonova, Tatiana, 182n34
Man Follows the Sun, 102, 103f3.5, 110
Man with a Movie Camera (Vertov), 97-98, 114n21
maps/mapping: in centripetal hierarchy, 82n15; in *The City of Great Fate*, 3f0.1; embodied, 11-14; in narrative movement, 109-10; panoramic cinema in, 34-35; of revolution, 68; transitional motion in, 9-10; in *The Unsent Letter*, 53-54
Margolit, Evgenii, 83
Markov, Mark, 64-65

marriage, 90-91, 98, 100-101
masculine space, 156
materiality: in architecture, 170; of cinema, 18-22; of cities, 106; elemental, 171; gender in, 183n38; of panoramic cinema, 32-33; of screens, 181n26, 182n37; of streets, 130f4.4; of time, 43-44; of walls, 150-51
maternal bodies, 171-72, 174-76, 177
megalography, 163-64
memory/memories: images of, 142, 148n33; as spatial experience, 126-27; spatiality and tactility of, 137-40, 138f4.8, 148n35; and walking, 139-45, 141f4.9; in *Wings*, 132, 134, 137-45, 138f4.8, 148n39
Metz, Christian, 74-75
Mikhailov, Nikolai: *My Russia*, 53
mimesis/mimicry: as approach to space, 51-52; discursive history of, 63-65; in *I Am Cuba*, 68; indistinction in, 52-60; movement in, 74-81; in participatory cinema, 20; in *The Unsent Letter*, 51, 60-63, 61-62f2.5, 65-66, 68
Minkowski, Eugène, 85n50
Mir movie theater (Moscow), 47n14
Mitta, Alexander, 101
mobility/movement: and architecture, 20-21, 88, 91-102, 109-12; in artistic perception, 74-75; in camera dynamics, 100; in containing memory, 143-44; embodied mapping in, 11-13; in mimesis, 74-81; in panoramic cinema, 20, 30, 36-41; and play, 101-105; representation of, 114n22; sense of, 95-101; and space, 80; transitional, 8-11; in viewer participation, 19. *See also* bodily movement
Mon Oncle, 112, 114n26
Moscow: aerial views of, 110-11, 111f3.7; in *The City of Great Fate*, 1-2; in *I Walk the Streets of Moscow*, 89-90; in *Leon Garros Searches for His Friend*, 12-13; neighborhoods of, 97; as playground, 101-102; in *A Sailor from "Comet,"* 12
Muratova, Kira: aesthetics of, 21, 159-60, 163-64, 166; feminism of, 154, 179-80n1; immersion in work of, 186; reductionism in, 151-52; spatial conception of, 166-67; still lifes of, 150, 158-60, 177. *See also Brief Encounters; Long Goodbyes*; still lifes
Murderers Are among Us, 143-44
My Russia (Mikhailov), 53

narrative: ejection of, 163-64; of heroism, 148n40; historical, 39-40; in *I Am Cuba*, 68, 70, 72, 74, 76-78; in *I Walk the Streets of Moscow*, 88-91, 107-109; monumentalization of, 145; movements of, 109-12; objects in, 180n10; and participatory effect, 49-50; space and time in, 50; spatial disorientation in, 82n20; in *The Unsent Letter*, 53-54
nature, 6-7, 8-9, 11-12, 52, 82n14, 83n24
neighborhoods, 5-6, 8fo.3, 97

objects: in *Brief Encounters*, 158, 159f5.5, 162-63, 164-66; material presentation of, 180n10
Once Upon a Time There Lived an Old Man and an Old Woman, 11-12
organization/reorganization of space, 5-8, 15-16, 54, 56-60, 65
otherness of space, 185-92
Over Tissa, 12

Palace of Young Pioneers, 93-94, 95, 113n14
panoramic cinema: Circular Panorama, 26-30, 27f1.1, 35, 36, 38-39, 45-46; ideology in, 29-30, 33-34, 36; immersion in, 19, 20, 27-29; kinopanorama, 30-41; perception in, 31, 48n37; reality and mobility in, 20, 28, 29-30, 36-41; screens in, 47n14; time in, 41-46; viewers in production of, 34-36
pantheism, 60-63, 64. *See also* mimesis/mimicry
Paperny, Vladimir: *Architecture in the Age of Stalin*, 25n3, 96
participation: in experience of space, 88; in panoramic cinema, 19, 31-32, 34-36, 39; physiological effects of, 50-51
participatory effect, 49-51
Pashkov, Alexander, 104
perception: ambiguities of, 90-91; camera dynamics in, 51, 97; of children, 101-105; of the flaneur, 127-28, 144-45; gender in, 153-54; and indeterminacy, 120, 122; mimesis in, 64-65; motion in, 74-75; in panoramic cinema, 31, 48n37; of spontaneity in urban space, 101-102; in still lifes, 163, 164-66; through long takes, 97; of time, 41-42; in *Wings*, 120-23, 121f4.1; of women, 128
peripheral spaces, 11-12, 53, 185, 186, 187-88
photography, 39-41, 43, 160-63, 161f5.6

Index 211

planar spaces, 166-74
Playtime, 21, 86-88, 90, 113n6
point-of-view shots, 61, 70, 72-74, 73*f2.8*, 119
politics: cultural, 158, 160-62; in embodied mapping, 11-12; in *I am Cuba*, 51-52, 67, 80-81; mimetic processes in, 65-66; spatial conquest in, 10; in spatial engagement, 14-15; of spatial use and appropriation, 4, 51
Pollock, Griselda, 155-56
porosity of borders, 10, 12
post-Soviet cinema, 187-91
private spaces, 153-54, 159-60
Production of Space (Lefebvre), 15
progress, rhetoric of, 16
psychasthenia and mimicry, 63-64
psychological affect, 51, 60
Ptushko, Alexander, 104
public spaces, 21, 142-43, 146-47n16
Punin, Nikolai, 96
Pylaiushchii Ostrov (Flaming Island), 84-85n49

Qualls, Karl D., 140

Rainer, Yvonne, 137
realism: everyday life in, 106; in panoramic cinema, 28, 29-30, 34, 37; technology in, 19-20; three-dimensional, 167-68
reality: disruption of, 13-14; impressions in, 74-75; in panoramic cinema, 36-41; reality effect, 19, 40-41, 48n43; regeneration of, 20-21
Reid, Susan, 95, 162, 180n9
Return, The, 189-90
revolution/revolutionary movements: in *I Am Cuba*, 70, 76-81, 79*f2.11*; mapping of, 68; spatial engagement in, 14-16; upheaval in, 79-81, 106-107
rhopography, 163-65
Ryklin, Mikhail, 46n3

Sailor from "Comet," A, 12
Saint Basil's Cathedral, 107-108
scientific management, 42-43, 48n47
screens: bodily integration with, 175; in *Brief Encounters*, 170-71; in *Long Goodbyes*, 174-75, 176*f5.12*; materiality of, 181n26, 182n37; in panoramic cinema, 47n14; urban, in *Wings*, 118-26; walls as, 170-71

Seriozha, 102
Sevastopol, 140-43, 141*f4.9*, 149n46
Shepitko, Larisa: on gender separation, 117; on image of memory, 148n33; immersion in films of, 186; use of memory by, 139-45; use of sound and voice by, 21, 134-36. See also *Wings*
Shitova, Vera, 120
Sierra Maestra mountains, 84n49
Silverman, Kaja, 136-37
Situationism, 21, 105-109, *108f3.6*
skyscrapers, Stalinist, 93-95, 101-102, 115n38, 115n43
Smith, Mark B., 8
social relations: ethics in, 189-90, 191; in *Leon Garros Searches for His Friend*, 12-14; space in transforming, 15-16; spatial relations in, 185-86; in the Thaw, 2; through embodied mapping, 13-14
social space, 4, 19, 106, 187-91
Soja, Edward, 17
sound: as cinematic material, 21; diegetic, 120-24, 137, 139; in *I Am Cuba*, 72; in panoramic cinema, 30; stereophonic, 135-36; in *Wings*, 134-39
space: domestic, 160-63, 161*f5.6*, 171-72, 175-77, 180nn8-9; empty, 98, 100, 142, 168, 178*f5.13*, 179, 182n36, 187; external, 86, 90, 92-94, 93*f3.3*, 113n10, 155, 170, 177; interior, 113n10, 151-52, 155, 164-66, 165*f5.8*, 187-89, 188*f6.1*; interrogations of, 14-18, 105-106, 186-87; otherness of, 185-92; social, 4, 19, 106, 187-91; spectatorial, 31, 40-41; and time, 50, 66-74, 107; volumetric, 167-68, 169*f5.10*. See also urban space/environment
spatial dynamics, 29-30, 33, 90, 101
spatial relations: ethics in, 191; human figures in, 68-74; in *I Am Cuba*, 76; immersion in, 185-86; revolution in, 68
spectatorial space, 31, 40-41
spectatorship, 33-34
Spring on Zarechnaia Street, 11
static composition. See still lifes
Staudte, Wolfgang, 143-44
Steamroller and the Violin, The, 101-102, 114n25
stereophonic sound, 19, 135-36
still lifes: in *Brief Encounters*, 150-51, 151*f5.1*, 154, 156-60, 157*f5.4*, 162-63, 165-66, 177-79,

178fs.13; in *Elena*, 187; in masculine subjectivity, 175, 177; perception in, 163; in peripheral spaces, 186; projection of, 175
stillness, 150-51, 186
streets: gendered experience of, 128; materiality of, 130f4.4; as place of transition, 104. *See also* flaneurs; walking
subjectivity: in camera dynamics, 67-68; feminine, 21, 124, 135-36, 145; immersion in, 186; masculine, 136, 175, 177; in mimesis, 64
subversion, 104-105, 151-52
Sum and the Remainder, The (Lefebvre), 15
symmetry, gendered, 187-88, 187f6.1, 188f6.1
synchronicity of image and voice, 135, 137

Tarkovskii, Andrei, 43-45, 101-102
Tati, Jacques, 111. See also *Playtime*
Taylorism, 42
technology, 18-22, 30-31, 84n47, 97-98, 113n12, 135-36
texture, 32, 39, 102, 150-51, 166
three-dimensionality, 167-70
time: and efficiency, 42-43, 115n28; in *Fairy Tale about Lost Time*, 115n28; in *I Am Cuba*, 50; linear, 18, 181-82n31; multiplicity of, 41-46; in narrative and description, 180n10; in panoramic cinema, 26-29, 41-46; in social transformation, 16-18; and space, 50, 66-74, 107; spatial dynamics of, 90, 101; subordination to, 108-9; in *The Unsent Letter*, 53-54
"Time League," 42
tourism, 9-10, 107-109, 115n39, 142
transience, 3fo.1, 18, 110, 144-45
Turvey, Malcolm, 114n21
Twenty-Second Congress of the Communist Party of the Soviet Union, 4-5
Two Sundays, 12, 147n19
two-dimensionality, 166-74

umheimlich (uncanny), 175, 177
unity, 34-35, 78-79, 96-97
Unsent Letter, The: aesthetics in, 51, 63, 81nn5-6; body-space relations in, 116; camera dynamics in, 60, 83n24; centripetal hierarchy in, 51-55; geography in, 53-55; ideology in criticism of, 81n6; indistinction in, 52-60; mimesis in, 20, 51, 60-63, 61-62f2.5, 65-66, 69; politics of appropriation in, 51; representational practice in, 50; space and time in, 50
urban movement, 1-2
urban planning and development, 5-8
urban space/environment: bodily movement through, 88; experience of, 100, 124-26, 125-26f4.3; flaneurs in, 127-34; movement in, 97-98; in narrative, 110; pedestrian movement through, 115n43; perceptual spontaneity in, 101-102; as playground, 115n32; sensory experience of women in, 120; Situationist critique of, 105-106; technology in, 97-98; transformation of, 11-12; walking in perception of, 144-45. *See also* cities
urban walkers. *See* flaneurs (urban strollers)
Urusevskii, Sergei, 19, 20, 49, 75-76, 84n44, 186. See also *I Am Cuba*; *Unsent Letter, The*
utopia, Soviet, 6-8, 26, 27-28, 116

VDNKH (Exhibition of Achievements of the People's Economy), 25-26
Veklenko, A., 38
verticality, 107-109, 115n38
Vertov, Dziga, 75-76, 97-98, 114n22
Vidler, Anthony, 18-19
viewers/viewing: environment in, 30-32; in panoramic cinema, 19, 31-32, 34-36, 39; physiological effects of, 50-51; sound in, 135-36
voice: gendered, 21, 147n30; in *Wings*, 134-37
volumetric space, 167-68, 169fs.10

walking: and memory, 139-45, 141f4.9; as narrative element, 129; in sensory experience, 128, 132-34, 133f4.7; in separation of gender positions, 117-18; in structural unity, 96-97; as substitute for flying, 127; as trope, 20-21. *See also* flaneurs (urban strollers); *I Walk the Streets of Moscow*
walls: in *Brief Encounters*, 150-51, 152fs.2, 166, 167fs.9, 172-74, 173fs.11, 183n38; materiality of, 150-51; as screen, 170-71, 176fs.12; urban, 131f4.5
wartime trauma, 142, 143-44, 148n38, 148n40
When the Trees Were Tall, 104
Widdis, Emma, 8-9, 11, 114n22, 166, 172n35
Wide is My Country, 30-33, 34-36, 41
widescreen format, 49, 51, 89, 94-95, 113n12, 135-36

windows, 120-22, 121f4.1, 124-26, 146n10
Wings: acoustic passages in, 134-39; flaneurs in, 117-18, 126-34, 144-45; gender separation in, 117-18; materiality of the street in, 130f4.4; memory in, 132, 134, 137-45, 138f4.8, 148n39; narrative of, 119, 132; screens and frames in, 118-28; urban walls in, 131f4.5; war veterans in, 145n4

With No Fear and Reproach, 101

women: in *Brief Encounters*, 153-54, 156-57; as *chora*, 172; in containing memory, 143-44; as flaneurs, 127-33; objectification of, 142, 153-54; spatial relations of, 21; in the USSR, 182n34; and walls, 173f5.11; as war pilots, 119, 146n7. *See also* bodies, female; gender

World War II history, 146n7

youth, Soviet, 89
Yurenev, Rostislav, 89, 91-92
Yusov, Vadim, 89-90, 114n25

Zavialov, Ivan, 84n47
Zelinsky, Konstantin, 96
Zemtsov, S., 170
Zlobin, A., 1-2
Zorkaia, N., 114n24
Zviagintsev, Andrei, 187-90, 192

Lida Oukaderova is Assistant Professor of Film Studies in the Department of Art History at Rice University. Born in the former Soviet Union, she competed her undergraduate studies at the Martin Luther University in Halle, Germany, and her PhD at the University of Texas at Austin. At Rice, she teaches a broad range of courses on the history and theory of film and has lectured widely on postwar Soviet cinema in the United States and abroad.

www.ingramcontent.com/pod-product-compliance
Lightning Source LLC
Chambersburg PA
CBHW070803230426
43665CB00017B/2468